MORE PRAISE FOR *THEM*

"*Them* provides a map back to a place where Americans can once again savor the unique freedoms that unite them instead of the politics that divide them." —GARRY KASPAROV

"Senator Sasse's *Them* is a cry from the heartland to remember who we are and what unites us. . . . He takes contemporary America to task for our tribalism, exclusion, reflexive attitudes, and outright harshness to one another. At its heart, his is a call to *community*— the best antidote to those who would divide our society and exploit our darkest angels."

—GEN. MICHAEL HAYDEN (US Air Force, Ret.)

"Through his inimitable historian's gaze, Sasse cuts through the self-serving partisan noise to jerk us back into focus on what's important: community. It's so much easier to blame each other than to remember it's 'each other' that makes us great, fulfilled, healthy, and moored. I don't care how old you are, where you're from or what you do—you need Ben Sasse to slap some sense into you. We all need to hear the hard truths of *Them*." —S. E. CUPP

"A wonderfully thoughtful—and wonderfully thought-provoking— book that challenges us to recognize and embrace, at a time of hyper-partisanship fueled by technology, the importance of what unites us as Americans over what divides us."

— GEN. DAVID PETRAEUS (US Army, Ret.)

Also by Ben Sasse

The Vanishing American Adult

THEM

WHY WE HATE EACH OTHER—
AND HOW TO HEAL

BEN SASSE

St. Martin's Griffin
New York

*To the Fremont Area Community Foundation,
Fremont Rotary Club, and Fremont Kiwanis Club,
which—along with groups just like them in hometowns
across our nation—daily demonstrate how to love a
neighbor. And to my parents for raising me to appreciate
community, and to Melissa, who is doing the same for
our three rowdies.*

Published in the United States by St. Martin's Griffin, an imprint of St. Martin's Publishing Group

www.stmartins.com

Designed by Meryl Sussman Levavi

ISBN 978-1-250-19368-1 (hardcover)
ISBN 978-1-250-19367-4 (ebook)
ISBN 978-1-250-19502-9 (trade paperback)

Our books may be purchased in bulk for promotional, educational, or business use. Please contact your local bookseller or the Macmillan Corporate and Premium Sales Department at 1-800-221-7945, extension 5442, or by email at MacmillanSpecialMarkets@macmillan.com.

First St. Martin's Griffin Edition: October 2019

10 9 8 7 6 5 4 3

Americans of all ages, all conditions, and all dispositions constantly form associations.

They have not only commercial and manufacturing companies . . . , but associations of a thousand other kinds, religious, moral, serious, futile, general or restricted, enormous or diminutive. The Americans make associations to give entertainments, to found seminaries, to build inns, to construct churches, to diffuse books, to send missionaries to the antipodes; in this manner they found hospitals, prisons, and schools. If it is proposed to inculcate some truth or to foster some feeling by the encouragement of a great example, they form a society. Wherever at the head of some new undertaking you see the government in France, or a man of rank in England, in the United States you will be sure to find an association . . .

As soon as several of the inhabitants of the United States have taken up an opinion or a feeling which they wish to promote in the world . . . , they combine. From that moment they are no longer isolated men, but a power seen from afar . . .

If men are to remain civilized or to become so, the art of associating together must grow and improve.

—ALEXIS DE TOCQUEVILLE, *Democracy in America*

CONTENTS

Preface to the Paperback Edition   vii

Introduction: More Politics Can't Fix This   1

PART I

COLLAPSING TRIBES

1. Our Loneliness Epidemic   19

2. Strangers at Work   47

PART II

ANTI-TRIBES

3. The Comforts of Polititainment   75

4. The Polarization Business Model   105

PART III

OUR TO-DO LIST

5. Become Americans Again   133

6. Set Tech Limits   167

7. Buy a Cemetery Plot   203

8. Be a Smarter Nomad   219

Conclusion: We Need More Tribes   239

Acknowledgments   255

Notes   257

Index   265

PREFACE TO THE PAPERBACK EDITION

NOT LONG AFTER THIS BOOK WAS PUBLISHED, I WAS ON MY way home to Nebraska from Washington on a Friday afternoon, with a layover in Minneapolis. I had been through the "order" half of the line, and was waiting at "pick up" for my burger when a man making a beeline toward me caught my eye. My mind went through the possibilities. What's he going to want to discuss? Trade wars? Border walls? Supreme Court confirmations? Taxes? The Middle East? But as he began talking, what he said surprised me:

"You're the guy who thinks we can fix politics just by being nicer to each other."

I was a little taken aback—because I *don't* think that. But before I could say anything, he went on: "That won't work! We're way too messed up for that."

I agreed with him, and told him so. But he was still frustrated with what he thought was the point of this book. *Them,* he said, "just argues that we need more civility."

But that's not what this book is about. (For one thing, my wife would never have let me write from 4 a.m. to 7 a.m. daily for a year for a thesis that lame.) So please take this as an advance heads-up: If you're looking for yet another call for decency in civil discourse, you should put this book down and move along.

* * *

I asked this peeved man if he'd read *Them*—and to his credit, he admitted that he hadn't. Fair enough. Plenty of us just read reviews of books or see segments about them on TV and come away thinking we understand what the book is trying to say. We're all busy. But I figured, since we both found ourselves in this airport with time on our hands, I had an opportunity to have a genuine conversation with someone who seemed to care as much as I did, who might want to see if we could find a common point of departure for a discussion about what's wrong—and about how we might fix it. He was willing.

There in the airport food court, as I waited for my burger, we kicked off from our point of agreement: that just "being nice to each other" is not going to be enough to solve our problems.

The truth is, we are facing challenges far more fundamental, which go to our very core as a society. Our challenges are unique—almost—to this particular moment in time that we're living through. Historians like to say that people, for the most part, are products of their times. Well, we live in some interestingly disruptive times, and we aren't sure yet what kind of people they are making us into.

Today, Americans are richer than we've ever been. Actually, we're richer than any people have ever been, anywhere. And not just today's super-rich. The median American household is richer than any general population has ever been. Annual median household income in this country is stunningly high—about $60,000 per family per year.

And yet—counterintuitively—all across the country, in cities and small towns, Northeast and Southwest, this racial group and that, despite our unprecedented wealth, we're stressed out and unhappy. A February 2019 Gallup survey found that a hefty share of Americans are worried "most" or "all" of the time about our financial present and future. But it's not just concerns about money—*happiness* is on the decline among Americans across all sorts of noneconomic metrics, too. How is it that we can be so well off and so ticked off at the same time?

Americans are also freer than we've ever been. By "freedom," in this sense, I don't just mean the freedoms fought for by the Founders, preserved in our Constitution, and protected by the men and women of our armed forces. I mean that we are also "free" to transcend our circumstances by means of the small devices we all carry around. Our smartphones have the ability to take us out of our surroundings, and give us the freedom to look up anything anywhere in the world, to talk to anyone in almost any country, to pull up thousands of years and scores of nations-worth of human knowledge. Only a few decades ago, the world's most expensive, gymnasium-sized computers, spitting out punch cards, could accomplish only a fraction of what the technology in your hand now does in milliseconds.

But—again counterintuitively—this freedom to shrink the world is actually making us *less* connected to each other and to our communities.

Our ability to be "free from" constraints is also making it harder for us to be "free to" participate in sustained, meaningful projects together. Our limitless technology is transforming us into nomadic, rootless people. How easy is it for any of us, instead of being present with a friend or a spouse, to tune out by getting lost in our isolating screens? How easy is it for us as parents to give our kids an iPad to drug them into silence for a bit? It's *so* easy to tune our world out, we often do it without even thinking. We look to pass the time rather than redeem it.

The old saying that "money can't buy happiness" is true. What really makes us happy is the security that comes from meaningful roots—our sense of connectedness to the people and places around us. As those roots erode, national happiness goes down. The data is clear about this. And if we're not careful, we can use the disposable income we get from being the richest people on Earth in ways that only further this rootlessness, hurting our neighbors and ourselves in lasting ways.

The damage is being inflicted in ways we may not even notice, but that doesn't make it any less deadly. The erosion of our roots is affecting our friendships, our jobs, our families, our health, and our very vitality.

In 1990, the average American had between three and four deep friendships. Today, the average American has fewer than two friends. How did we manage a reduction in friendships by nearly 50 percent in only thirty years?

First of all, it helps to know what we mean by friendship. I certainly don't mean Washington friendships, like when senators refer to "my good friend, the distinguished senator from Vermont" when they and everybody watching knows the only reason they stood up in the first place was to rip the face off of the senator from Vermont. And I don't mean Facebook "friends," either, whose interaction with us is based on clicks and "likes" and emojis sent back and forth. That can be passing fun, sure, but it's not true friendship.

I'm talking about what Aristotle called "the friendship of the good," or "perfect friendship." He didn't mean you have to be a perfect person, or even a perfect friend, to enjoy this kind of relationship. What Aristotle describes is a kind of friendship among people who respect one another, who share common values, who want to help each other and see one another succeed not for their own advantage, but for the other person's sake.

That kind of friendship is proving harder to cultivate in a digital age. Aristotle himself recognized that "such friendship requires time and familiarity." You have to be intentional about making it work in the first place, and diligent about maintaining it. The data show that these kinds of friendships get harder to maintain as we get older. Tragically, 40 percent of Americans have just one confidant, or none at all.

By age 65, nearly two-thirds of men say their wife is their best friend, but fewer than one-third of women at the same age say the same thing about their husbands. Why the gap? It turns out that most men have been in atrophying relationships for decades by retirement age, and replacing few of them. So they typically just have fewer candidates for deep friendships. For most men, it turns out, a significant share of their close friendships are forged with the folks they work alongside. And as the experience of working in America tends to become shorter in duration, and more rootless, we risk losing the friendships that come with working side by side toward a common purpose year after year.

A rootless work experience is a product of the "disruption" that has become a byword for today's economy. When I was a kid in the 1970s, primary breadwinners stayed at the same firm for an average of two and a half decades. Today, that average is down to four years, and the trend is pointed further downward. The major reason for this is that we—as natural problem-solvers now armed with bigger tools—are systematically innovating ourselves out of our jobs. The technological revolution we're living through is allowing humans to find ways to make machines do more and more of our work for us. As automation expands to more and more sectors of the economy, our output goes up (which is good) but more and more people find their careers in upheaval (which is not good).

This has far-reaching consequences besides some folks simply losing their job. Having to change jobs means a gap in your health insurance, usually for nearly six months. If you change jobs every four years like the average American, that means you're likely spending up to one-eighth of your time walking around without insurance, which just might be when a car accident or cancer diagnosis rears its head.

What's harder to measure, but just as important, is the loss of the idea of calling—of vocation—of finding a profession or trade or craft that you could devote yourself to for most of your working life. During the last upheaval of this scale, the Industrial Revolution, the concept of adolescence changed radically. Teenagers' mission became finding the job they wanted to take when they left school, the paid calling they would stick with for the next several decades until they retired. Now, with an increasingly rootless work culture, it follows that a longer-term identity crisis, a pervading sense of unease, is plaguing the American workforce. All of us yearn to be called to something bigger than ourselves, yet most of us, most of the time, aren't hearing that call at work.

The crisis is hitting us at home, too. What we know as the "nuclear family"—Mom, Dad, and kids—is crumbling across America. And it's partly because American fathers are increasingly rootless. Today, 40 percent of American children are growing up without a dad. That cuts across all races, socioeconomic classes, geographical areas, and every other distinction. It's even worse among younger adults. When a woman aged 30 or younger gives birth, there is now a majority probability that that baby will have no meaningful, consistent connection to their father.

I can think of no greater looming crisis in American life than this spiking fatherlessness. Our next generation is being hobbled in ways we can only imagine. There are obviously many single mothers out there who do a wonderful job against the odds, but American men are drifting away from their ultimate responsibility at an alarming rate. We are setting ourselves up for a generational crisis, and I pray for the kids who find themselves in this situation through no fault of their own. They're going to need our help.

The family crisis is going to make itself most felt in the next generation, but our own isn't doing so well either. If you are reading this, you have just lived through the first three-year consecutive decline in life expectancy for Americans in a century. Maybe you know someone who didn't live through it.

From 2016 through 2017 to 2018, we've seen the worst decrease in American life expectancy since we've been keeping track of this data. The closest we came to this was a two-year dip in the early 1960s, and that was because of a freak flu pandemic that swept the nation from the fall of 1962 to the spring of 1963. And this decrease over three consecutive years is in spite of us being the richest, most powerful nation in the world, and in spite of individual Americans being richer than ever.

This unexpected downturn is confusing, because most of our typical health indicators paint a better picture: Longevity for 80-year-olds is up. Longevity for 85-year-olds is up. Infant mortality rates are flat. Heart disease and cancer—by far our two largest killers—are being beaten by better treatments. Fantastic medical innovations are saving and prolonging more lives. And yet life expectancy in the United States is headed in the wrong direction. Why? How?

The sad reality behind our life expectancy decline is an increase in deaths of despair. Americans, particularly American men, are killing themselves, either directly with suicide or indirectly through the abuse of opioids and other addictive substances. Males between 20 and 55 years old—men in the prime of life—are dying at unprecedented rates, and they're doing it to themselves. They're doing it because they lack hope. We lack purpose. In many communities, there are no jobs, stores have shut down, and everybody seems to have given up. This, for many, is the end of rootlessness: homelessness.

It's easy for people in Washington or elsewhere on the coasts to think of this as a problem confined to places like Appalachia and the Midwest. But it is happening everywhere. It's easy enough for many Americans to keep this disastrous national trend at arm's length until some "nice kid" from a "good family" in an upscale suburb dies of a heroin overdose. The truth is, it's all of our problem. And the communities where it is most rampant are the ones at the forefront of our crisis of rootlessness. They offer a warning for our future.

I hate to paint a grim picture, but when we're living through an epidemic of suicides—both intentionally and gradually—we should be digging into what is happening. And as I agreed with the gentleman in the airport, there's no way all of us just saying "please" and "thank you" more often will solve any of this. The strictest observation of all decorum and protocol is not going to build a true friendship, give hope to an unemployed 50-year-old worker, bring back an absent father, or save a life threatened by addiction.

* * *

This book doesn't pretend to have all the answers, but we should get to some common agreement that our political problems are downstream from bigger economic, technological, and cultural problems. If we're going to take some steps in the right direction, we're going to need to have a lot more communities engaged in a much bigger conversation about root causes.

For many of our neighbors in the most disrupted communities, facing addition and with divided families, these challenges seem almost insurmountable. And for us collectively, it often feels like we're so divided that we can't possibly deliberate on any of this effectively together. I believe that we can—but we should also acknowledge that the guy at the airport food court was right: Just being a little more civil to each other isn't going to fix the underlying causes of what ails us. We have genuinely hard work in front of us.

History can be a bit of a guide—because it turns out that we've faced a crisis of social capital amid technological disruption with

xiv   PREFACE TO THE PAPERBACK EDITION

parallels to our present struggles once before. When I said earlier that our moment is "almost" unique, that was on purpose.

In the first two decades of the twentieth century, America was in crisis. Average Americans—everyone but the Gilded Age plutocrats—were adjusting to the economic effects of the Industrial Revolution. Our society was undergoing a massive shift from an agrarian economy to an industrial one, and that meant a mass expansion of our cities, the industrial centers. Socially, we had a hard time catching up with the changing nature of work and the massive migrations from thick local communities to anonymous cities anchored on imposing factories. Alcohol abuse exploded. Social capital collapsed, people had difficulty adjusting to their new jobs and new environments, and they turned to the bottle, especially teenagers and young adults.

And what happened next? In 1919, prohibition was enacted by constitutional amendment. Then, as now, the process of getting any amendment passed is extraordinarily difficult, just as the Founders intended. To pull it off, the measure has to have massive popular support. There wasn't much in the way of opinion polling then, but some historians estimate that perhaps 85 percent of the public was in favor of prohibition. Clearly, the people felt drastic action was necessary.

I'm obviously not calling for a ban on booze today. But I am calling for us to recognize that people faced with a similarly daunting social and cultural crisis responded by turning to politics with greater zeal and less patience. We shouldn't be surprised that so many of our neighbors are again looking to Washington with a strange mixture of hope and rage.

In my humble opinion, while politics obviously matters, most of what we're dealing with right now doesn't originate in politics—and thus cannot be solved by politics either. The power to tackle the social capital deficit plaguing us is going to need to come from the people, rebuilding in hundreds of ways in a hundred thousand communities. And our roots are strongest when they're fused together.

Oh, and two more places where the guy in the airport and I also agreed: Being civil is definitely better than being uncivil—but being civil is much more a consequence than a cause of a healthy citizenry.

MORE POLITICS CAN'T FIX THIS

IF THEY EVER FIGURE OUT TIME TRAVEL, I HAVE MY LIST ready.

There are certain moments in history I would love to see and hear. Socrates teaching in the marketplace in Athens. Luther nailing his ninety-five theses to the door at Wittenberg. General Cornwallis surrendering to the upstart American rebels at Yorktown. Harriet Tubman whispering across the fence to a soon-to-be-freed slave for the first time. There are certain moments that changed history forever.

I'm not supposed to say that, as a historian. The job of the historian is usually to be a spoilsport. It says so right there on the back of our "Professional Historian" identification card. I'm supposed to point out that these moments are few and far between, that most of human history has been pretty ho-hum, that the odds that the times we happened to be born into are genuinely world-changing are . . . slim, and that the only reason we think our times are special is because we're narcissists, every last one of us. Lots of historians are now even certain the great moments weren't all that great: Socrates was just another wise guy trying to scrape together a buck, et cetera. It's a profession of party-poopers.

But here, in this book, I'd like to propose that we really do, in fact, live during one of the most extraordinary moments in human history. We're living through a revolution that is going to utterly transform the ways we live and work. We're living through an up-heaval that will arguably dwarf the disruption our nation experienced a century and a half ago, when we morphed from an agricultural society into an industrial one. We're living through an unprecedented explosion of innovation.

Just take a quick inventory of what's in your pocket: namely, a supercomputer.

At this moment, you're connected to 2 billion people worldwide through Facebook—over one-fourth of the population of the planet. Have a question for someone in Argentina? Four hundred years ago, a message from the king of Spain to his royal governors in the Americas took months to arrive. Today, it takes seconds. (In fact, the king of Spain is on Twitter: @CasaReal.)

Do you need turn-by-turn directions through Timbuktu? No problem. (And you'll need them—I've been there, and the sand is constantly in your eyes—among other places.) You can even have those directions read to you in Morgan Freeman's glorious voice. But if driving is too much of a hassle, you can just order a ride from your phone ("Phil is arriving now!"), and use real-time satellite imagery to give him tips on dodging police on your journey.

Are the in-laws driving you crazy? You can catch the seventh inning from Wrigley under the table. (Just nod politely every now and then.)

It's all there, and more, in your hand.

At the height of the Cold War, MIT had big contracts from the Department of Defense to help manage our targeting exercises to prepare for a nuclear exchange with the Soviets. The computers they created—at the time, the most sophisticated machines ever invented—were the size of a gymnasium. And they were 2 percent as useful as the average iPhone or Android. (Additional fun fact: there's more computing power in the average digital washing machine today than was used to put the first man on the moon in 1969.)

We've become accustomed to instantaneous answers and moment-to-moment connectedness. But the digital revolution that is making it possible was unthinkable just fifty years ago.

We're the richest, most comfortable, most connected people in human history.

And yet . . .

In the midst of extraordinary prosperity, we're also living through a crisis. Our communities are collapsing, and people are feeling more isolated, adrift, and purposeless than ever before.

We're not talking much about this crisis. Nonetheless, we all have a sense that something's not right. Our marriages aren't satisfying, our kids seem hypnotized. We quietly feel that adulthood has been a disappointment. We sense that somewhere along the way, everything went off the rails.

* * *

We have a crisis in this nation, and it has nothing to do with regulatory reform or marginal tax rates. This book is not going to be about politics. (Sorry to disappoint.) It's about something deeper and more meaningful. Something a little harder to quantify but a lot more personal.

Despite the astonishing medical advances and technological leaps of recent years, average life span is in *decline* in America for the third year in a row. This is the first time our nation has had even a two-year drop in life expectancy since 1962—when the cause was an influenza epidemic. Normally, declines in life expectancy are due to something big like that—a war, or the return of a dormant disease.

But what's the "big thing" going on in America now? What's killing all these people?

The 2016 data point to three culprits: Alzheimer's, suicides, and unintentional injuries—a category that includes drug and alcohol–related deaths. Two years ago, 63,632 people died of overdoses. That's 11,000 more than the previous year, and it's more than the number of Americans killed during the entire twenty-year Vietnam War. It's almost twice the number killed in automobile accidents annually, which had been the leading American killer for decades. In 2016, there were 45,000 suicides, a thirty-year high—and the sobering climb shows no signs of abating: the percentage of young people hospitalized for suicidal thoughts and actions has doubled over the past decade.[1]

We're killing ourselves, both on purpose and accidentally. These aren't deaths from famine, or poverty, or war.

We're literally dying of despair.

And this is not even to mention the data about how we're having less sex and making fewer babies—both of which are, across history, signs of diminished hope in the future.

It turns out that the massive economic disruption that we entered a couple of decades ago and will be navigating for decades to come is depriving us psychologically and spiritually at the same time that it's enriching us materially. The same technology that has liberated us from so much inconvenience and drudgery has also unmoored us from the things that anchor our identities. The revolution that has given tens of millions of Americans the opportunity to live like historic royalty has also outpaced our ability to figure out what community, friendships, and relationships should look like in the modern world. As reams of research now show, we're richer and better-informed and more connected—and unhappier and more isolated and less fulfilled.

There is a terrible mismatch here.

We're in crisis.

* * *

I love to run with my kids.

In a uniquely memorable half-marathon two years ago, one of my daughters, then age 12, projectile-vomited just short of mile thirteen. I don't mean she got down on a knee behind a tree; I mean she made a giant splash in the middle of a crowd. But this kid has a will of steel; I knew she wasn't dropping out that close to the end. I was proud of her as she dug deep and continued to put one foot in front of the other. But I was also scanning the road ahead for water stations. It's important to stay hydrated even if you haven't decorated your shoes, but I knew water was going to be new life for her. When we saw a table up ahead—manned by friendly people extending encouragement along with their paper cups—it was like seeing an oasis in the desert. We knew we were among friends.

When the Lincoln (Nebraska) Marathon came around last year, my team and I set up a water station like we do every May. We like to greet and encourage the 14,000-plus Midwesterners who lace up. I enjoy the marathon vibe: people coming out of their houses with coffee in hand to cheer on the runners, neighbors high-fiving strangers as they struggle by, dogs taking advantage of the Gatorade dribbling from discarded cups in the streets, homeowners setting up lawn sprinklers to provide some relief from the heat. Although I would have preferred to be running with my kids, I admit that sometimes it's nice to be the one handing out the water rather than the one in desperate need of it.

We had an ideal spot on Sheridan Avenue, a beautiful old boulevard with tall elms and oaks lining the road. Our station was just past mile marker four, so some runners slowed down to enjoy the shade before tackling the miles ahead. I often have my kids with me as I work across the state, and my 6-year-old son was there that morning. Some of our friends had brought their kids with them as well. Our dozens of volunteers delighted in the race, and the kids delighted in the challenge of keeping the water cups filled.

Shortly before the first runners arrived, a small group of people set themselves up across the street from us. Protesters, with signs—a familiar sight for anyone in office. But this was different. As the first runners approached our water station, holding out hands for a cup, the protesters began to shriek, clutching at their throats: "It's poison! It's poison! Don't drink it! He wants you to die!"

The runners flinched. The shrieking continued, as waves and waves of runners arrived. Some ignored the scene, but many declined a water cup with a soft, uncomfortable "I'm sorry." Nothing sours the occasion like murder charges.

Thinking back on it more than a year later, that morning still leaves a bad taste in my mouth. I've now had enough nasty experiences in my nearly four years in office to develop a thick skin. I've had property vandalized and blood thrown on my office door. I've had death threats credible enough to require police visits. I've had interview video selectively edited and then pushed on social media. A conspiracy theory circulated that I had masterminded a human trafficking network in Omaha (the rocket scientists behind that narrative failed to catch that the alleged ring began before I was born). My wife has had angry constituents show up at our front door; my kids have heard me cussed out during family meals at restaurants. But that marathon moment was uniquely painful.

These folks planned and organized to show up in the morning at a water station at an amateur race to scream at runners that they were *being poisoned*. Why? Because we don't see eye-to-eye on every policy issue? How do you explain that to a bunch of confused young kids?

Something is really wrong here.

But truth be told, I don't think the protesters were actually yelling like that because we have different positions on policy. Something deeper is going on.

* * *

In 2007, my wife had a fluke aneurysm, which in turn produced three strokes. For two months, there was a decent chance Melissa would die.

We'd been married twelve years, and I was in shock that my best friend and the mother of our young children might not survive. For the first couple of weeks, I sat in the hospital day and night beside her, my life frozen. I wasn't paying my bills, getting the mail, sleeping, showering enough. The list of ugly was long. I forgot that I had left my car—back on day one at the hospital—in a spot that would become part of a rush-hour lane the following morning. After tickets and towing, that mistake ended up running to about $800. Life was suddenly too big for us, even the small stuff.

One night, I decided to get some fresh air. I went to a TGI Fridays a block from the hospital, so I could order some food that didn't come on a metal tray. I stood in the waiting area—and stood—and kept standing. The host had overlooked me, several times, and seated other parties. All I wanted was to get my name on the list, so I could eat some food and get back before the doctor returned. Yet, there I stood—alone in the dark waiting area. Ignored. Suddenly, the anger welled up.

"Excuse me," I said, my pulse humming. "Don't you see me?" Then, I proceeded to let him know how he'd mistreated me and exactly what I thought of it. This wasn't any YouTube–worthy, viral video rant—but it was still a mistake. As a kid and then in college, I had had a bunch of jobs—from stadium vending to retail to painting dilapidated houses—that required me to interact with angry folks on occasion. I'd resolved not to be one of them. I've never once sent food back in a huff with the chef. I've always felt solidarity with any TGI Fridays server, not with the jackwagon reaming him out. But . . .

. . . there I was: the jackwagon. As the host rushed to put me on the list, I felt embarrassed. I hadn't yelled, but I'd been rude to a guy for a simple mistake. I needed to apologize to him.

This stranger wasn't my problem. My problems were the stacks of bills and the confused kids and the uncertainty. *My wife might die.* I felt lonely and powerless. I didn't mean to get upset—but here, finally, was a problem I could fix. I could get my name on the dang list. I could get something to go my way. For a few seconds, I had the relief of a scapegoat, someone I could blame.

* * *

One of the rewarding things about being an elected official is getting to meet and listen to Americans who love our country and are concerned for our future. But the most common conversation I have with patriotic Americans these days—the most common, by far—is depressing rather than uplifting. I get the question endlessly when I'm out and about in Nebraska: "Why can't you guys in D.C. just get some commonsense stuff done?" (Sometimes it's an order: "You people need to do your eff'ing job!")

When I talk with people one on one or in small groups, it becomes clear how the dysfunction in D.C. is affecting their lives: "I don't know what to plant if I don't know if there will be crop insurance this summer. You get that, right?" "Why can't you all do a commonsense infrastructure investment bill without breaking the bank? I'm a trucker, but I'd pay more gas tax for better roads and bridges." "How is it fair to kids brought here as babies—through no choice of their own—to wonder if they're gonna get deported? And how is that complicated mess an excuse for not securing the border?" "Shouldn't my son, who's been deployed to Afghanistan *three* times, know what our actual plan is in a war that started seventeen years ago?" "Why do we *never* have a budget?" "Will the annual spending bill happen in the middle of the night on the eve of a government shutdown *again* this year?"

This book is not about politics—but it is at least tangentially about the question "Why can't you guys in D.C. get anything done?"

Citizens are right to be discouraged. Governing really does always seem to take a backseat to partisan screaming and point-scoring. I see it up close every week, and nearly a dozen different senators (from both parties), just in recent months, have confessed to me that they wonder if we're "wasting our lives." Contrary to a popular misconception, no one runs for Senate to get rich, and the near-constant travel away from family makes most of the thoughtful folks here wonder things like—to quote one of my colleagues—"whether this is a responsible way for a grown-ass man to spend his time."

But I notice, too, that constituents are rarely just interested in solutions; they're also interested in assigning blame. I have been regularly informed by Nebraskans that our dismal situation is the fault of Mitch McConnell ("boo!") or Elizabeth Warren ("hiss!")—or any of a dozen others, on either side of the political spectrum, whose names have taken on a sort of talismanic role: shorthand for all sorts of diabolical scheming.

Political discontent is nothing new in American history, of course. But there's something different about the way Americans view policymakers today. Answer honestly: Do you have a visceral reaction when you read any of these names: Nancy Pelosi, Paul Ryan, Harry Reid, John Boehner, Chuck Schumer? Many people do. The assumption now isn't just that folks are incompetent but that they are evil.

We *really* don't like each other, do we?

There's an interesting military phenomenon that applies to this political moment—and even to my TGI Fridays outburst. In urban combat training, there is a well-documented tendency to shift our focus from a distant but important target to a less important but closer target. If you're being attacked and your threat is fifty yards away, but a closer target pops up, you'll turn your attention to the new target—even if it's less of a threat. We tend to want to knock down the easier stuff. Conversely, we want to ignore or deny challenges that are farther out or more difficult.

It seems clear that in America today, we're facing problems that feel too big for us, so we're lashing out at each other, often over less important matters. Many of us are using politics as a way to distract ourselves from the nagging sense that something bigger is wrong. Not many of us would honestly argue that if our "side" just had more political power, we'd be able to fix what ails us. Fortunately, we can avoid addressing the big problems as long as someone else—some nearer target—is standing in the way of our securing the political power even to try. It's easier to shriek at the people on the other side of the street. It's comforting to be able to pin the problems on the freaks in the pink hats or the weirdos carrying the pro-life signs.

At least our contempt unites us with other Americans who think like we do.

At least *we* are not like *them*.

I'm not sure what caused those protesters to tell marathon runners that I was feeding them poison, but I am sure it wasn't my position on the omnibus spending bill. (I was against that monstrosity, by the way.)

We're angry, and politics is filling a vacuum it was never intended to fill. Suddenly, all of America feels marginalized and ignored. We're all standing there in the dark, feeling powerless and isolated, pleading: "Don't you see me?"

Why are we so angry?

* * *

Melissa and I married just after college in 1994, and my first postgraduation job took me all over the country. Because we didn't want to be apart, and since she was eminently employable as a science teacher willing to work in rough schools, we decided to follow my gigs from place to place, rather than hassle with constant commuting. And so, for our first decade of marriage, we bounced back and forth across the country, two nomads with frequent-renter cards at U-Haul. In just over ten years, we paid taxes in a dozen states.

However, when we started thinking about the children we hoped to bring into the world, we knew we didn't want them growing up on the move. We wanted them to grow up in a close-knit neighborhood. We wanted our kids to live where they knew people, and where they were known. We envisioned other parents helping keep an eye on them. We saw, in our mind's eye, Little League and Main Street and familiar faces in the church pews. I imagined something similar to my own childhood.

In Fremont, Nebraska, in the 1970s and 1980s parents had a sort of informal alliance—adults versus kids, the community versus chaos. While my friends and I were free to roam the whole town on bikes, we knew that lots of the adults in town had been empowered by our parents to guide and correct our behavior. Twice in the first few weeks after I learned to drive, I arrived home to find Dad ready to quiz me about choices I had made at specific intersections. Other adults in town had already phoned in my ill-advised decisions. I didn't enjoy getting caught, but there was a sense of "we." The town was in it together.

Now, ready to begin our own family, Melissa and I wanted to find a place like that. But it seemed to exist only in my memory.

At first, we wondered if we couldn't find it because we had been wandering for too long. Maybe we were like the characters in a dozen country music songs, doomed to ramble because we'd warped our souls.

But as we met with college friends who were also looking to "settle down," we discovered that they were wrestling with the same anxiety. Perhaps it was because they, too, had been transients. But then I started talking about things with high school friends, some of whom had never left our Nebraska farm town—and they offered their own troubling reports. They said that if you go to a game at our high school gym on the weekend something's different—less community, less enthusiasm. Elementary school kids aren't packed in the stands, imagining what it'll be like when they're old enough to wear the black and gold. They're not off to the side, working on their own crossover dribble with friends. And, after 2007, if kids huddled together at all, it was just each child "parallel playing" with their own phone or iPad—"alone together," to quote social scientist Sherry Turkle.[2]

What was going on? What had happened to the tight-knit places so many of us had called home? Had the new popularity of sports like soccer and lacrosse—and the rise of year-round sports specialization—fractured the hometown basketball and football crowds? Is our disjointed feeling caused by having too many cable television channels, so that no one watches the same shows anymore? Has social media "friendship" changed our understanding of, and attention to, real-life friendship? Do the bigger houses we live in today—more than three times as large as sixty years ago, on average—offer us comfort but also generate isolation? Has our upsized real estate contributed to the rise of messy exurban sprawl at the expense of small towns and inner cities, with their town squares and neighborhood centers? I started looking into the studies of consumerism and "overchoice."

All these factors are part of the complicated explanation, but the net result is simple: Most Americans just don't have community cohesion like we used to. We don't feel that we're connected to our neighbors in any meaningful ways. We don't feel like we're part of something bigger. No longer are parents keeping an eye out for the roving bands of kids, making sure they aren't up to no good. No longer is the town packing the stands for the game.

This isn't a nostalgia-induced lament that can be condensed to the old adage, "You can't go home again." Rather, it's an exploration of why America seems to be tearing apart at the seams. This isn't primarily about Republicans or Democrats. Most policymakers don't seem to understand what's happening—and they certainly don't have any grand answers. It has to do with the deep bonds that join people together, that give their lives richness and meaning—and the fact that those bonds are fraying.

We can't fix this with new legislation. We don't need a new program, a new department, one more election. If our 2016 presidential election was the most lurid and dismaying election of our lifetime—and it was, without a doubt, a five-alarm dumpster fire—it was still only the consequence of deeper problems, not their cause. If we could wave a magic wand and make all of the political acrimony disappear, it might bankrupt some of the cable news networks, but it wouldn't do much to fill the hole millions of Americans feel in their lives right now. Getting rid of political strife would be like whitening the yellowed teeth of a smoker. It would simply erase one characteristic of a toxic situation, camouflaging problems that go much deeper.

What we need are new habits of mind and heart. We need new practices of neighborliness. We need to get our hands dirty replenishing the soil that nourishes rooted, purposeful lives. But how?

* * *

While Melissa and I were coming to the gut-punch realization that the in-it-together community in which we wanted to raise our babies might no longer exist, I happened across an article in *Sports Illustrated* that used the beautifully bizarre compound adjective, "that hometown-gym-on-a-Friday-night feeling."

That was it.

The "hometown-gym-on-a-Friday-night feeling" was what I'd known as a kid. My dad was a football and wrestling coach, and he had keys to the basketball gym, so my buddies and I logged enough hours there that it came to feel like an extension of our homes. (When President Trump accused me in 2016 of "looking like a gym rat," my family beamed with pride. There is no higher compliment.) On Friday nights, my family would pile into the car and we'd drive down to Fremont High. The community assembled in the gym. Those game nights were the best.

Obviously, we cared whether the basketball team had a winning or losing record—but there were more important concerns. The gym was packed either way—with bankers and farmers, nurses and preachers, teachers and parents who the teachers wanted to "have a word with." There were no rich and poor there—there were only Fremont Tigers. Everyone showed up for games, not just families of current athletes. I used to think of those bleachers as "homeroom" for the town: the place where everyone gathered, made plans, swapped news and gossip, and solidified friendships. I have faint recollections of discussions of Ronald Reagan and Jimmy Carter, but I always had the sense that those discussions were far subordinate to the stuff that really mattered.

People walked away from political conversations without thinking ill of each other, because that kind of talk *happened in the context of actual relationships* centered around local things that were a lot more important.

Right now partisan tribalism is statistically higher than at any point since the Civil War. Why? It's certainly not because our political discussions are more important. It's because the local, human relationships that anchored political talk have shriveled up. Alienated from each other, and uprooted from places we can call *home*, we're reduced to shrieking.[3]

So, the first third of this book is about the collapse of the local tribes that give us true, meaningful identity—family, workplace, and neighborhood. It's about the evaporation of social capital—the reservoir of relationships that help us navigate the world—and about the precipitous decline in recent years of the institutions that Alexis de Tocqueville, nearly two hundred years ago, saw as the heart and soul of America. It's about the waning influence of the Rotary Club and the Scouts, the VFW and the local bowling league. It's about the mountain of data showing that shut-ins are getting fewer casseroles with instructions written on a notecard: *Bake at 325 until brown on top!*

This book is not about legislative failures in Washington, D.C. This book is about the death of Little League in River City.

The second part will gesture toward some of our cultural fights, but I'm not trying to persuade anyone about politics in this book. Rather, we'll explore how *anti-tribes*—of news consumption more than political activism—have cropped up to try to fill the void left by the collapse of the natural, local, embodied, healthy tribes people have traditionally known.*

These anti-tribes aren't succeeding at addressing our emptiness, and they're poisoning our nation's spirit in critical ways. But lacking meaningful attachments, people are finding a perverse bond in at least sharing a common enemy.

The third and final part of the book asks what we can do about it. If America is going to survive—and that's never an assumption to be taken for granted in a republic—we will have to find a way to restore the bonds of community that give individuals a place in the world where they can enjoy the love of family and friends, express their talents, and serve others in fulfilling ways. Chapter 5 explores what it would look like to recommit to America's history of principled pluralism. We want an America with free speech, religion, press, assembly, and protest—even for those we disagree with. In spite of the endless disagreements that flow from diversity, we want to be *free to* build local communities where we shoulder one another's burdens in compassion and generosity. Chapter 6 looks at the habits required to live in community in a digital age that constantly promises us we can be *free from* real places and real people. That's a sham. If we really want to be happy, we must plant roots and tend them. That means, in large part, thinking carefully about how to get the best out of the technology that liberates us from inconveniences—without letting our devices cut us off from the richest parts of life. (As we'll see, that task is becoming especially pressing as genuinely bad actors look to exploit our problems by manipulating new technologies to further undermine our interests.) Chapter 7 wrestles with the ways our lonely generations are segregating themselves from one another—and the refusal, among many, to accept the reality of aging bodies and ultimately death. Finally, Chapter 8 suggests how we might

---

* Most of my examples in these chapters (both explanatory and critical) will come from the right. They will also come from small towns, and often involve sports. That's entirely a product of circumstance. I'm a sports-loving Republican from a small town and I represent a state that's gone overwhelmingly Republican in every presidential election cycle since 1968. I simply know the world of the right better. But liberals and non-sports fans from big cities should rest easy: I'm assured, usually with a shake of the head and a long, frustrated sigh, that we are all sharing the same noxious issues.

rebuild our crumbling institutions over the coming decades. Just as institutions were rebuilt to accommodate the urbanization and industrialization that swept the country 150 years ago, so too will we need to go about rebuilding institutions of community and trust for our mobile age. We will focus here primarily on how housing might be adapted to a mobile age, but soon we will also need to ask: How might secondary and higher education lend themselves better to our new economic modes? How might we rethink midcareer retraining as job turnover becomes more frequent and as more people become permanent freelancers? And as life expectancy increases and workers retire earlier, how will people more meaningfully benefit from productive service to friends and neighbors in their golden years?

* * *

Above all, this book is an urgent call to name the problem that's ripping us apart.

It's not taxes or tweets; it's not primarily politics or polarization; it's neither an unpredictable president nor the #Resistance that wants to impeach him. It's not a new bill or a blue-ribbon commission. The real culprit has less to do with us as a polity and everything to do with us as uprooted, wandering souls.

Our world is nudging us toward *rootlessness*, when only a recovery of *rootedness* can heal us. What's wrong with America, then, starts with one uncomfortable word.

Loneliness.

PART I

COLLAPSING TRIBES

Without friends no one would choose to live, even if he had all other goods.

—Aristotle

1

OUR LONELINESS EPIDEMIC

Why the Chicago Heat Wave Isn't Capitalized
Loneliness Kills ⚘ Not All Depression Is Depression
The Prophet of Social Capital ⚘ The Scissors Graph Society
Haves and Have-Nots ⚘ Fathers and Margins for Error
Can We Admit the *Goodnight Moon* Gap Yet?
The Parent Lottery ⚘ How to Be Happy

IN THE SUMMER OF 1995, CHICAGO EXPERIENCED THE DEADLI-
est heat wave in U.S. history. For seven days in July, the upper Midwest sweltered under three-digit temperatures, and the Windy City
had no wind. The *Chicago Tribune* compared the humidity to "roasting under a wet wool blanket." On Thursday the 13th, the mercury
sat at 106 degrees, but the heat index cracked 120 at Midway Airport. Temperatures fell at night, but only to the high 80s. I've been
in Middle Eastern cities on 115-degree days, but this was worse.[1]

Chicago wasn't built for this kind of heat. Many residents didn't
have air conditioning, and those who did ran their units so relentlessly that parts of the power grid collapsed. Electricity went out
around the city, leaving people to bake in brick apartments.

Heat exhaustion takes a terrible toll on the body. An elevated
heart rate, muscle cramps, and nausea can be accompanied by

fainting, seizures, and hallucinations. Most people can manage 48 hours of intense heat, but after that the weakened body begins to fail. Without medical attention, the kidneys and other vital organs shut down.

Chicago's hospitals and morgues filled, and the Cook County medical examiner was forced to store human remains in rented freezer trucks. Coroners initially counted 465 dead, but many of the dead weren't discovered until weeks later, when the stench of decomposition oozed from homes and apartments. Researchers would eventually tie 739 deaths to the week's weather.

Chances are, you've never heard of this extraordinary episode, and I likely wouldn't have either except that Melissa and I were living in Chicago at the time. We'd just gotten married and moved into a tiny apartment in Evanston, across the street from Northwestern University's football stadium. We were fortunate: Our window airconditioner managed to alleviate the scorching heat. The only ill effect we experienced was when the dashboard of Melissa's eighteen-year-old clunker cracked from daily baking in the sun.

Why the Chicago heat wave Isn't Capitalized

Researchers from the Centers for Disease Control, descending on Chicago, hoped to prepare for future heat waves by identifying which populations were most vulnerable and why. Many of their findings were unsurprising: those who lacked air conditioning died at higher rates; the elderly and the sick were at greatest risk; and among the elderly and the sick, those without caretaker relationships, or without ready and reliable access to transportation, fared worst.

But sociologist Eric Klinenberg found himself puzzled by one part of the story: How was it that so many people could die unnoticed in a city of 2.8 million citizens? Klinenberg began an investigation that lasted more than five years. His initial findings simply echoed those of the CDC. But then he struck on something surprising: At a glance, three of the ten neighborhoods with the *lowest* number of heat-related deaths, Klinenberg found, looked demographically just like the neighborhoods with the highest number—predominantly poor, violent, and African-American. Race and poverty could not fully account for who died and who survived.

The crucial variable, Klinenberg discovered, was social relationships. In neighborhoods that fared well during the heat wave, residents "knew who was alone, who was old, and who was sick," and took it upon themselves to do "wellness checks." They "encouraged neighbors to knock on each other's doors—not because the heat wave was so exceptional, but because that's what they always do." By contrast, areas with high death tolls were areas that previously had been "abandon[ed] . . . by businesses, service providers, and most residents"; only "the unconnected" remained. They died alone because they lived alone. In the final analysis, the difference between life and death, Klinenberg's *Heat Wave: A Social Autopsy of Disaster in Chicago* concluded, was *connections*—or what he labeled "social infrastructure." Isolation turned something dangerous into something deadly.[2]

More than two decades later, schoolchildren across the country still know the tale of how in 1871 Mrs. O'Leary's cow kicked over a lantern, igniting a blaze that devoured Chicago, but few will ever learn about the (never capitalized) heat wave of 1995—even though it killed twice as many people as the (always capitalized) Great Chicago Fire. Why?

Part of the answer is that Currier and Ives's images of the Chicago conflagration were impressed onto the imagination of nineteenth-century America. But that's only another way of saying that the heat wave victims died out of the nation's eye, just as they lived out of their community's eye. Their deaths have gone unremembered because their lives went unnoticed.

Loneliness Kills

In classic works of literature, people often die from extraordinary rejection or loss. Shakespeare's King Lear, Ophelia, and Lady Montague die from grief; Hugo's Jean Valjean dies after losing Cosette; Tolstoy's Anna Karenina is so convinced she's unloved that she throws herself under a train.

Though it might be tempting to chalk these deaths up to literary melodrama, the American Heart Association says that death-by-heartbreak is in fact quite real. In "broken heart syndrome" (technical name: takotsubo cardiomyopathy), rejection or loss causes stress hormones to flood the body, mimicking the effects of a heart attack. "Tests show dramatic changes in rhythm and blood substances that are typical of a heart attack," the AHA reports. And, though rare, it is possible for otherwise healthy people to die from this condition. Everyone has heard of elderly couples who die within weeks or months of each other.[3]

But is loneliness an out-of-the-ordinary event? Must its consequences take the form of sudden death? What happens when loneliness builds over time? It turns out that this is precisely what is happening in the United States today, in epidemic proportions.

Eric Klinenberg's research inaugurated the "loneliness literature"—sociological and medical research into the effects of community on well-being. Scientists are now showing that loneliness affects the brains and bodies of millions of people, in measurable and alarming ways.

Breakthroughs in imaging technology are producing an explosion in what we know about the human brain. For example, neurological scans using functional magnetic resonance imaging (fMRI) show that our response to emotional rejection lights up the same brain region that registers emotional response to physical stress, giving rise to the same health effects: increased stress hormones, decreased immune function, and heart problems. So it comes as no surprise that lonely people get sick more often, take longer to recover from illness, and are at higher risk of heart attacks. According to researchers at Ohio State University and the University of Chicago, emotional stress causes us to age faster—and it turns out that chronically lonely individuals are more prone to Alzheimer's disease and dementia. Studies suggest that one lonely day exacts roughly the same toll on the body as smoking an entire pack of cigarettes.[4]

Among epidemiologists, psychiatrists, public-health officials, and social scientists, there is a growing consensus that the number one health crisis in America right now is not cancer, not obesity, and not heart disease—it's loneliness. And with our nation's aging population, it's only going to get worse.

Shakespeare and Tolstoy, it seems, were on to something. Loneliness is killing us. According to a seminal report from the Dahlem Workshop on Attachment and Bonding, "Positive social relationships are second only to genetics in predicting health and longevity in humans."[5] Brigham Young University's Julianne Holt-Lunstad has been studying data from 3.5 million Americans over nearly four decades. According to her findings, lonely, isolated people are somewhere around 25 percent more likely to die prematurely—not just from suicide (which has been spiking across multiple demographic categories in the United States in the last two decades), but from any of an array of health problems. Similarly, University of California–Irvine social ecologist Sarah Pressman has been comparing the mortality effects of loneliness to various better-understood causes, such as obesity, heavy drinking, and smoking. Persistent loneliness reduces average longevity by more than twice as much as heavy drinking and more than three times as much as obesity (in fact, loneliness drives obesity, not vice versa, as previously thought). The research of loneliness experts John T. Cacioppo and William Patrick confirms that loneliness alters behavior and physiological response in ways that are "hastening millions of people to an early grave."[6]

Men are especially at risk. One comprehensive study of 67,000 American men found that bachelors under the age of 45 were far more likely to die in a given year than their married male peers. It turns out that men, unlike women, tend to stop forming friendships once they begin careers or marry—for most men, by their early thirties—which makes them particularly susceptible to disruptions in their social networks later in life. For most men, marriage and children constitute their chief points-of-entry in adult life into any broad community, and their sources of social support atrophy quickly when those vanish. Elderly men are the loneliest demographic group in the United States. Of the lonely dead discovered in the wake of the Chicago heat wave, there were a stunning *four times more men than women*.[7]

Doctors are sounding the alarm about what public-health experts now call our "loneliness epidemic." Former U.S. surgeon general Vivek Murthy speaks widely about the physical toll of persistent loneliness. As he told the *Boston Globe*, the conclusion is clear: "The data is telling us . . . that loneliness kills."[8]

Not All Depression Is Depression

How widespread is our problem? A fifth of Americans volunteer that loneliness is "a major source of unhappiness" in their lives, and a full third of those over the age of 45 confess that "chronic loneliness" is a fundamental challenge with which they are struggling.[9]

These numbers are huge, but they actually understate the problem. Part of the difficulty of capturing the gravity of the crisis is that our terminology is fuzzy—for example, we don't consistently differentiate between "social isolation" and "loneliness." "Social isolation" is when a person objectively lacks relationships. Klinenberg and other researchers found that it's entirely possible, as in Chicago in the summer of 1995, to be socially isolated even while surrounded by millions of people. But loneliness is a more expansive category than isolation. According to psychologists, loneliness is not merely isolation or an individual's "perception of being alone and isolated," but rather the "inability to find meaning in one's life." Sociologists sometimes describe the concept as "a subjective, negative feeling related to *deficient* social relations," or the "feeling of disconnectedness" from a community of meaning. It's hard to measure, and perhaps even harder to talk about clearly.[10]

Jacqueline Olds and Richard S. Schwartz, clinical psychiatrists who also happen to be married to each other, argue in their important book, *The Lonely American*, that much of what is called "depression" might actually be chronic loneliness. They observed in their practices that many of their patients' descriptions of depression were tied to accounts of isolation. "We began to notice how hard it was for our patients to talk about their isolation, which seemed to fill them with deep shame," they write. "Most of our patients were more comfortable saying they were *depressed* than saying they were *lonely*" (their emphasis). After reading Olds and Schwartz, I began to ask psychiatrists and psychologists whether they had noticed anything like this in their own work. A flood of agreement followed.

One therapist exclaimed: "Oh, heavens, yes! The number one reason people think they're coming into my office is self-diagnosed depression. But most of the time, my conclusion is that their challenge is lack of community and healthy relationships. My fear is that my profession is just prescribing them a medication, because that's the easiest path out of the appointment."

Before continuing, let's be clear: Lots of Americans do, indeed, suffer from depression, and breakthroughs in psychotherapy methods and pharmacology have changed lives—and surely saved many. My purpose here is simply to relate what many mental-health professionals have observed: that sometimes what patients think is depression is actually a response to deep-seated loneliness.

Loneliness is surely part of the reason Americans consume almost all the world's hydrocodone (99%) and most of its oxycodone (81%). Recently, in *New York Magazine*, journalist Andrew Sullivan laid out how these drugs are often used to dull something more than physical pain—what he calls "existential pain." Explains Sullivan: "The oxytocin we experience from love or friendship or orgasm is chemically replicated by the molecules derived from the poppy plant. It's a shortcut—and an instant intensification—of the happiness we might ordinarily experience in a good and fruitful communal life." Sullivan describes a scientific experiment that compared how rats in different situations responded to the presence of an artificial stimulant (water with morphine: rodent heroin). A rat alone in his cage drank five times as much morphine water as a rat whose cage included food, colorful balls, an exercise wheel, and attractive lady-rats. "Take away the stimulus of community and all the oxytocin it naturally generates," Sullivan writes, "and an artificial variety of the substance becomes much more compelling." Every day in the United States, 116 people die from an opioid-related drug overdose. According to the CDC: "In 2016, the number of overdose deaths involving opioids (including prescription opioids and illegal opioids like heroin and illicitly manufactured fentanyl) was 5 times higher than in 1999."[11]

The natural, healthy stimulus of community is vanishing, and the damaging health effects of persistent loneliness are being compounded—by drug overuse and abuse, which now claim more lives in a year than diabetes, liver disease, pneumonia, or the flu. This is very bad and very new.

The Prophet of Social Capital

What is causing this pervasive experience of alienation? Why are so many more Americans isolated and alone than half a century ago?

To help answer these questions, there's no one better to consult than Harvard social scientist Robert Putnam, who has been chronicling the collapse of neighborly America for a quarter century. Putnam asks the big questions: What makes life livable in a big, diverse democracy like ours? What are the ties that bind us together? What causes those ties to fray or unravel? Why are so many indicators of social collapse currently spiking?

In the early 1990s, Putnam took note of a curious phenomenon: While there were more bowlers in America as a share of the population than at any time before, fewer of them were joining bowling leagues. People were *doing* various things—but they weren't doing them *together*. Putnam was teasing out the connection between community life and personal fulfillment: "Though all the evidence is not in," he wrote, "it is hard to believe that the generational decline in social connectedness and the [associated] generational increase in suicide, depression, and malaise are unrelated."[12]

Putnam used bowling leagues as his shorthand, but he found similar trends across many types of social and service organizations. From bridge clubs to alumni groups and veterans' associations, memberships were aging and nobody was joining. Between 1975 and 1995, membership in social clubs and community organizations such as the PTA, Kiwanis, and Rotary plummeted. Same with labor union membership and regular church attendance. (Recently, overall participation in youth sports leagues has dropped as well.) Locally organized churches declined, with more anonymous, commuter megachurches absorbing their members.

Some have called Putnam the "philosopher of neighborliness." He might be better described as the prophet of "social capital," the soil of meaningful relationships that helps individuals and societies flourish. Putnam noted long ago that as membership in social clubs dropped, so did socializing with friends. People stopped having friends over for dinner. Between 1975 and 1999, the average number of times Americans reported entertaining at home annually fell by nearly half—from just over 14 times to approximately 8. Likewise, inside families, there has been a marked decline of families eating and vacationing together. And with access to cheaper televisions and more square footage, families started sequestering themselves in different parts of the house to watch television separately. According to Roper poll data, even sustained conversation with friends and family fell precipitously. "It is hard not to read these figures as evidence of rapidly loosening family bonds," says Putnam. Obviously, these trends did not apply to every family. But survey after survey reveals an indisputable decline over the last three decades of the twentieth century.[13]

These trends in declining family life coincided with a broader erosion of trust in nearly every American institution—altogether, a remarkable shift from thirty years earlier. In 1965, "disrespect for public life, so endemic [previously] in our history, seemed to be waning. Americans felt increased confidence in their neighbors. The proportion that agreed that 'most people can be trusted,' for example, rose from an already high 66 percent during and after World War II to a peak of 77 percent in 1964." (Today, Pew Research puts that number closer to 30 percent, and confidence in the trustworthiness of government and government officials is somewhere in the teens, on average.) The 1950s and 1960s were hardly a golden age, of course. Segregation was the norm, infant mortality was relatively high, and strong local community sometimes entailed suffocating conformity. Nevertheless, people *across demographic categories* were optimistic about their futures, individually and collectively. "Engagement in community affairs and the sense of shared identity and reciprocity," Putnam writes, "had never been greater in modern America." The key word in Putnam's summary is *shared*. This was not mere individual optimism about economic prospects; there was shared optimism and a "sense of shared identity."[14]

Putnam's 2000 bestseller, *Bowling Alone*, brought the country's social-capital crisis into sharp relief. We're familiar with the valuable role of physical capital (e.g., land, machinery) and human capital (e.g., knowledge, skills) in a given project. "Social capital" has to do with the valuable role of human *connections* and relationships. Putnam defines it as "the connections among individuals—social networks and the norms of reciprocity and trustworthiness that arise from them." Social capital is nurtured by communities with thick bonds of trust. One of the effects of the diversification of American society in the 1960s and 1970s, which introduced new voices and interests into the national conversation—a good thing, in important ways—was to divide communities and undermine the sense of collective trust among neighbors. Putnam notes that trends in social differentiation parallel "almost precisely the decline in social capital." We are living in the aftermath of that upheaval.[15]

At first glance, it might seem that technological breakthroughs promise to mitigate our social-capital deficit. Social media companies promise new forms of community and unprecedented connectedness. But it turns out that at the same time that any Billy Bob in Boise can broadcast his opinions to thousands of people, we have fewer non-virtual friends than at any point in decades.

We're hyperconnected, and we're disconnected.

Since 1972, the General Social Survey—the gold standard dataset for American sociologists, run by the National Opinion Research Center at the University of Chicago—has kept tabs on how, and with whom, American adults live their lives. In the mid-1980s, the survey began asking people for details about their friends and confidants. According to Duke University social scientist Miller McPherson, between 1985 and 2004, Americans reported that the number of people they discussed "important matters" with dropped, on average, from three to two. Other analyses from the "friendship literature" suggest something similar.[16]

The average American has gone from more than three to fewer than two intimate, flesh-and-blood actual friends over the last three decades.

More alarmingly, the number of Americans who count no friends at all—no one in whom they confide about important matters, no one with whom they share life's joys and burdens—has soared. In the mid-2000s, one-quarter of Americans said they had no one with whom to talk about things that matter. That was *triple* the percentage from the 1980s. These trends have not slowed. McPherson and his team, by the way, had intentionally set out to disprove Putnam's arguments in *Bowling Alone*, but they were forced to admit that the broader data reinforced his troubling findings—and that the situation was perhaps even worse than he let on.

Putnam's most recent book, *Our Kids*, builds on his previous discoveries. Putnam argues that our understanding of the term "our kids" has changed in recent decades. When he was growing up, in the 1950s Midwest, if an adult said, "We need to build a pool for our kids," listeners would have heard a challenge to the moms and dads of the neighborhood to raise money for a *neighborhood* pool. The Rotary Club would have jumped into action. "Our kids" meant the children in the community, for whom parents felt a collective responsibility. But today, Putnam suggests, the same sentence refers to a *personal* pool—a construction project in the backyard, preferably fenced in from prying eyes. "Our kids" used to indicate a sense of neighborhood responsibility, in which parents kept an eye out for all the kids on the block, not just their own. Now, we retreat from the common, and the term has been pared down.[17]

The Scissors Graph Society

The confidence and trust that, according to Putnam, characterized the 1950s and early 1960s were part and parcel of a widely distributed social-capital surplus. But as social capital has vanished, certain groups have suffered disproportionately and are at risk of being thrown into multigenerational cycles of poverty and underachievement. Putnam's data make it indisputably clear that America is being split into "haves" and "have-nots," and the gap between them is growing. Children at the top have many more opportunities than children at the bottom, and—in a stark departure from the middle half of the last century—it's increasingly difficult to move up. He observes that many Americans no longer believe that hard work is enough to climb the ladder of success. From these various data, he concludes that "the American Dream [is] in crisis."

Putnam tracks and summarizes a broad range of social indicators: educational attainment, unemployment, earnings, financial worry, birth rates, family structure, extracurricular activities, diet and weight, incarceration, marriage failure, neighborhood trust, institutional trust, and more. Measure after measure shows erosion since the 1960s and 1970s.

But when Putnam takes a harder look at his data, the true state of the union comes into focus. There's been serious erosion, but it hasn't been uniform. In reality, the top one-third of Americans are doing very well, while the bottom two-thirds are in free-fall. Needless to say, life looks very different depending on which group you're in. We are not all moving in the same direction; we are "coming apart."[18]

One clear-cut example of this divergence is the rapidly expanding gap in out-of-wedlock births—a phenomenon statistically linked to poverty, low levels of education, and criminal convictions—between women with and without college degrees. Of births to women with a high school diploma or less, 20 percent were out of wedlock in the 1970s; today, it is just shy of 70 percent. However, nothing like this upward arc happened for women with college degrees over this same period. A higher percentage of college-educated women are having kids outside of marriage today than forty years ago, but the rate remains under 10 percent of births to this group of mothers. This new divide on family formation amounts to two almost entirely different cultures. Not surprisingly, trends in the number of children being raised in single-parent homes follow the same pattern, as do divorce rates and rates of marital infidelity.[19]

One of Putnam's key insights is the ever-starker contrast between "most people" (the bottom two-thirds) and "rich people" (the top one-third), and the division is made strikingly clear in the book's charts—what Putnam's readers and commentators have come to call his "scissors graphs."

Consider the following representative sketch:

THE SCISSORS GRAPH

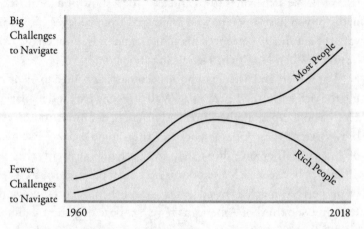

Let's unpack this a bit: The horizontal axis is time, moving from 1960 at the left toward the present. The vertical axis in his charts is a measure of something that we do or (usually) don't want: teenage pregnancy, school dropouts, divorce, or fatherlessness. The y-axis (vertical) shown here moves from "fewer challenges to navigate" at the bottom to "bigger challenges to navigate" as we ascend. As the curves move from left to right, they tell a profound story—in effect, the story of community collapse in American life over the last half century. Nearly everyone encounters some serious difficulties as the 1960s became the 1970s. But then Putnam's two key groups unexpectedly diverge. The affluent third recovers, endures some bumps, then stabilizes—and in some cases starts to improve—up to the present. By contrast, the bottom two-thirds suffer some initial bumps, followed by a much broader and continuing spike of unhealthiness. Whether the subject is out-of-wedlock births, fatherlessness, obesity rates, "financial worry," "neighborhood trust"—name the metric—the same basic pattern holds: in each case, things are going relatively well for the top one-third—but heading into disastrous territory for everyone else.

Haves and Have-Nots

Since we've been throwing around terms like "rich" and "top third," it might be useful to pause and clarify what we mean, especially because the definition is likely to surprise. When Putnam lectures on this topic, he sometimes stops and asks for a show of hands: "How many of you have a parent who graduated from college?" That's invariably around 99 percent of his audience. Hands shoot up. "Okay," he says. "When I say 'rich,' I'm talking about you."

For readers and listeners who've become accustomed to identifying the rich with "the 1 percent"—Wall Street hedge fund managers, Hollywood types, Forbes-listers—Putnam's definition raises eyebrows. Aren't these folks at a book lecture "middle class," like most of America? They sure think they are. Putnam's answer is that the difference between rich and poor is no longer determined by wages or property as much as by education—and then by social network. Roughly one-third of Americans have a college degree, and almost all the gains of recent decades have accrued exclusively to this "educational elite." For these families, life tends to be easier all around. College-educated parents are more likely to read to their children, more likely to drive them to extracurricular activities, and more likely to encourage them to pursue higher education than parents who aren't college educated. The benefits of these practices multiply with network effects, so that the well-off become even better off—and everyone else is left farther behind.

Almost everyone holding this book (or, just as likely, scanning it on a tablet) fits into this "upper third" category. You are readers of books, and that habit is now—unlike throughout most of U.S. history—largely a habit of an institutionally educated elite. For most of our history, a high school diploma was sufficient to get a job writing for the local paper.

To be clear, although I served as a college president for five years, I do not believe that a college education is at all necessary for a thoughtful, meaningful, or happy life. In fact, the cartel-like hold of universities on the American imagination and American economy has throttled alternative paths to flourishing and forced people with no interest in it or need for a degree into a costly four-year investment. Nonetheless, there's an increasingly clear correlation between a college diploma and being among the "winners" in contemporary America. Conversely, those without a diploma are increasingly cut off. Putnam observes that it is becoming rare to see intermarriage between college-educated and non-college-educated people. This is new and odd. But, then, this declining intermarriage is really just an echo of the fact that college-educated and non-college-educated people mix socially less and less today.

What Putnam is identifying, with his distinction between the top one-third and the bottom two-thirds, is a difference in the creation and availability of social capital. The top one-third has thick social networks. Children in generally stable families not only have an inner ring of support, made up of family and close friends; they also have access to an outer ring of "friends of friends," tutors, mental-health professionals, and a variety of mentors who assist them physically, intellectually, and emotionally.

Crucially, these networks are imbued with a sense of trust. People know there are others they can turn to for help. That does not exist for most people in the bottom two-thirds, whose social networks are thin and whose lives are more precarious. Their situation cannot be reduced to economics, although that is obviously an important factor: "Unemployment, underemployment, and poor economic prospects discourage and undermine stable relationships," Putnam allows. But his key variable is social capital.[20]

Fathers and Margins for Error

The primary form of social capital is family. "All of these changes in family structure," Putnam writes, "have produced a massive, class-based decline in the number of children raised in two-parent families during the past half century or so." The educational, economic, and social consequences have been huge. Educational attainment now relies heavily on family support and tracks closely with family stability. Educational struggle, meanwhile, correlates tightly with having a dad who has only a high school education or less. A particularly formidable knot of challenges for America's future, then, involves the rapidly growing number of children whose fathers are only intermittently present, or absent altogether.

My dad is a recovering adrenaline junkie—an occupational hazard for football and wrestling coaches. One of his pastimes was amateur racing (mostly motorcycles and cars, but I've also seen him do really ill-advised stuff on go-carts and unicycles). Growing up, we collected an endless supply of racing metaphors for life: "To finish first, you must first finish." "Eventually, we all drive not by thought but by instinct." "It's better to race for a moment than watch for a lifetime." "It's useless to hit the brakes when the car's already upside-down." "Racing, wrestling, and bullfighting are the only real sports—all the rest are games." At my house, "behind the curve" meant being too late to begin navigating a turn or an obstacle—not being located on the left side of a statistical bell curve.

But the most important bit of racing wisdom in our family concerned the value of having a safety shoulder on a road or racetrack: "It's worse to make a mistake without a shoulder than with one." If you're driving down a road with rumble strips and a big shoulder, you can drive a bit more casually. If you drift too far to one side, you're alerted to it, and there's time to adjust. No problem. But the same careless driving on a steep road with no guardrail, shoulder, or rumble strip can be deadly.

To extend the metaphor: Life is smoother and safer when you have some shoulder to work with. If you do, a bad decision, an error in judgment, or a moral lapse means merely that you have a learning opportunity. If you don't, the same mistake means hitting the wall or going over the cliff.

Much of what Putnam is concerned with can be summarized as the importance of having a shoulder or cushion—"a greater margin"—to work with in life.

It turns out that this is especially important in our increasingly complex world. In a hunter-gatherer society, the death of a father was painful, but it didn't mean that a child would grow up without elders to protect him, to teach him how to hunt, and to usher him through all the rites of becoming a man. The rules of the society were simpler

OUR LONELINESS EPIDEMIC   35

and widely understood. Our world is different, which means that
today mistakes that are insignificant for the well-networked individual can be disastrous for the young man or woman lacking any
margin for miscalculation.

Yet despite the complexity of contemporary society, there are
still some simple formulas we can use to distill the path to social and
economic flourishing. One of these, labeled the "Success Sequence,"
and credited to Ron Haskins and Isabel Sawhill of the left-of-center
Brookings Institute, proposes a three-step rule book for modern
American life:

1. Finish high school.
2. Get a job. (Any job. Because working leads to more working,
   which leads to better jobs.)
3. Get married before having children.

When people follow this pattern—and crucially, in this order—
life generally turns out pretty well.

Many family advocates, such as Wendy Wang, a demographer
at the Pew Research Center and director of the Institute for Family Studies in Charlottesville, Virginia, have touted the findings as
showing an effective pathway for "have-nots" to become "haves."
Those who follow the Success Sequence tend to see their situations
and their prospects rise—while those who don't, don't.

Critics of the Success Sequence, who target it as oversimple, are
right to observe that there are many reasons people end up poor—
for example, economic structures, government policy, racism, institutional failures, and more. These critics worry that cultural and
behavioral choices can be emphasized to the point that economics
and public policy are neglected altogether. Some proponents of the
Sequence exacerbate this problem by arguing in ways that conflate
cultural and racial issues.

Debate over the importance of family has been hung up on
this point for half a century now, with little to show for the back-
and-forth arguing. We won't take the time here to chronicle the

decades-long debates surrounding the "Moynihan report," which in 1965 documented the nationwide breakdown of the African-American family. But I want to note that I, a conservative Republican, intentionally sit on the Senate floor in the desk of Daniel Patrick Moynihan, the liberal Democrat who represented New York in the Senate for more than two decades. I requested his desk for three reasons relevant to the themes of this book: first, he grasped that legislating requires not just political maneuvering but also, and more importantly, a common understanding of what overarching challenges we face and what specific problems we are working to tackle; second, he is the author of the oft-cited (and as oft-misattributed) quote—"You are entitled to your own opinion, but you are not entitled to your own facts"; and, third, his report on the collapse of the black family in the 1960s underscored the causal link between family structure and poverty in America—and, by implication, the absurdity of thinking that poverty can be tackled without addressing family brokenness.

Professor-Senator Moynihan endured harsh criticism for the third of these; he was regularly attacked for taking a "victim-blaming" approach to the painful problems in African-American neighborhoods. These attacks were mostly silly. The right answer is that *both* culture *and* economics matter; this shouldn't be this contentious. And I suspect that if Moynihan were alive today, his attention would be on the collapse of places like Appalachia—afflicted by drug abuse, inadequate education, government dependency, and unemployment. He would likely make three points:

1. Family structure, out-of-wedlock birthrates, and marital failure are at the root of so many of these other social ills.
2. This is not to deny that economic-structural issues (such as the evaporation of coal and industrial jobs) have also contributed to the cultural breakdown we are observing.
3. None of this has anything in particular to do with race. Whether one looks at the black family of the 1960s or the white family of the 2010s, the sources of dysfunction are largely the same.

What's increasingly disappearing is the shoulder on the road. Kids with intact families and all the social capital associated with intact families tend to be able to navigate the bumps and disruptions that life inevitably brings. But kids raised without stable families and without that crucial source of social capital are often crippled by even modest impediments.

If we are going to make any lasting difference in the lives of our neighbors struggling in poverty—or wrestling with loneliness—we must tell the truth about the irreplaceable role of family. The most important shoulder in life is a parent's.

Can We Admit the *Goodnight Moon* Gap Yet?

Some of this is difficult to talk about. We need to get more comfortable admitting the truth that there are, today, effectively two different Americas—and that the challenge of moving from the bottom two-thirds to the top one-third is getting objectively harder.

Perhaps we could begin by admitting that most of us regard questions of how one ought to live as moral questions—and moral questions make for particularly fierce disagreement. But guess what? We don't need to agree on every complex moral issue to begin a discussion. For our purposes in this book, we can work strictly from the fact that, as the research indisputably shows, American neighborhoods are now more fragmented and less unified, and we can ignore potential disagreements about precisely why this should trouble us morally. As a matter of plain fact, Americans have less and less in common, and that has day-to-day costs.

Consider two examples—one about the Success Sequence and another about the typical age of first childbearing today. Personally, I believe there are many moral issues at play in the Success Sequence—for example, in the decision to have sex, to get married, or to pursue one line of work over another. I value the nuclear family for moral and traditional reasons, not just practical ones. But even if you disagree with me about any of these matters, we should be able to agree that having narrower margins or no shoulders, as discussed above, are getting more costly for our neighbors. At a minimum, then, talking honestly about the Success Sequence is a way of making wider margins more likely in the lives of that bottom two-thirds.

So here's a practical reality that every American ought to be able to acknowledge: *If you follow the Success Sequence, you won't be poor. But if you fail to follow the Success Sequence, it's 50/50 that you (and your kids) will be poor.* That's what the data teaches, plain and simple. If you finish high school, get a job, and get married before having children—in that order—you have only about a 3 percent statistical chance of ending up poor. By contrast, life is really, really hard for most folks who forgo these basics. Admitting this has nothing to do with "liberal" or "conservative" perspectives. It's just the reality, backed up by a mountain of research.

Here's a second reality that we could start talking about today: Depending on their level of education, women now start bearing children at very different ages. Fifty years ago, better-educated women experienced their first pregnancy at about 21 years of age, versus 19 years of age for women with a high school education or less. Today, college-educated women are giving birth for the first time at age 27, while non-college-educated women are giving birth for the first time earlier than in the past—right around their eighteenth birthday. The education gap is producing a pregnancy gap of nearly a decade, compared to a gap of just two years half a century ago. There is no need to have a grand moral debate here before simply recognizing the difference that this decade is making in the lives of children.

Another of Putnam's provocative discoveries is what he calls the *"Goodnight Moon* Gap," alluding to the popular read-aloud book for babies. At issue is how much, and how differently, parents in the top one-third invest in nurturing their children, compared to parents in the bottom two-thirds. In the early 1970s, there was no measurable American divide by class or education level on this metric. Today, however, we know that college-educated parents not only use more-sophisticated vocabulary when they're talking to their children (which has major implications for brain development), but also that college-educated parents simply spend much more time—perhaps upward of 50 percent more—*talking with* their children. They read to them, help them solve problems, and engage in moral reasoning with them. Children in social-capital-rich families thus receive both quantitative and qualitative advantages.

Some of this "*Goodnight Moon* Gap" is driven by economic challenges for poorer Americans that leave them with fewer discretionary hours to invest in meaningful time with their children. But, again, the problem is deeper than economics. As Putnam demonstrates, poorer, less-educated parents tend to believe that their primary task is getting their children to obey, as opposed to better-educated parents, who emphasize helping their children understand *why* they ought to obey a given rule. Reading, reasoning, and problem-solving with their parents help children develop the higher-order skills that make them better equipped to face the challenges of a fluid, complex world.

Unfortunately, identifying the difference that parenting makes has become controversial in some quarters. Ian Rowe, who runs a group of charter schools in New York City, is a former senior scholar on education at the Gates Foundation. Last year, after Bill Gates announced in a long essay that the billions of dollars invested by his foundation in secondary education have made little difference in outcomes, Rowe responded with a public letter to his former boss. Moving his private questioning into the public, Rowe asked how it was that the Gates Foundation could systematically "overlook the vital role that families play in shaping the academic" and broader outcomes of students. At the same time that Gates purported to assess all possible causes of educational struggle, not once in 3,000 words did he mention the role of family and parenting. Rowe makes clear why this is a major omission:

> It's simply stunning considering the foundation's legendary and deserved reputation for expertly using data to inform its policies and find the true causes of the ills it tries to remedy.

Five decades ago, the enduringly relevant Coleman report established the primacy of family structure and stability in driving educational outcomes for children. At the time of that publication, 6 percent of American children were born to unmarried women. Since then, that number has skyrocketed, especially among women and men under the age of twenty-five. . . . According to a recent CDC report, 2016 was the *tenth consecutive year* that 40 percent of American children of all races were born outside of marriage. . . . [This is] an almost certain recipe for poverty, stress, and poor educational outcomes for the single mom and (typically) her children.

This "new normal" of permanent, staggeringly high nonmarital birth rates is a catastrophe for our country. . . . Of course, there are extraordinary single parents whose children defy the gargantuan odds against them and succeed in life. . . . [But] the data are clear on the myriad difficulties facing these kids. Children from poor, unstable families led by unmarried young women and men are, for example, more likely to suffer cognitive impairments as infants, to be chronically absent in elementary school, and to have repeated disciplinary issues. And they're much less likely to attend an effective preschool and read proficiently by third grade.[21]

In short, Rowe argues that we are simply refusing to tell the truth about what the data clearly reveals about the central driver of educational attainment.

I've put this question to dozens of teachers over the past two years. As the son of a public school teacher, and as the husband of a former public school teacher, I've been in countless discussions with teachers about what, at bottom, makes students thrive or flounder. I've never heard a teacher answer these questions with anything besides "parents" or "families." Yet our public policy discussions try to treat students in isolation—and tend to pretend that the key factor is whether they have the most up-to-date technology in their classroom, or whether teachers are instructed in the latest pedagogical methods. These simply aren't the core missing variables.

Brad Wilcox, a sociologist at the University of Virginia, has labeled this elite unwillingness to admit the importance of family structure and parenting "talking left, walking right." What he's put his finger on is the difference between what so many college graduates tend to preach for others versus what they actually practice in their own lives. At the same time that the upper third of modern America is proclaiming its open-mindedness on matters of family life and sexual ethics, most of us are actually living staunchly "conservative" or "bourgeois" lives.

The clearest examples are comparative rates of divorce and marital infidelity. In the 1970s, no-fault divorce laws proliferated, and television programs and movies like *Kramer vs. Kramer* normalized marital collapse. Across classes, the traditional notion that marriage was a permanent or lifelong commitment, characterized by duty and sacrifice, began to wane. Across all classes (at first), divorce rates climbed. The same period saw wealthier Americans embrace fads such as swinging, and as the long-standing taboo on extramarital relationships began to weaken, Americans of all classes became more likely to seek sexual partners beyond their spouse. However, the statistics suggest that, over the subsequent decades, many elites intuited that their doctrines had ugly real-world consequences—and so, while they did not change liberalized laws, their own *behavior* became very conservative. Today, the top one-third of Americans once again have significantly lower rates of divorce and marital infidelity, and that has been a crucial element of their social and economic success. Ironically, their conservative behavior is part of what makes elite (and mostly liberal) Americans so successful.

But, as Charles Murray demonstrates in his monumental book *Coming Apart*, the bottom two-thirds often *do* now live by those more commitment-skeptical doctrines, and the results have been catastrophic. Lacking the social capital to absorb the consequences of high rates of divorce and fatherlessness, the socioeconomically lower classes experience outcomes that lock them into a cycle of further poverty and family brokenness—a context in which generating sufficient social capital becomes much less likely. This is the deepest "haves versus have-nots" divide of our time.

The Parent Lottery

We've described the Success Sequence as "simple," but that shouldn't be confused with "easy." Even children who grow up with adults modeling this behavior often have a hard time pulling it off. That's why the most important "decision" anyone can make, Putnam quips, is "choosing their parents." If you "choose" affluent, well-educated, married parents, then in today's America, you're going to be fine. But if you "choose" poor, less-educated parents, no matter how talented you may be, "you're not going to be fine," Putnam worries.[22]

This isn't how America is supposed to work.

And it wasn't always so.

Robert Putnam grew up in Port Clinton, Ohio, a middle-class town on the banks of Lake Erie. He writes vividly about the late 1950s, when income and class divisions weren't as sharp as they are today. One of Putnam's classmates, "Don," came from a poor family but didn't know it. He said he "went to college and took Economics 101 and found out that I had been 'deprived.'" Despite modest circumstances, Don was his high school's star quarterback. "You met everyone as an equal through sports," he says. Another classmate, "Frank," came from one of the wealthiest families in town. But Putnam notes that Frank lived just four blocks from Don, yet was basically as unaware as Don that they were from different classes. The classmates' neighbors included "a truck driver, store owner, cashier at the A&P, officer at a major local firm, fire chief, gas station owner, [and a] game warden." All the kids played together. Nobody seemed to know or care whose parents made more money. "Everybody just got along."[23] The third baseman needed to be able to throw a rope to first base, not report on mom and dad's bank balance.

Fremont, Nebraska, in the 1970s and 1980s, wasn't much different than 1950s and 1960s' Port Clinton in terms of the relative insignificance of class. The more memorable difference was that in my hometown teenagers from all walks of life detasseled corn, whereas in Putnam's hometown kids from rich and poor families alike worked at the factory or caddied at a lakeside golf course.

I grew up in a middle-class home. Some of my friends had more than we did, some had less—but socioeconomics had basically no bearing on friendships in our 25,000-person town. At the Fremont Wrestling Club, I cared only who threw the best headlock and who had the quickest sweeping single-leg shot; I honestly didn't know whose mom and dad had higher-status jobs. There was only one Little League baseball association, and there was only one Jaycees football league, and everyone was in both.

This is no longer true. As across the nation, class divides are now fairly deep in Fremont. The town has declined economically in the decades since my upbringing here—and as in America as a whole, there is considerably less socioeconomic mixing. Not only do Americans no longer know their neighbors, but in many cases they simply don't know many people who *aren't like them.* Fewer people know people across class divides. Bill Bishop and Charles Murray have shown how people with high levels of income and educational attainment no longer live spatially near their less-educated, lower-paid peers. We sort ourselves out geographically in ways that ensure we rarely rub shoulders with people outside our social class.[24]

Putnam sees here a "savvy gap" that compounds the *Goodnight Moon* Gap: "Kids from more privileged backgrounds are savvier about how to climb the ladder of opportunity." An 18- or 19-year-old from a low-income background, with little social capital, walks onto a college campus at a profound disadvantage. By that point, it doesn't matter much how many remediation programs the campus may build to help ease his transition. "These kids are baffled about school practices, two- and four-year colleges, financial affairs, occupational opportunities, and even programs (both public and private) specifically designed to assist kids like them," says Putnam.

Today, counterintuitively, intellectual preparedness has actually become statistically less important to ultimate success in college than the amount of social capital with which a freshman arrives. In short, there's a massive quantity of data to support Americans' well-documented, growing worries that who gets ahead in America

now has less to do with how hard you work than simply with who
you know.

Something is tragically un-American here in the decline of hard
work, and the return of class.

How to Be Happy

Every human being wants to be happy. From the philosophical classics of Plato and Aristotle to the great texts of the world religions,
to poetry and song-writing down to the present day, we find this
permanent truth inscribed in the great works of men and women,
because it's inscribed in our hearts. America's Founding Fathers
understood this. A right to "the pursuit of happiness" was given by
God, they wrote in the Declaration of Independence, and it can not
be stripped away by any king or potentate who happens to wield the
sword of state for a time.

Happiness has never been easy to come by, let alone hold onto.
Even to say precisely what happiness is presents a challenge. Nonetheless, when life brings us joy and contentment, we know it. The question is whether we can play an active part in making that happen.

Social scientists have identified four primary drivers of human
happiness, which we can put in the form of four questions:

1. Do you have family you love, and who love you?
2. Do you have friends you trust and confide in?
3. Do you have work that matters—callings that benefit your
   neighbors?
4. Do you have a worldview that can make sense of suffering
   and death?

Think of these four components as the legs of a chair. When all four
are in place, things are sturdy. When one goes missing, your happiness begins to wobble.

In this chapter, we've discussed the importance of family and of
friends. In the next chapter, we will turn to the question of work.
People long to find ways to express their unique skills and talents, to

provide for themselves, and to serve people around them. But the un-precedented changes that are beginning to roil the global economy are making that more difficult than ever before. Figuring out how to navigate this revolution of work—which is arguably the most funda-mental anchor of human identity—is one of the biggest challenges heading toward America over the coming decade.

Two are better than one,
because they have a good return for their labor.

For if one falls down, his companion can lift
him up; but pity the one who falls
without another to help him up.

—ECCLESIASTES 4:9–10

2

STRANGERS AT WORK

When America's Number One Job Dies 🐾 Frankenstein Faster and Faster
The Unexpected History of ATMs 🐾 How the Future Might Work
Could Half of Work Disappear by 2030?
Naming the Monster That Haunts Us
I Need You to Need Me 🐾 The Shift from Nouns to Verbs
Confessions of a Digital Nomad
The Hometown-Gym-on-a-Friday-Night Feeling

WE LIVE—AND WORK—IN UNUSUAL TIMES.

For thousands of years, most people had one primary community for their whole life. They grew up in a village or town, married from the small number of choices on offer there, worked alongside neighbors they and their families had known since birth there, raised children there, grew old there, and were buried there. Work, faith, recreation, and family were bound up together. Even nomadic hunter-gatherers, who hunted their buffalo and gathered produce over vast swaths of land, took their network of relationships with them as they roamed. They re-pitched their tents in a new place many nights, but their social network was immovable. Whether nomads or settled farmers, most people have known worlds with a common way of work, and therefore a common way of life.

People have always naturally had, for lack of a better word, a *tribe*.

The arrival of modern economics, and especially the Industrial Revolution, disrupted all that.

The way we work now is new in ways we rarely pause to appreciate. Historically, most workers were either jacks-of-all-trades in rural subsistence economies or worked lifelong jobs in the city. They had one role, one title. Whether rural or urban, they found their identity in large part from their work—and because many people did the same job, that identity was shared widely. For a number of people, their work even bequeathed them a name: the Smiths and Millers, the Coopers and Bakers.

Whenever these settled worker identities were destroyed, a period of angst and turmoil inevitably followed.

As modern technologies emerged and industries developed a century and a half ago, many young people were pushed from the farm or pulled across the Atlantic into America's emerging cities with their giant factories. These enterprising migrants were seeking better ways of life, but they often ended up finding conditions much harsher than they expected. Friends were few and far between, and the anonymity of the city spawned not just outward crime but inward alienation. Frequently, these lonely fresh-from-the-farm and fresh-off-the-boat workers turned to the bottle for comfort.

Prohibition, those fourteen years when producing, distributing, and selling alcohol was illegal nationwide, looks in retrospect like a quaint artifact of a more innocent time. We have a picture in our mind of some uptight scold—perhaps Mrs. Oleson from *Little House on the Prairie*—plotting to spoil a bit of good, clean fun. But in reality, passing a constitutional amendment is incredibly hard, and at least initially Prohibition was enormously popular. How did that happen?

Simply put, people were afraid. Business was booming, and America was making money hand over fist. But something was wrong. Amid the chaos and uncertainty of an economic and migratory boom, moms and aunts, dads and uncles and neighbors, were worried that America wasn't paying sufficient attention to the social consequences of urbanization. Alongside spiking profits in each city, there was also spiking inequality. Our nation was experiencing massive poverty—as well as waves of crime, prostitution, and alcoholism. The situation didn't feel sustainable, because it wasn't.

(Disclaimer: Because I'm contractually obligated to love everything corn-based, I like a glass of bourbon as much as the next guy. I'm therefore thrilled that the Volstead Act was repealed. Prohibition was terrible public policy. My point here is thus obviously not to defend Prohibition; it is to puzzle over why an idea that seems so foolish, even outrageous, to us now was so massively popular a hundred years ago.)

It turns out that the cultural shifts that were so unsettling then have much to teach us about what we're experiencing now: namely, a revolution in *work*, a transformation of the ways we provide for ourselves and our families and express our skills and talents. One hundred years ago, a rapidly urbanizing world was a world in which everything was in flux. Imagine leaving your parents, siblings, and friends—and not knowing if you'd ever see them again. That was common. Nothing was certain. People did not know what to expect, and they were scared.

And right now, as a result of a new but analogous set of economic forces, we again don't know what to expect—and lots of us are scared. In the 1970s, average duration at a firm for a head of household was two and a half decades; today the average American remains at a firm barely four years. What we do now—in our highly differentiated, independent, faster-churning jobs—is about to ramp up another notch of change frequency, as a huge share of American workers evolve into project-work freelancers with no set, long-term company relationship.

When America's Number One Job Dies

"Driver" is the number one job in America. And it is currently the number one job in thirty-seven of the fifty states. People serve their neighbors as UPS deliverers, cabbies, big-rig operators, school bus drivers, pizza delivery guys, and on and on.

Though the job of "Uber driver" (as I have been) is modern, the general function of a charioteer is centuries old. Our term "car" is just shorthand for "carriage," meaning something carried or pulled, something that needs to be steered or directed. Obviously, the introduction of the internal-combustion engine to a mass market was a big disruption. (Fun fact: Winston Churchill basically refused to acknowledge the invention of cars. In World War II, when his chauffeur was waiting for him, he would ask: "Is the coachman upon his box?") Ultimately, though, whether the carriage is pulled by one dreary mule, two stallions, or the electric equivalent of hundreds of horses, a driver is required. Right?

Not so.

According to estimates, two-thirds of driving jobs could evaporate inside the next decade, as autonomous vehicles become reality. Of course, to the people developing these technologies, to commuters who will benefit from their efficiencies, and to older people no longer able to drive, the rapid progress of self-driving vehicles and drone delivery promises to liberate lives. My wife can't drive because of an aneurysm that left her partially blind, so the prospect of self-driving vehicles brings smiles to faces in our house. There is, too, the obvious lifesaving potential: About 35,000 people die in automobile accidents annually, 94 percent of which are the result of human error.

But the movement toward autonomous and semi-autonomous vehicles will also rattle the lives of millions of workers, tens of millions of family members, and thousands of communities. If you know truckers like my Uncle Chuck, you've heard the quiet panic of workers who drive to provide for their families. Millions of our neighbors find a substantial part of their identity in the title "driver." If the technology eliminates even a fraction of the number of driving jobs that analysts are predicting, the economic effects will be felt nationwide.

Many social psychologists fear this job disruption will usher in a staggering level of cultural disruption. Think about how the collapse of the coal industry over the last decade affected Appalachia. Although the number of miners is tiny compared to the number of professional drivers (tens of thousands versus millions of drivers), we might be slower to notice the shocks of the driver disruption because of their geographic and political dispersion. But we should be on the lookout. The disruption in communities all across the country when the number one job begins to evaporate could be calamitous. The opioid and meth crises that are tormenting many coal communities could similarly seep into many driving families.

Frankenstein Faster and Faster

There was one popular novel that nineteenth-century Americans almost invariably knew: Mary Shelley's *Frankenstein*. In the story, a cunning scientist stitches together dismembered corpses to fashion a new creature. At first, the creature is both smart and sensitive—not just intellectually gifted but gentle. But the gentleness doesn't last. He becomes increasingly brutal as the reader turns the pages.

Is that what urbanization was—a once-promising creation that astonishingly turned on its makers? The new technologies and bustling cities promised grand transformations, but people began to worry that the process might be spinning out of their control. There was no OFF switch. Would the relentless march of new machines devastate the texture of tight-knit communities?

Cultures are gardens, and factories felt like mindless weedwhackers.

At the end of the Civil War, more than 80 percent of Americans still lived in and around farming communities. But then the big tools of industry became irresistible magnets pushing America into cities. By World War II, 60 percent of the nation lived in urban areas. Even so, nearly half of Americans were still farmers or ranchers as recently as the start of the twentieth century. But today, less than two percent of us are.

That's a breathtaking pace of change—a wholesale transformation of the American economy and geography—and, what is more, total U.S. agricultural output has been shooting *up* through the whole process. Substituting technology for labor meant farmers could produce far more crops than ever before, but in less time, with fewer hands, and with less backbreaking work. In ways that would surprise city dwellers, farming today is much more an exercise in brains than brawn.

Manufacturing has followed a similar pattern—but the transformation has gone even faster. The simplest way to think of a factory is as a giant, complex tool. The high-water mark of American "big-tool" employment was the mid-1950s, when more than 30 percent of the American workforce performed industrial jobs. That was, in some sense, a historical accident. From 1945 to 1970, America produced almost everything for both North America and Europe, because European industrial capacity had been decimated by the Second World War. By the late 1960s, Europe had rebuilt its industrial capacity and begun to outpace American factories, helping to create the stagflation pains of the 1970s and early 1980s. But American factories retooled, and our total annual output began climbing again—and with even less labor required. Today, less than 8 percent of American workers perform industrial jobs, and—the false promises of politicians notwithstanding—large-scale manufacturing is never going to be the cornerstone of American work again.

America's productivity boom could not have happened without lower tariffs and freer global trade in the postwar period, but that is only part of the story. The primary reason we can do more with less—first in agriculture, then in manufacturing, now in everything—is simpler: humans are smart. And we use our smarts to identify tasks that can be routinized. We then fashion robots and other machines to do those tasks for us. New technologies displace humans over time, because humans plan it that way. We literally think ourselves out of our jobs.

The transformation of the industrial and agricultural sectors is the obvious result of more sophisticated technological capabilities, and we can hardly be surprised that automation is now creeping into areas that require cognitive abilities like making tacit judgments and sensing emotion—or making the snap decisions required of drivers every few seconds in traffic. Technology adapts to accommodate more and more complex roles. There's no turning back. Artificial intelligence and more automation are inevitable.

Of course, the ascendancy of machines is not just awe-inspiring; it's also more than a little concerning. Sometimes it can seem like Mary Shelley's monster is huddling with Alexa and plotting for your job.

The Unexpected History of ATMs

But wait. We've heard similar predictions from prophets of doom and other technology skeptics countless times. Consider the rise of ATMs in the 1970s and 1980s.

My mom, Linda, was raised on a little family farm about an hour northwest of Omaha, outside a thousand-person town settled by immigrant homesteaders after the Civil War. No one in her family had ever even contemplated going to college, so it was never really an option for Mom.

While she was in school, she worked on the farm or at a shop in town, but after graduating from high school, Mom took a job as a bank teller at Nebraska Savings and Loan at 6th and C Streets in my hometown of Fremont, twelve miles from her childhood farm. She loved the idyllic town. Between her work and her apartment, there was a courthouse and a Woolworth's, a post office and a barber shop, the gate of a Lutheran college and the ominous Pathfinder Hotel, named for our city's honorary founder, John C. Fremont, who led five westward expeditions through the region in the 1840s and 1850s. Mom enjoyed her customers, and she never imagined that the job of making change could be displaced.

But in 1967, tellers began worrying about job security. In London, a Barclays branch that wanted to stay open on Saturday created a "vending machine" for paper money, to give customers after-hours access to their accounts. Two years later, the new cash machines came to the United States.

At the time, a typical branch needed twenty-one tellers to operate. Further, those tellers devoted a significant portion of their time to checking for mistakes, because at the end of the day, their cash box and their balances had to line up. ATMs didn't make errors. Suddenly, banks could run efficiently with only thirteen human tellers, a reduction of nearly 40 percent, and keep longer hours.

The additional options were great for customers, and great for banks' bottom lines. But what about for workers? My mom told me that when rumors of the first ATM bound for Fremont arrived, she and her fellow tellers spent a good bit of their break time speculating about who among them would lose their job to the tireless machines that never made mistakes. What they didn't know was that the opposite would happen. Over the next thirty years, the number of tellers in America actually increased. Tens of thousands of Americans would find new work as bank tellers—and the quality, value, and stature of the role went up, too.

How could this be? It turns out that fewer tellers per branch meant banks could create new branches more cheaply—so they did. Those of you who've grown up with the expectation of an ATM on every corner and in every gas station would bristle at the inconvenience of banking in the early 1970s, when a trip to the bank meant sacrificing your lunch hour or your Saturday morning. You had to take out enough cash to hold you over until the next visit. But as new "microbanks" arose, you not only had access to your cash at all hours, you had a shorter distance to go to get it. And people like my mom were still in high demand.

Counterintuitively, "labor-saving" technology created many more jobs. As importantly, the nature of the jobs changed. The position "upskilled," meaning that tellers had to develop new, higher-level skills. Instead of simply handling cash, tellers learned to sign people up for credit products. They taught newlyweds about loan and investment vehicles. Many of Mom's coworkers soon found themselves happily navigating more complicated and higher-paying jobs. Coincidentally, the proliferation of ATMs was a boon to women's prospects and opportunities in the workplace. As female tellers upskilled, they were often promoted to become loan officers, an occupation previously dominated by men.

What might this unanticipated history of the ATM suggest about the coming disruption of millions of driving jobs over the next decade?

We can imagine a sequence of events in the driving industry that parallels what happened at banks over the last few decades:

unexpected opportunities, upskilling, and more. The crucial recognition, though, is that it is difficult to predict what will happen when technology upends an industry. Many times, even if we're right about the magnitude of a workplace technological disruption, we can't really predict technology's effect on workers by category.

How, then, can we begin to think about what comes next? How worried should we be?

How the Future Might Work

Conventional wisdom is a powerful drug. This is one of the central insights of James Manyika, chairman of the McKinsey Global Institute. Manyika is one of the world's foremost experts on technology, the digital economy, and the future of work. He advises heads of state, chief executives of Fortune 500 companies, and others seeking to navigate economic disruptions and technological change. He's one of my favorite brains on this topic. (Full disclosure: I'm a former McKinsey senior advisor and have worked for the McKinsey Global Institute, which Manyika now runs.) I regularly seek him out for his thoughts on big questions: How will rapid technological change and artificial intelligence transform the U.S. labor market? How will these changes affect income inequality and the concentration of wealth, domestically and globally? How fast is the world going to change?

When Manyika is advising power players on large-scale trends, he makes use of a decision-making grid that begins by asking a simple question: "How certain can we be that we know the magnitude of a coming change?" We're all prone to misjudge the size of a problem, for a variety of reasons: maybe it's politically polarizing, or maybe it affects us personally. We need to step back and carefully assess. If there are compelling reasons to think the change is going to be relatively small, then there's no sense spending much of our time and energy on it. But if there are compelling reasons to think it will be serious, then we need to dig deeper. As Manyika points out, in the case of big changes, it's rarely true that they're uniformly good or uniformly bad; they're good, and bad, and neutral all at once, and it's important to be able to disentangle the predictable and unpredictable elements.

We should state Manyika's bottom line up front. It's this: Disruption is coming, and it's going to be gigantic. Moreover, many of the massive changes are arriving soon—with many irreversible changes likely visible well inside the next decade.

But he and other McKinsey experts think most people are only seeing one part of a very large and complicated picture. Many people, typically from more privileged backgrounds, believe that predictions of significant disruption are overblown—that we've always had tectonic economic shifts, but the dust settles quickly. Many of these people observe that their own jobs don't look much different from their parents'. There have been lawyers and engineers and financiers and journalists for a long time.

Are they wrong? Yes and no. Manyika suggests that this response is a problem of perspective. People from well-to-do backgrounds are well positioned to absorb the benefits of economic disruption and to avoid its worst convulsions—and there will be *a lot* of benefits from the coming disruption, especially for them. "The net economic value of more automation—of data-aided, digital automation—is going to be off the charts," Manyika told me. (When I talked to him about this, he emphasized "off the charts" by throwing both hands up, referee-signaling-a-touchdown style.) Artificial intelligence and machine learning are poised to increase productivity, expanding the goods and services on offer globally. But the bounty of the digital and automation revolutions will include not just greater *quantities* of good and services, but also higher-quality, lower-cost, and more tailored innovations, from genetically targeted cancer treatment and trauma care to individualized architecture and energy-efficient construction. Experts are already on the lookout for revolutions in fields as wide-ranging as micro-lending, meatpacking, philanthropy, crop irrigation, elder care, and property insurance.

We will also continue to see the "Uber-ization" of existing industries and the expansion of the "sharing" services that have already become staples in the lives of many. The Sasse family, like a whole lot of others, regularly uses these services for lodging, tutoring, and food preparation, and we're grateful for convenient, high-quality, low-cost, waste-eliminating tools. (We've forgone on-demand mowing-and-weeding services, though. That's what the kids are for.) Countless dazzling-yet-economical products and services are in the offing. If you think the iPhone is amazing technology, well: *you ain't seen nothin' yet.*

But because big distortions are often "good and bad all at once," it remains the case that much of the hyper-rationalization of production and distribution is going to come at the cost of existing industries and jobs. The consumption side of this revolution is going to be great—but how bad could things get for those on the wrong end of the job revolution?

Could Half of Work Disappear by 2030?

McKinsey analysts have been modeling 800 job categories across the globe in industries comprising just over 90 percent of world GDP, with a special focus on the United States, Mexico, Japan, China, India, and Germany. The central takeaway of one of their major, yearlong reports, *Jobs Lost, Jobs Gained: Workforce Transitions in a Time of Automation*, is a blockbuster: "50 percent of the activities that people are paid to do in the global economy have the potential to be automated by adopting *currently demonstrated* technology" (italics added). To reiterate, half of all jobs in the global economy could be automated not just by speculative technologies but rather simply by the broad dissemination of already existing technologies.[1]

They further predict that up to one-third of workers in the United States and Germany—and 800 million total workers across the globe—could see their jobs disrupted *within the next twelve years.*

That's genuinely breathtaking—so it's not surprising that newspaper headline writers have been going straight for the exclamation marks. The problem is that they often misstate findings: "McKinsey: Automation May Wipe Out ⅓ of America's Workforce by 2030," one representative article warned.

But if that's not quite right, it nonetheless helps us understand a second error in the conventional wisdom about economic disruption. As we've seen, some people tend to downplay the potential downside of the disruption because they're so focused on its fruits. That's one of two common mistakes. The other mistake, though, is to assume that *whole jobs* will simply evaporate overnight—much like what people thought would happen to bank tellers in the 1970s. If one group sees only upside, another group sees only instant apocalypse.

McKinsey's analysts predict something different, something more nuanced. Only a small fraction—perhaps one in twenty—job categories will be entirely eliminated in the next decade. Rather, the major action will take place at the level of the many individual *tasks* that make up any given job. Think about it like this: Every job involves several distinct activities. A person who sells shoes, for example, might help customers find the right size, organize stock, advise customers on competing features, arrange products attractively in store windows, ring up sales, and reorder from suppliers, all in the same shift. These are the various tasks within the job of a shoe salesperson.

McKinsey suggests that most jobs (probably about 60 percent) have about 30 percent of their activities that could be automated. In other words, only a small number of today's jobs will simply vanish. But *most jobs* will begin to look significantly different. It is more accurate, then, to speak not simply of jobs lost and gained, but also—and primarily—of *jobs remade.* The activities that will be automated more easily are rote, repetitive activities like operating machinery, counting, or filing. Tasks that can't be easily replicated are those like, in McKinsey's words, "interfacing with stakeholders, applying expertise to decision making, planning, and creative tasks, or managing and developing people." So, the shoe salesperson's inventorying skills are going to become less relevant—but he'll still be needed to tell a customer that she was made for those heels, or that that particular cut of suit demands loafers *with* tassels.[2]

Most jobs will be "unbundled" and "rebundled." Many jobs will absorb parts of the job above or below them on the totem pole, and most jobs will see substantial horizontal combination. And such changes will likely happen fast. This is true for shoe salespeople, truck drivers, and factory workers, and also for accountants, lawyers, and other white-collar workers. (Technology is beginning to transform even the ultraconservative profession of law.) McKinsey's experts say the upheaval will affect just about everyone: "Automation now has the potential to change the daily work activities of everyone, from miners and landscape gardeners to commercial bankers, fashion designers, welders—and CEOs." Emotional intelligence, communication skills, and creative problem-solving will be increasingly demanded.

If we return to the question of perspective, we can see how the degree of disruption, and the magnitude of the threat or promise, changes depending on where you sit—and how different lenses help us see the picture more clearly. If we stipulate that everyone is going to be affected, it's obvious that certain job categories will fare better than others. For example, big-tool factory workers are at greater risk than, say, palliative care nurses, because a machine can haul and measure and polish, but care robots (which Chapter 6 will show are coming fast) will not likely be able to provide sufficient comfort to the large number of Baby Boomers needing additional services during their declining years. So from the factory worker's perspective, the disruption poses a threat, both to his or her paycheck and status (factory work remains a comparatively "high-status" position, a holdover from the mid-twentieth century). But from the palliative care nurse's perspective, the same large-scale economic disruption is likely to provide entirely new categories of higher-end work managing emerging machines. With the U.S. population aging rapidly, he or she will be in high demand, and her job will likely become higher status.

Now look at the disruption from the perspective of workers by age, rather than by job category. Again, taking as a given that the revolution will affect everyone to some degree, it seems likely that midcareer workers (regardless of industry) are at the most risk. The 55-year-old probably has more financial responsibilities (e.g., family, mortgage, car, etc.) and, for that reason, less flexibility to change jobs or pursue fundamental retraining. An older worker, on the other hand, is very near retirement and will be able to take advantage of his transition from being primarily a producer to primarily a consumer. Younger workers are more adaptable to large-scale economic changes—and nowadays are being trained for them up front.

We're twenty or thirty years into a digital revolution that will almost surely continue for another half a century before we have any settled sense of our "new normal." Some experts think that, by just four years from now, fully half of American workers will be *freelancers* who cobble together multiple projects rather than have any one defined position as a permanent employee. We can use various perspectives to try to get a better handle on the changes that are coming, but there are too many variables for anyone to pretend we can predict with certainty what a "typical" job arrangement will look like.

Still, one thing we can reliably predict: What we're going through now will likely end up being at least as disruptive to community as were the agricultural and manufacturing revolutions of the last century and a half. Thoughtful analysis will require distinguishing and naming both the good and the bad. And genuine wisdom will require not just acknowledging the disruption of our ways of making a living, but also of our ways of thinking about ourselves, our identities, and our places in the world.

Naming the Monster That Haunts Us

For a minute, let's assume the most benign, least disruptive version of what comes next. Let's assume that the explosive productivity growth from automation is broadly distributed and that the majority of workers are able to transition from disrupted jobs to new, well-compensated positions. I think that, even with all the new goods and services, most of us, in the backs of our minds, would still worry that we've lost something significant.

When we read about the era of farm-to-city migration in late-nineteenth- and early-twentieth-century America, it isn't nearly as frightening for us as it was for them, both because the uncertainty has passed and because we now experience on a daily basis the benefits this transformation yielded. That is to say, we can be optimistic about what happened because we know how the story played out. We ended up calling the era "industrialization" and "urbanization."

But imagine for a moment if we called it "post-agriculturaliza-tion," instead. That is, imagine if we named the era for the old thing that was passing away, rather than for the new thing that was born. That would signal chaos, uncertainty, nostalgia, and decline.

What many Americans are experiencing today is probably best captured by "post-industrialization." At one level, the term sounds like unhelpful academic jargon. But admitting that *we-don't-know-what-to-call-this-so-we'll-call-it-the-"After-the-Last-Economy-Economy"* seems pretty honest. Venture capitalists and others who are likely to surf the wave of these economic changes tend to refer to this emerging era with enthusiastic, forward-looking terms like the Tech Economy, the Mobile Economy, the Knowledge Economy, or the Digital Economy. These cheery-shiny labels do, indeed, cap-ture important developments, but none of them captures the spirit of our age for most workers. While the product offerings of Super Bowl commercials or the latest Amazon product launch might dazzle us, what most workers are feeling is uncertainty. And uncer-tainty is scary.

Mary Shelley knew that it is unsettling not to have a label or a name. She used this natural fear of ambiguity to profound effect in her novel. These days, people remember her demon-creature as "Frankenstein." But that's wrong; that was actually the name of the scientist-creator. Shelley never gave the monster a name. This was a purposeful omission, which has now become a convention in horror movies. A powerful entity with no name is unnerving. By contrast, naming something gives us a handle on it. Adam brought the Garden of Eden under his dominion by the act of naming the animals.

Our not-quite-named "post-industrial economy" is probably the best shorthand for what many workers are feeling today, because it starts by identifying what has been lost: the assumption of lifelong employment at one firm and in one place—the assumption that what we have and where we are is a permanent anchoring around one institution in one place.

We feel lots of work ache, but we have little shorthand for iden-tifying and naming precisely the hollowness that flows from not having shared projects with lifelong coworkers. All we know for sure is that technological and economic changes seem to be coming faster and faster, and our roots seem shallower and shallower.

I Need You to Need Me

I've asked hundreds of entrepreneurs and tech funders about the challenges they think our future holds. Most of them, even the giddily optimistic, eventually acknowledge that the disruption we're going through—this migration from industrial-era jobs to whatever comes next—raises questions that are much bigger even than income inequality or class mobility. The deepest, most provocative questions are about callings—about identity and meaning, purpose and place.

Work, after all, isn't merely about providing for one's family. It is certainly that, but it is also about having a sense of purpose, a means of serving one's neighbors, a place to fit in.

We need to be needed. This is true in love, it is true in friendship—and it turns out that it is true in work. People need a vocation. We have a widower in our neighborhood who mows his lawn basically every weekday. This is because we are made to work but are often so disconnected from real community that we don't have anything *necessary* to do. There's genuine tragedy in how we've cut ourselves off from being needed—and the consequent loneliness runs deep.

I generally differ with Democrats on what precisely the federal government's role should be in the next economy, but we're often aligned on something much deeper than government policy: We agree that meaningful work is part of how human beings find genuine fulfillment. Former president Bill Clinton preaches it this way: "Work is about more than making a living, as vital as that is. It's fundamental to human dignity, to our sense of self-worth as useful, independent, free people."[3]

My colleague Chuck Schumer, with whom I wrestle on just about everything in our day jobs, puts this idea beautifully in the dozens of commencement speeches he gives each spring. He tells graduates entering the work world that, while their new diplomas are lovely, their happiness will depend largely on whether they can answer what he calls the "Monday morning and Friday evening questions": On Friday evening, are there family and friends waiting for you to show up—people with whom you've shared many years and meaningful experiences who yearn to spend time with you? And on Monday morning, do you have important work to do? This isn't about whether you make lots of money, but rather: Is there something important that a neighbor needs me to do?

I grew up in a household where these two identities or contexts had a good bit of overlap. My dad was a football and wrestling coach, and because he also refereed six different sports, Friday evening was typically a work night for him—with me tagging along as a gym rat. Most of his friends were teachers, coaches, and refs, as well, but to everyone he was "Coach Sasse."

Dad's work defined him in positive and fulfilling ways. Everywhere we went, people recognized him and greeted him with shouts of "Coach Sasse!" I heard him called that so many times that as a 5- or 6-year-old, I suspected his first name might be "Coach" instead of "Gary." It was who he was.

He'd earned this honorific through years of work on the field and in the gym. I can still see him running drills, painting fields and diamonds, driving vans through snowstorms, riding buses home late from away games, scheduling matches, printing out statistics, breaking down film, drawing up plays, photocopying depth charts, going to camps, organizing postgame meals and postseason banquets, washing loads of towels that stank so badly they could've walked to the washing machine on their own, exulting with kids in a victory, visiting the hospital after an injury, and—most of all—putting his arm around a player's shoulder and urging him to persevere after a painful loss. He earned his title by investing in our community and in the lives of young men—by yelling at boys when they needed it and by offering an encouraging word when it was of use. He helped lay a foundation of character and fortitude in his players.

Three decades later, when I accepted a post as a college president back home, men would regularly approach me to ask if I was related to Coach Sasse. When I said yes, he's my dad, time after time they'd open up to me—a stranger—about the ways my dad had changed their lives.

On a dozen occasions, men have become emotional telling me how my dad stood in, at some time in some way, for their missing dads.

I grasped little of this when I was in elementary school, but there was still a hint of recognition in my decision, in third-grade flag football, to ask to have "Lil' Sasse" instead of "Ben" on the back of the hoodie we all got for cold games. Dad didn't coach any elementary-grade teams, but I still wanted to be tied to his identity as a coach. I wanted to be connected to his work.

After he had retired, I would take him to Lincoln's Memorial Stadium for Nebraska football games (the Huskers being the winningest team of the last half-century, as you probably know). Nebraska hasn't had an unsold seat to a home game since October 1962—by far the longest sellout streak in college sports—so it's important to get there early to navigate 90,000 fans. But as meaningful as it is to buy a Runza (a uniquely Nebraska Russian-German food), to join in the "Husker Power" chants, to cheer the Tunnel Walk to the deafening sounds of the Alan Parsons Project's "Sirius" blasting from the loudspeakers, to review a video montage of the Big Red's five national championships since 1970, or to salute the military flyover, there's a different sound that I'll probably remember best in my old age. And that is when some guy inevitably shouts, as Dad and I are working our way up the stands: "Hey, Coach Sasse! Over here!" No matter their age, you can hear the respect and affection in their voices. Some of them haven't seen him since junior high, but they carry their own football and wrestling stories in their hearts. Some of it can surely be chalked up to their personal nostalgia about their youth rather than to his exceptional instruction, but he still held a role in their narrative: He was "Coach."

What we discover, when we put our skills and talents to use in work, is that our occupation links us to other people and gives us an identity and a sense of meaning. It doesn't matter whether a person is a CEO with her corner office or a server with his name embroidered on the restaurant-issued apron, a job gives us a place in the world.

This came home for me quite profoundly when I heard the story of Rick Norat. Rick was raised by a single mom in a family of drug addicts. By the time he was 8, he was getting high. Unsurprisingly, he ended up in trouble at school, then homeless, and ultimately in prison. While behind bars, he began to change his life by learning to read and write. He earned his GED and saved the money from his dollar-an-hour job in prison so he could buy a radio. He began listening to NPR and started improving his vocabulary. When he was eventually released from prison, he took advantage of a transitional program and went into pest control.

Arthur Brooks, a social scientist serving as president of the American Enterprise Institute in Washington, D.C., interviewed Norat in connection with his research on happiness. Getting right to the point, Arthur asked Rick if he was happy. The ex-convict enthusiastically dug into his pocket, pulled out an iPhone, and showed Brooks a recent email from his boss.

He excitedly told Brooks about an urgent bedbug outbreak: "They *needed* someone desperately. Right now," he explained. "They called *me*. I've become a go-to guy for the company. I am *needed*. I have a purpose. Do you understand?" He beamed: "These people *need me*. I've never had that."

Brooks had found the most enthusiastic bedbug exterminator in America. But he wasn't surprised by Rick's delight. Read that declaration of purpose again: "These people *need me*. I've never had that."

"Work gives people something welfare never can. It's a sense of self-worth and mastery, the feeling that we are in control of our lives," Brooks wrote in his book *The Conservative Heart*. "Work is where we build character. Work is where we create value with our lives and lift up our own souls. Work, properly understood, is the sacred practice of offering up our talents for the service of others." This is some important truth. We're made to connect to others, we're created to solve problems, and we can achieve these ends in part through our occupations, our work.

The Shift from Nouns to Verbs

What my dad did for a living and who he was were, in important ways, the same thing. We can debate the merits and demerits of collapsing Monday morning and Friday evening too tightly in my childhood household, but one thing was certain: He knew, and those of us who depended on him knew, a sense of certainty, solidity—there was a permanence about what he did when I was young. Kids and parents all through town had a relationship with my dad, and those relationships were roots that planted us firmly in place. He helped us recognize what it meant to be *home*, to be a part of a *community*. A lot of people my age and older will recognize this experience. But it's becoming increasingly rare.

As mentioned at the beginning of the chapter, the average breadwinner in the 1970s stayed at a single company for two and a half decades, whereas the average employee today will stay at any one job for little more than four years.

That means that the strong, long-lasting relationships—the years of coworking—that characterized previous generations are not being created by more recent generations. For many understandable reasons, we are now more open to sliding from opportunity to opportunity, using social media to keep "in touch" with people across the country or across the world.

There are many benefits of cheap and reliable travel, and of telecommunications and the potential of telecommuting, but one of the downsides is less overlap of people from the different spheres of our lives. Coach Sasse knew his kids and parents well—partly because he saw them not only on the field and in the stands but also at the supermarket or at church. Most people today will not have that kind of work. A typical corporate worker may very well live in Omaha but work for a company based in Seattle, "alongside" coworkers who live in San Francisco, London, and Hong Kong. Maybe she forms a meaningful friendship there—but it's unlikely, especially if she departs in thirty-six months.

Bill Gates has suggested that the distinguishing mark of what we're going through right now is that this is the first broadly *intragenerational* economic transformation in human history. In previous moments of transition, the effects were *intergenerational*: parents lived one way, their children would adapt to a disruption to live another way. But in our case, massive job churn is happening within a single generation, so that the same people will need to be able to work quite differently at age 55 than they did at age 35.

Put differently, our work used to be a noun: Mr. Smith. Coach Sasse. But work is likely going to become a verb. We will do many different important things but rarely with permanence. And that means we're losing the sense of identity that a job once brought. As jobs last a shorter time, and become less connected to tangible communities, we can hardly be surprised that people are feeling more detached and rootless.

Here again, we are feeling the pangs of loneliness.

Confessions of a Digital Nomad

In the previous chapter, I told the story of the 1995 Chicago heat wave. Recently, I tried to tell the tale in a couple of speeches, only—embarrassingly—to lose my composure at the same spot: When neighbors and city personnel began discovering the decaying corpses of people—generally men—who had died alone, they sometimes found next to them stacks of handwritten letters to estranged children.

The notes asked for forgiveness—for their lack of involvement, for events they missed, and for the neglect of long ago. (It was Harry Chapin's song "Cat's in the Cradle" come to life. "Please come see me," fathers begged, years too late.) But the notes were unsent. The horrifying letters asked for reconciliation that never came.

The fact that this kind of thing happens in America is unthinkable. And the fact that it happened in the town in which Melissa and I were living at the time should have been unbearable. But we didn't know; we had no deep sense that Chicago was "our" town. It was just a place we kind-of-sort-of lived for less than two years, and we probably always assumed we were just passing through. Decades later, I find myself in Chicago a couple times a year. Invariably, as I walk out of O'Hare or Midway Airport, I feel a mild pang of regret that I'm not flooded with feelings of familiarity more closely approximating nostalgia. We made our "home" here, but we never really invested in neighbors. We had many warm relationships, but they were with other people passing through. We were two of the nomads in the emerging "digital economy."

I should back up and tell you why we moved to Chicago to begin with. Weeks after we were married, we moved there for my job and for Melissa to attend graduate school. We had employment offers and educational opportunities in other places as well, but we chose Chicago partly because we had fallen in love there. For a summer in college, I had run a community service project in some of the poorest and loneliest neighborhoods on Chicago's troubled South Side. Melissa was a girl from the University of Alabama working on the same project. Witnessing poverty, drugs, deprivation, and despair that summer caused us to wrestle through some big problems together. Wrestling and questioning together is intimate, so it often brings people close.

I had watched the way she cradled the heads of weeping children. We were stopped by police multiple times because we were white, and there simply were no white people in the neighborhoods where we were spending our days. At a church where we worshipped, a 6-year-old boy asked if he could poke us because he'd never touched anyone white before. We wrapped our arms around a prostitute as she wailed that though she kept bathing she didn't think she could ever wash the filth off her body. These were neighborhoods that we got to know—some of the same neighborhoods that, two years later, would be "roasting under [the] wet wool blanket" of the heat wave. Yet on our return as a married couple to the city, we no longer had any real connection to these places.

After our honeymoon, we moved into our little apartment and began to set up home. However, before we had even gotten all the boxes unpacked—twelve days after we arrived—the phone rang. It was a Sunday afternoon, and my boss told me the "good news" that I needed to be on a 6 a.m. flight to Minneapolis the following morning to help turn around a company careening toward bankruptcy. I'll never forget putting the phone back on the receiver and having to tell my bride that I had to pack up and go. And it wasn't just one trip. I had to travel almost every week, often Monday through Friday, for the next nine months. The look on Melissa's face did not scream "idyllic, newlywed bliss." Suddenly, she was going to be living in the city virtually alone, grappling with graduate school studies, while her new husband disappeared most of every week. Plus, our dog (Husker) would soon grow from twelve pounds to 120 pounds. (To those of you asking, What kind of morons get a Rottweiler when they're first married?, I hear you.)

Not only did my work upend our plans for a romantic first year of marriage, it also disrupted our intentions to get to know our neighbors and city. When I was back on weekends, I was trying to spend as much time as possible with Melissa. We didn't intend to isolate ourselves, but we had too little time to do any of the community-building we had intentionally done when we'd been together on the South Side. Embarrassingly, given our beliefs about the importance of the local church, we did not even join a congregation, so we missed out on the fellowship of friends in the pews.

After less than two years, we were gone—off to southern California for a new consulting venture. Although we didn't know it yet, we were on the leading edge of life in the new mobile economy. Ultimately, we ended up living all over—we paid taxes in a dozen states—and we still carry some guilt over the fact that in those early years of life together, we didn't take the time to connect to or really serve our communities. We slid right over them. We did interesting work during those years, but we were what can only be described as "placeless."

The Hometown-Gym-on-a-Friday-Night Feeling

Urban studies theorist Richard Florida divides Americans into the mobile, the rooted, and the stuck. Community is collapsing in America because the rooted are vanishing; the stuck have too many crises in their lives to think about much else; and the mobile are too schizophrenic to busy themselves with the care and feeding of their flesh-and-blood communities.[4]

Most of us reading (or listening to) this book are mobile. We're free from the constraints of place—its annoyances and inconveniences, its potentially burdensome obligations—and we're free to see more of the world, with its extraordinary richness and color. But what have we lost in the process? Increasingly, we're shackled to the feeling that we don't belong anywhere, and we're not bound to people who can anchor us in a place we can call home.

This was the feeling I had during those two years in Chicago. This wasn't my place; these weren't my people. And on autumn weekends, as fans poured into the football stadium across the street, that feeling grew worse. I grew up around football—working the chain gang and selling food in a stadium fits me like a glove—and there we were next to Chicago's Big Ten team. But it just wasn't "home."

About that time, as mentioned in the Introduction, a *Sports Illustrated* writer referred to the "hometown-gym-on-a-Friday-night" feeling. It would be another five years—as we chased jobs and dogs and further education from L.A. to Annapolis to New Haven and beyond—before I realized that that compound adjective captured exactly what I was missing. I missed the easy shared cause of a town in the stands during a game; I missed my dad's coaching buddies gathered in our kitchen after a game; I missed knowing there were people we could turn to if things got tough. I missed the sense of "we."

I'd grown up in a thick, rooted community. Now I was learning the costs of mobility—and, ironically, the costs of having too many opportunities. Everything was thin.

An opposite problem afflicts those Richard Florida calls "stuck"—unable to escape communities rotting around them. The Robert Taylor Homes, which once stretched almost two miles along State Street on Chicago's South Side, were the largest housing project in the nation. That is not a compliment. They were a picture of hell on earth. While perhaps well intentioned—the federal government supposedly designed the twenty-eight sixteen-story housing towers to give the poor a temporary leg up to move out of poverty—the complex ended up being a racist, dehumanizing monstrosity. Permanently ensconced in poverty, 25,000 residents lived in what became cesspools of crime, molestation, gang violence, unemployment, and general brokenness. The urine-soaked elevators rarely worked, apartments were charred by arson, dealers sold drugs in dim hallways, and police frequently refused to go into the buildings at night. People had to bring their wounded outside to receive assistance. At one point, postal workers refused to deliver the mail. The dealers were the closest thing to a local authority.

The first time I approached these projects, it was a midday in June. We heard gunfire inside one of the northern towers and decided to retreat. The community service project I was heading in connection with some local churches had rented housing three blocks away. To escape the rising summer temperatures, a bunch of guys from my floor began lugging mattresses up a fire escape to sleep on the roof at night. Every evening we would fall asleep to sirens, and a number of times to gunshots. This was not a neighborhood where any mom or dad would choose to raise children.

This landmark of segregation and urban destitution has since been demolished, razed by the government that created them. When they were torn down, a whopping 96 percent of the residents—that's 24 out of every 25 people—were unemployed. The slums didn't give a hand out of poverty; they helped to entrench it.

The stuck are not just in inner cities, of course. Many of the people who still reside in the Rust Belt and coal-mining communities that have declined precipitously in recent decades are similarly stuck, unable to find ways to escape the downward spiral or to restore productive vitality to their communities. We don't know precisely what comes next, but many people elsewhere are also likely to find themselves stuck as the economy disrupts what they have always known, and as they struggle with unemployment or underemployment in the context of hollowed-out towns and neighborhoods.

Between the mobile and the stuck are the rooted—a small and diminishing minority. Rootedness, of the kind many of you readers were fortunate to have known growing up, requires cultivation. We have to make the decision to prioritize it. For some people that's difficult—whatever the reason—and it's up to friends, neighbors, and community leaders to help rebuild the conditions where they can flourish. What sustains people, really, is sharing a common cause, a common purpose—a sense of being in it together.

People yearn to belong. They want to be part of a tribe, to have roots. That desire will never be stamped out of the human heart. What it means, though, is that when healthy forms of belonging vanish, people will turn to more troubling forms.

In the next chapters, we will examine the rise of *anti-tribes*. We're meant to be *for* things and people, but absent that, most of us will choose to be *against* things and people, together, rather than to be alone.

PART II

ANTI-TRIBES

The enemy of my enemy is my friend.

—FOURTH CENTURY BC PROVERB

3

THE COMFORTS OF POLITITAINMENT

Loved by My TV Family ⟐ The Great Wahoo Traffic Light Debate
Tell Me What I Wanna Hear ⟐ Brains Ache for Order
Echo Chambers Everywhere ⟐ A Brief History of "Who Started It?"
Renaming Religious Liberty "Bigotry"? ⟐ Our Missing Serial Killer
Who Fact-Checks the Fact-Checkers? ⟐ Alone in the Electronic Glow

MY PARENTS USED TO INSIST THAT WE HAD AN ALMOST
moral obligation to follow the news. In their view, this was part of
being a responsible citizen. And the directive made clear that this
meant that our time with the newspaper was about spinach rather
than French fries—current events, not comics. They expected us to
be up to date on the major national and local events, to be able to
talk knowledgeably about them and offer informed opinions.

At breakfast as a kid, this meant I had to force myself to read
the *Omaha World-Herald*'s front page and one editorial before
turning as fast as possible to the sports page, which in those days
was the only way to find out what had happened in the games that
had been played the day before. Then, after sports practice in the
evening, our family would gather around the TV in the living room

for the first fifteen or twenty minutes of the six o'clock news. We'd
hear the latest about the Iran hostage crisis, air traffic controller
strikes, faraway earthquakes, Chrysler bankruptcy, and, always, the
Cold War. Only then could I zip back outside to the serious business of being a kid aspiring to lead Nebraska past Oklahoma in a
November football game.

Now, you could argue that the news in those days didn't always
go deep enough, or offer truly international coverage, but at the very
least the combination of the morning newspaper and the evening
broadcast news gave each of us a pretty good sense of the major
stories affecting our nation and our state. News was what people
needed to know to go about their day or to begin thinking about
their upcoming voting. It was information that was supposed to help
us make responsible decisions about future civic duties.

Today, I am a parent trying to teach my three children how to be
responsible citizens. But they face a problem I didn't. The challenge
today isn't catching the news; it's figuring out what even *is* news.

Because technology now guarantees that the news, or at least
stuff purporting to be news, is ever present and always on. Today,
"well-informed" people don't just know that there was an earth-
quake. Heavy news consumers know which buildings collapsed,
minute-by-minute casualty estimates, who is suing whom over
faulty construction, the divorce details of the lawyer doing the suing,
which celebrities emoted, which celebrities made unsympathetic
comments, and which politicians offered the quickest slap-downs of
the celebrities' earthquake-related insensitivities. It's all coming out
of the firehose jumbled together, 24 hours a day, 7 days a week, 365
days a year.

From the moment we wake up, we're plugged in. We check our
notifications before crawling out of bed, we scroll through headlines
during the workday, Facebook alerts pop up, Twitter messages flash.
At my local gas station, a nasty thing called "Gas Station TV" starts
yelling as soon as the pump starts flowing. When we get home, we
watch the talking heads clamoring on our news network of choice.
We watch the ten o'clock news. Before we turn out the lights, we
check to make sure nothing else has happened. All day long, it's

BREAKING NEWS and "think pieces." And when professional content fades, social media from my second cousin's high school ex-boyfriend insists there's no limit to new news I should be angry about. It's hot takes on hot takes on hot takes.

There's just one problem: There aren't enough legitimately important segments to fill every hour, every day, every week with news we actually *need*. There's no sense that we're watching this together, that there is news that the whole nation needs to hold in common as we make decisions about where "we the people" think we should be going next. But because we're willing to tune in, the production side is all too eager to pretend there's something urgent you just need to know (after the commercial break, of course).

Deep down, we know this isn't healthy. We want distance from it. We need room to breathe.

Yet if we're honest, many of us will also confess that we consume information this way on purpose. It's not just background noise to our lives but is rather a one-stop shop for keeping ourselves both informed and entertained. We approach it as "polititainment." We were raised to be well informed, but few of us would claim with a straight face that the way we take in news nowadays has much to do with a dutiful preparation for carrying out our obligations as citizens.

No, the gossip and bickering and witty put-downs are tasty. We're not eating our daily helping of vegetables. We're snacking on potato chips as comfort food.

Loved by My TV Family

Why do we have this constant need to be in the loop, up to the minute? In the previous chapters, we discussed the inbuilt desire for a tribe—the instinctive need to belong, to be part of a community, to know we're *home*. But what happens when we lose that sense?

We start hunting for substitutes. In contemporary America, the most powerful substitute is very often our TV "family."

Thirty years ago Vanderbilt professor Cecelia Tichi described how ABC television executives cleverly rebuilt *Good Morning*

America's set to resemble a living room with a crackling fire next to a big-screen monitor. Every Monday through Friday, Joan Lunden and Charles Gibson—as surrogate mom and dad—interviewed people by electronic hookup, their faces warm and ruddy on the screen next to a fireplace that glowed no matter the season. As Tichi put it, the "hearth and the color monitor were strategically positioned side by side to convey a distinct message. Viewers were asked to grasp and to accept the analogy of the hearth with the television, and in turn to associate their own TV sets with a glowing hearth." This setup is now a staple of morning and midday news programs.[1]

Today, social media enables two-way, interactive television viewing. Hosts invite viewers at home to tweet in suggestions for the next segment. They read clever comments from people across the country. They interact in ways that make Charlie from Urbana and Natasha in Tacoma feel like they're both part of one big family, in the same way that millions of Americans saw Walter Cronkite as "Uncle Walter." It turns out that television is not very good at giving us the news we need—no one is getting an in-depth analysis of a tax proposal or health-care reform plan in a four-minute segment—but it's exceptionally good at selling a kind of cut-rate comfort.

It's an insight going back to Plato that certain modes of communication are better equipped for certain types of messages—or, as media theorists say, the *form* of communication dictates the *content* that's communicated. The great media theorist Neil Postman uses the example of smoke signals. Like the lanterns in the bell tower of Old North Church that prompted Paul Revere's ride, smoke signals were a form of communication, but they were obviously good for only a certain type of message—namely, a very simple one. As Postman wrote: "Puffs of smoke are insufficiently complex to express ideas on the nature of existence, and even if they were not, a Cherokee philosopher would run short of either wood or blankets long before he reached his second axiom. You cannot use smoke to do philosophy. Its form excludes the content." Postman argued that with the arrival of TV, "the content of politics, religion, education, and anything else that comprises public business must change and be recast in [shallower] terms that are most suitable to television."

Put differently: The traditional understanding of "news" shifted to accommodate the new medium. The overriding concern was no longer the message itself, although that was (usually) still important, but making sure the message could be tailored to television's unique capacities.[2]

We can see a more recent example with the rise of Twitter, where messages must fit into 280 (originally 140) characters. Twitter is another message delivery system that is good for some things and bad for others. It's good for advertising articles and flinging pithy one-liners (Mark Twain would have been a first-rate Twitter user). It's lousy for in-depth policy debate. A tweet is more like a smoke signal than an essay.

(In Chapter 6, we'll explore how social media not only affects the content of our conversations, but also harms our moral and emotional lives by shifting our focus away from family and neighbors and local spheres of actual influence and toward faraway spheres where we're far more likely to be passive, and therefore to conceive of ourselves as victims of distant, malevolent actors.)

Of course, new media arrive and are adopted before we have time to think through their big-picture consequences, so as we've leapt to embrace insta-commentary, we've failed to recognize that the medium is good only for certain types of messages. In the process, we've obliterated the gatekeepers who helped to ensure that information was important and reliable; we've erased the distinction between "news" and "opinion"; and we're losing the habits that could help us make calm, considered decisions. When it comes to consuming news, we're miles wide and an inch deep.

Professor C. John Sommerville, author of *How the News Makes Us Dumb: The Death of Wisdom in an Information Society*, saw this coming two decades ago, in 1999, when "tweeting" was still something only birds did: "If news were just one of many things that we read each day, it wouldn't have the same impact. If we would read science, the classics, history, theology or political theory at any length, we would make much better sense of today's events."[3]

When we consume something poisonous from the flood of news now flowing over us daily—say, a story that is subtly but significantly biased, or an argument that is unsupported by strong evidence—we are often unable to tell. We don't have the resources, or the patience, to pause and evaluate what we're hearing. As news has become faster, and everyone with an internet connection has become a "news-maker," we've become overwhelmed by titillating information from every neighborhood at once, and more susceptible to spectacular claims.

For example, parents today are far more worried about kidnapping than in the past—even though child abductions are at an all-time low. Similarly, voters in the last election cycle believed that violent crime was spiking—but it simply wasn't true. Violent crime was at a forty-five-year low. Emotion trumps data. Some national security analysts suggest that al Qaeda and other jihadi groups with international reach use our media consumption habits to help select their targets for maximum emotional impact.

What is happening is that we're seeing lots more images and news about each specific tragic shooting or kidnapping than in the past—despite the fact that there are objectively fewer such tragedies. Moreover, as discussed in earlier chapters, because we rarely share experiences with people who are different from us, especially in terms of socioeconomic class, this lack of familiarity with other ways of living and working makes it less likely that we'll empathize with other communities' emotional responses to the images. We can worry or we can get angry based on our own experience, but we don't have many avenues for constructive action or mutual understanding. Civil society suffers as a result.

When you combine rapid-fire, 24/7 news—coming not just from a few sources, but from hundreds of thousands of "sources," from the *New York Times* to Henry Hipster live-streaming the "breaking news" from his Brooklyn walk-up—with the loneliness we've discussed previously, it's little wonder that people turn to the loudest voices. Think of how you feel when your cable news host of choice rips into the opposition. Even if they don't always speak for us, their presence is nonetheless familiar in a lonely living room.

Polititainment inevitably distorts our political foes like a gigantic funhouse mirror. But we're not fully aware of this contemptuous misshaping of our fellow Americans, partly because the contortion has a calming effect on our lonely souls. It's comforting to tune in and hear the somber tone of our favorite media personality during a tragedy. On mundane trivialities, their sarcasm is soothing. And during political scandals, their indignant tone is cathartic. Even if you know the story probably isn't quite as black and white as they're saying, it's reassuring to hear that what you believed to be true about the presumed bad guys is "true."

Many of our television hosts are modern-day carnival barkers. We can get dopamine, adrenaline, and oxytocin all at once. It's an adult video game.

But instead of expertly separating us from our wallets, they're separating us from things much more valuable: our time, our sense of perspective, and our judgment. And they're separating us from each other.

The Great Wahoo Traffic Light Debate

One reason for the ever-growing chasm is that almost all of us are convinced that our position is 100 percent right, and the other side is 100 percent wrong—no matter how silly it seems, when you think about it, to assume there are only two sides to all big debates. We like being told that there are black hats and white hats. It's cleaner that way.

My father and grandfather spent a good chunk of my childhood arguing about a traffic light on Highway 77, in the little town of Wahoo near my home. This debate, about what was then the only traffic light in this farm town, was the "Who was the best James Bond?" of stoplight debates. It inspired very strong feelings on both sides. Gramps couldn't recall ever having stopped at the intersection. The light was always green for him. Dad, on the other hand, swore it was red ninety-plus percent of the time. He was stopped at that intersection so many times that he began to imagine that the red light bore him malice.

After years of this bickering, I decided to answer the question once and for all. In June 1991, after my freshman year of college,

I pulled over by the intersection and pulled out a stopwatch. As it turned out, the stoplight ran exactly the same amount of time each way: just under two minutes green, just under two minutes red. So, not only were both Dad and Grandpa wrong, they were wrong to the exact same degree—despite years of looking at the same traffic light. (And my dad, "Coach," almost always had a stopwatch with him.)

How could they both be so wrong? For a while, I chalked it up to my grandfather's sunny disposition, whereas dad was perhaps a bit more—let's say "analytical." Eventually, I realized this was an example of what psychologists call "confirmation bias," which shapes both memory and imagination. My dad and my grandfather both had jobs that required them to spend endless hours on highways—Dad as a coach, referee, and summer bus driver for farmworkers; Grandpa raising money for and overseeing the athletic department at a local college. Both of them had surely hit that intersection at both red lights and green lights hundreds of times. For whatever reason, though, one had enough early experiences with a green light to expect that pattern and to overlook red lights encountered later, while the other one paid more attention to his early red light experiences. Over time, they discarded or forgot the occasions that didn't fit the pattern. In reality, both probably saw about a 50/50 split between red and green lights, but they paid attention to different experiences. As a result, they were both perfectly, equally wrong.

What does a dumb family dispute over rural Nebraska commutes have to do with collapsing community in America? Actually, a lot. Because confirmation bias and motivated reasoning (we'll discuss this later) have become the organizing principle of our media consumption and our political discourse.

Tell Me What I Wanna Hear

Like my father and grandfather at the traffic light, people filter out most information that conflicts with their presuppositions or desired conclusions. We've all had friends in the midst of a self-destructive cycle who sincerely want advice, then resist when you tell them something they don't want to hear. I've had friends like that, and I've also been that friend. You've been both, too.

Researchers have spent decades coming up with experiments to demonstrate how confirmation bias operates in human psychology. One famous study had participants listen to talks on various topics. The lectures, however, had poor audio quality, like listening on a staticky old radio, so subjects could only really catch everything being said if they slowed down the tape. The catch was that they were allowed to slow down the audio only a certain number of times. The researchers wanted to see what information sparked enough interest to induce the listener to pay special attention. It turns out that smokers were eager to slow down the audio for information that downplayed the links between smoking and lung cancer. By contrast, nonsmokers were unlikely to take the same information seriously.

More recently, a pair of researchers at Ohio State University gave 156 people the chance to read articles that affirmed or contradicted their political ideas. The participants spent far more time reading articles that confirmed what they already thought than articles that might have taught them anything new. In other words, academic research is confirming what most of us see every day: people work hard to confirm their biases, not to challenge them.[4]

The desire to make sense of the world, and to build on things we think we understand, is not a function of perverse attitudes or inferior education or a low IQ. In fact, the watershed exposition of confirmation bias and motivated reasoning comes from a complex consideration of how professional scientists tend to go about their research. "Normal science, the activity in which most scientists inevitably spend almost all of their time, is predicated on the assumption that the scientific community knows what the world is like," Thomas Kuhn wrote in his 1962 book, *The Structure of Scientific Revolutions*. That is, most scientists think they *already* know how the world works at the macro-level. Once in a while, a Newton or Einstein discerns some new law of nature. But most scientists are not trailblazers; most of them, most days, work *inside* a given paradigm—the shared set of assumptions that follow from Copernicus's revolution, or Newton's mechanics, or Einstein's relativity theory.

Kuhn was attacking the pristine (that is, naïve) view of the scientific method, according to which scientists are neutral, dispassionate actors just searching for truth, who compile facts in a sort of heap, each new fact one step closer to Truth™. But generally, that isn't how things work at all. Most scientists are constantly collecting new data and trying to work it into a prevailing framework. This is what Kuhn calls "normal science." They are trying to support the current model. But as they work, they also regularly find facts that don't fit neatly into the dominant theory. These "anomalies" are set aside. Over time, the junkyard of anomalies might get really big—but most of the folks working in "normal science" are willing to ignore it. The important thing—especially emotionally—is how many of the new facts continue to confirm the theory "all of us" have believed for so long. However, at some point, an innovative thinker comes along and introduces a new model, which can account for *more* facts—including the anomalies resting uncomfortably in the junkyard.

Kuhn calls this period when one model collapses and another takes its place "revolutionary science." The new model will have problems, too, but it wins if it can explain more of the troubling facts than the extant model—*and* critically, if the champion of the new model is able to overcome the "political" commitments that the established order has to the prevailing model. Crusaders for a new model rarely win, because big change is hard, but when they do succeed, it produces a "paradigm shift"—a new outlook on the world.

Brains Ache for Order

What's true for scientists is true for everyone. Most of the time, the path of least resistance is confirmation. This isn't necessarily selfish. In order to make progress, it's prudent to start from certain assumptions, even if they're not perfect. We can't restart from square one every day.

Another way to think about this is by distinguishing between coherence and correspondence theories of truth. When I map out a problem I'm wrestling with, I want two things at once: I want my map to correspond to whatever actually exists in the external, real world; and I also want my map or theory not to contain any internal contradictions or untidy riddles.

Kuhn's key insight about human psychology is that we usually yearn for internal coherence far more strongly than we yearn for external correspondence with reality. Sure, when I come across a new and complicated fact I like to tell myself that I'll allow the fact to triumph over my theory. But, truth be told, I'm more likely to doubt the pesky fact, or at least find a way to explain it away, than to doubt my theory. We're all like the scientists who are looking not to upend their theories but to confirm them. We are more interested in coherence—or internal consistency in our worldview—than to correspondence with the facts we encounter in the world beyond our heads.

In simple terms: We're biased.

Our mind's order-seeking need is responsible for "motivated reasoning," which describes our tendency to accept what we want to be true much more easily than we accept apparent new "facts" that we don't want to be true. If you happen to be someone who generally agrees with my politics or my worldview, you are probably inclined to read the pages of this book sympathetically. But if you are on the other side of the political aisle (and let me pause to thank you for giving this book a shot), you might be scanning these pages, looking for a sentence or paragraph that you can use as a justification to dismiss the rest of the book. I get it. I do it, too.

What this ultimately reveals is the centrality of intellectual traditions, intellectual frameworks, and intellectual *communities*. It turns out that no people—not even scientists—are disembodied automatons. We have beliefs and jobs and mortgages. Scientists have deadlines and a schedule and scholarly discussion partners and buddies in the break room. We all bring self-justifying biases to bear at the beginning of every day.

Psychologists in the 1950s demonstrated how our community bias works by asking Ivy League students from different schools to watch a football game. The students were more likely to see genuinely close or controversial officiating calls as right when they favored their school and wrong when they penalized their school. Yale Law School's Dan Kahan explained, "The students wanted to experience

solidarity with their institutions, but they didn't treat that as a con-
scious reason for seeing what they saw." Humans aren't automatons.
We come from communities and places, and we have passions and
experiences and investments.[5]

This is not an argument against the existence of objective reality,
nor should it dissuade us from seeking to align our subjective judgments with objective truth. But it should nudge us toward more humility about even those things we think of as unquestionably true. If
we're being honest with ourselves and each other, we know that our
views are shaped by a whole lot more than "just the facts, ma'am."

Echo Chambers Everywhere

No one is exempt from the human condition—and that includes
journalists, even with their claims to objectivity. Most members of
the media aim to do their jobs in an unbiased, dispassionate manner.
But like all of us fallible beings, they often fail. In the real world,
most reporters adhere to various paradigms in their work. These
lenses have been formed through education, experience, and the cost
of late nights finishing stories at the office. Like the rest of us, reporters tend to build new insights on top of old ones—new stories tend
to try to confirm old ones—and so they struggle to take seriously
new facts that appear to contradict the narrative they've already produced. They almost inevitably (and understandably) end up wedded
to storylines they've previously believed and therefore told.

Most reporters judge that the media as a whole is doing a decent
job of "calling balls and strikes," but survey data suggests that most
of America (66 percent, according to a recent Gallup poll) disagrees.
The point of this chapter is not to establish who's right on this or that
debate about objectivity, but rather to examine why such a chasm of
perception exists—between reporters and their reading and viewing
public—and how that exacerbates our current cultural divides.[6]

For starters, our national political reporters are highly homo-
genous—and very different from median America in terms of educational attainment, political perspective, cultural commitments,
and geographic base. Ninety-two percent of journalists have at

least a bachelor's degree—compared to less than a third of Americans. Seven percent are Republicans—compared to about a third of Americans. Most national political reporters live in one of two cities, both of them wealthy, liberal, and on the East Coast.

Does this mean a Columbia-educated liberal laboring for life as a D.C. reporter is intentionally skewing his or her reporting? Of course not. But it does mean he or she is likely to have a difficult time appreciating the assumptions shared by the patrons in a suburban Nashville or rural Nebraska diner—and that makes it harder to write well about them. The lack of diversity of reporters' average experience—especially in terms of socioeconomic class and years spent around college campuses—often means they only infrequently meet people holding different views, even on topics where the dissenting views are the national majority. Indeed, perhaps counter to what they and you might think, there is actually much greater experience of socioeconomic diversity in most small towns in America than in the "super-ZIP" East Coast neighborhoods in which most reporters live, work, and go out.

This journalistic bubble inevitably creates distance between reporters and their audiences; sometimes it creates outright hostility in both directions. The detachment frequently comes into stark relief on social media—and sometimes centers merely on consumer rather than political preferences. "The top 3 bestselling vehicles in America are pick-ups," John Ekdahl, a conservative blogger, tweeted one evening in January 2017. He's right. The Ford F150 and the Chevy Silverado have sat unchallenged for decades at the top of the annual lists of all vehicles sold in America. "Question to reporters: do you personally know someone that owns one?" It was an interesting question. Trucks and SUVs suggest a certain lifestyle, with certain expectations about weather, terrain, and work—and that often has political consequences. Where I live, for example, nearly every day someone in my household will be driving on unpaved roads, some of which will not see a snowplow anytime in the first twenty-four hours after a snowstorm. Conversely, finding parking is never a challenge within an hour of our house. Some of that different geographical experience ends up being translated into political alignment with vehicle purchasing choices—Republicans like four-wheel drives; Democrats prefer compact and more eco-friendly cars.

This question about our hypothetical relationships with truck owners need not have been a cause of shouting—but the query sparked another of Twitter's inexhaustible supply of minor controversies. *Mediaite*'s David Bixenspan's response was representative: "With 'the media' as we think of it heavily concentrated in New York, with its massive public transit system, it's not entirely the most fair question."[7]

But that was the entire point. Many of the reporters who were so stunned by Donald Trump's victory over Hillary Clinton have never paused to consider how disconnected their experiences are from the daily lives of many—perhaps most—Americans. Bixenspan's retort was reminiscent of *New Yorker* film critic Pauline Kael's (in)famous remark that she had no idea how Richard Nixon had won the presidency: "I don't know anyone who voted for him!" Nixon in 1972 carried every state except Massachusetts, and tied for the largest popular vote in U.S. history (61%), and yet in many liberal neighborhoods in Eastern cities, his victory was utterly inexplicable.

It turns out that, as across all of human history, city and country values differ a lot—and journalism is largely the domain not only of people who live in urban centers but who *prefer* to live in urban centers. It's not wrong, but it is different. Unfortunately, the failure of some journalists to notice and challenge the assumptions of their particular echo chamber imposes a significant cost on everyone—because all of us need the insights and perspective that rigorous, thoughtful reporting produces.

A Brief History of "Who Started It?"

This brings us to the question of who is responsible for the extreme polarization that now plagues our national politics. I want to suggest, hopefully without losing sight of my own biases, that the dominant media explanation does not tell the full story.

I'll take a piece written by Jim VandeHei, the talented founder of popular political news sites *Politico* and *Axios*, as an example of what I'm talking about. In 2017, VandeHei wrote a history of polarization in American politics under the headline, "How American Politics Went Batshit Crazy, Starting with Newt Gingrich." VandeHei provided what might, at a glance, seem like a plausible timeline showing that Republicans are primarily responsible for creating our toxic contemporary political climate. "Gingrich ushered in a good-versus-evil style" of politics, he wrote. Then Fox News "monetized" it, causing MSNBC and CNN to follow suit. In 2008, the screaming infected presidential politics, as John McCain debased himself by selecting Sarah Palin as his running mate. Republicans thereby, in VandeHei's analysis, "celebritized rage politics." Sarah Palin, combined with the emergence of Facebook and Twitter—a kind of accelerant for political anger—paved the political path for Donald Trump, with his special genius for stigmatizing and "othering" his little, lying, low-energy opponents.

It's a tidy story, but, as any Republican with a memory of those years would argue, Gingrich's energetic coalition did not appear ex nihilo. He was tapping into an angry constituency that was already there.

So who was that base? And why were they angry?

It is impossible to understand the 1994 Republican takeover of the House of Representatives without understanding conservative anxiety over two Supreme Court confirmations in the years just prior. In one of the more influential speeches of twentieth-century America, liberal lion Ted Kennedy declared to the public in a planned, nationally televised speech that Robert Bork—President Ronald Reagan's nominee to fill a high court vacancy in 1986—was, quite simply, a monster:

> Robert Bork's America is a land in which women would be forced into back-alley abortions, blacks would sit at segregated lunch counters, rogue police could break down citizens' doors in midnight raids, schoolchildren could not be taught about evolution, writers and artists would be censored at the whim of government, and the doors of the Federal courts would be shut on the fingers of millions

of citizens for whom the judiciary is often the only pro-
tector of the individual rights that are the heart of our
democracy.[8]

In my view, this was a gross and malicious mischaracterization. Antonin Scalia and Bork had very similar views of the role of a justice—
yet Ted Kennedy himself had voted to confirm Scalia. In fact, Scalia
had been confirmed *unanimously* by the Senate, just *one year* earlier.

Bork's problem was one of timing: Liberal activist groups had
decided, for the first time in American history, to wage an electronic-
era political campaign against a Supreme Court candidacy—and the
media aided the effort, covering the nomination not as a debate over
competing ideas of the American judiciary but as a battle of good
versus evil. It is unusual for a sitting justice to comment publicly
on politics at all, let alone on a court confirmation battle. But left-
of-center Justice John Paul Stevens not only defended Bork against
Kennedy's accusations but recommended his confirmation: "I personally regard him as a very well-qualified candidate and one who
will be a very welcome addition to the court."[9]

Stage management was a key part of this made-for-TV political
drama, and one of the central cast members was the Senate Judiciary
Committee chairman: Delaware senator Joe Biden. His former staffers later admitted that Chairman Biden hatched a plan to work with
outside advocacy groups to heighten the visibility of the Bork hearings. Biden thought a Supreme Court fight could be a key lever to
boosting his name recognition in advance of the 1988 Democratic
primary: "The Bork nomination was going to be the opportunity
for Americans to see Joe Biden and for the first time really thinking
about him as a president," Biden's former chief of staff confessed.[10]

In the final tally, fifty-two of fifty-four Democrats voted against
Bork, sinking his nomination, and "*to bork*" was entered into the
Oxford English Dictionary, defined as: "to defame or vilify a person
systematically"—character assassination intended to keep someone
from assuming public office.

In the summer of 1987, I was a 125-pound, 15-year-old wrestler
focused mostly on bench-pressing 225 pounds before school started

back up. I cared little about politics and watched none of Judge Bork's hearings. But at the gym, at the river, at McDonald's, and at church, I overheard endless conversations among frustrated adults about it. People in my town believed that dirty pool tactics were warping the process and railroading an acceptable nominee—and significantly, for the polarization of American life that was to come, they believed that the reporters had thrown their lot in with Democrats.

Biden and Kennedy's "fight legitimized scorched-earth ideological wars over nominations at the Supreme Court," Court watcher Tom Goldstein has written, and, indeed, four years later, on the occasion of another Court vacancy, Democrats and outside political groups—and, to the adults in my childhood town, the media as well—returned to the successful anti-Bork playbook. Though most confirmation hearings are about as riveting as standing in the DMV line, Clarence Thomas's 1991 made-for-TV hearings included porn movie character "Long Dong Silver," strange stories about pubic hair on Coke cans, and murmurings about the sexual preferences of black men. Broadcast networks carried the hearings live all day, and *Saturday Night Live, Designing Women,* and *Murphy Brown* satirized them at night.[11]

Thomas would ultimately be confirmed to the Court, but many Republican staffers and operatives found their view of politics as a form of warfare permanently cemented by the Thomas hearings—famously described by the justice himself as a "high-tech lynching." To them, Newt Gingrich was a reaction to, not the first cause of, ugly political tactics. Similarly, many Republicans began to feel that political reporters, having opted for sensationalism over hard-nosed reporting, could no longer be trusted as dispassionate chroniclers of American public life.

VandeHei makes no mention of the Bork or Thomas hearings in his history of contemporary American political polarization—and in that, he's like many in the mainstream press. His account is plagued by omissions that, to conservatives like myself, are crucial to relating the story at all accurately. Many on the Right have grown so accustomed to selective histories and arguments of this sort that they've come to dismiss the mainstream media entirely. Reporters need to grasp this history when so much of the public seems open to the idea of "fake news." When you consistently do not see your perspective mirrored in the national media, you're likely to think that media is hopelessly out of touch.

Interestingly, I would not typically count Jim VandeHei among those inclined to be biased. He is not only one of the most entrepreneurial minds in journalism but also an exceptionally fair reporter in his own right. He started as a D.C. political reporter just as Gingrich was becoming an insurgent Speaker, and he worked as the *Washington Post*'s national political reporter through most of the George W. Bush years. He left the *Post* to found *Politico* in 2006—an enormously successful project—and launched *Axios* ten years later. His talent and breadth of experience are reasons this alternative history is so interesting: It's an illuminating example of how people filter out some information and emphasize alternative plot points. By locating the origin of "good versus evil" politics with Gingrich's Republican Revolution—a moment that was central in VandeHei's budding career—he reassures liberals that they are victims and inadvertently confirms the widespread conservative belief that reporters are not interested in presenting their perspective.

Renaming Religious Liberty "Bigotry"?

I was skeptical of Donald Trump's candidacy through the primary and general elections in 2016. As a conservative, I worried that Mr. Trump neither embodied nor much cared about the principles that have long animated conservatism. And though I am critical of the national media's frequent inability to frame issues from perspectives other than their own, I nonetheless believe that candidate and now President Trump's blanket attacks on the press as an institution (as opposed to critiques of specific bad stories) are constitutionally troubling and politically foolish. Because of my doubts about Trump's understanding of constitutional principles, I announced that I would be writing in a different Republican on my general-election ballot.

Many of my constituents were livid. I received thousands of messages criticizing my decision. I was formally rebuked by the Nebraska

Republican Party in an overwhelming vote. What in particular were my home-state Republicans angry about?

The number one complaint I received in the following months—and I mean upward of 90 percent of the comments that flooded in—was that the election was ultimately about who would be picking federal judges and Supreme Court nominees. My constituents had divergent views on immigration and health care and environmental policy, but on the Court they were of one mind. Why?

Judges can potentially curtail the Second Amendment or rewrite social policy, and they never stand for election, so battles over judicial selection and confirmation are obviously important to people across the political spectrum. But for Nebraska Republicans, as for many conservatives, the judiciary was the last remaining bulwark of religious liberty—which, to them, is being rapidly eroded, not least by a national media that frequently presents "religious liberty" as little more than a code word for right-wing bigotry.

Here's a representative note I received:

> What the hell do you expect [me to do in the general election]? What do you expect anyone who cares about religious liberty to do in this case? So let me get this straight, because I don't like the fact that Trump is a reprobate and a known perv, I have to now be OK with destroying religious liberty? With killing unborn babies? . . . Vote your conscience all you want, vote Third Party all you want, but ultimately, someone has to decide who leads this country. Trump didn't make this country immoral, he just took advantage of the fact that it already was.

The writer went on to explain that among his family and friends the 2016 election was *exclusively* about judges. It was about who would decide the future of the First Amendment in general and religious liberty in particular. In his view, by the end of a Hillary Clinton administration, America "would have been hunting Christians in the street for sport under a 7–2 Hillary Court." The fear that religious liberty is under assault was the central issue that drove votes in his circles.

What spurred this thinking? Consider this contemporaneous example: In September 2016, the U.S. Commission on Civil Rights, founded in 1957 to end the disgrace of Jim Crow laws, released a report titled, "Peaceful Coexistence: Reconciling Nondiscrimination Principles with Civil Liberties." The report puts "religious liberty" in scare quotes and calls for curtailing the First Amendment in the service of "social justice." Here is a snapshot of the majority's position, in its own words:

> Progress toward social justice depends upon the enactment of, and vigorous enforcement of, status-based nondiscrimination laws. Limited claims for religious liberty are allowed only when religious liberty comes into direct conflict with nondiscrimination precepts. . . . Religious exemptions to the protections of civil rights based upon classifications such as race, color, national origin, sex, disability status, sexual orientation, and gender identity, when they are permissible, significantly infringe upon these civil rights.[12]

Commission chairman Martin Castro continued: "The phrases 'religious liberty' and 'religious freedom' will stand for nothing except hypocrisy so long as they remain code words for discrimination, intolerance, racism, sexism, homophobia, Islamophobia, Christian supremacy or any form of intolerance."

The Commission's report makes no effort to understand the unique role of religious liberty across American history. It fails to acknowledge the benefits of religious liberty at present—to people such as Simratpal Singh, a Sikh-American and decorated Afghanistan War combat veteran whose request to wear a turban with his uniform for religious reasons recently won an accommodation from the Defense Department; or to Samantha Elauf, a Muslim-American who triumphed over retailer Abercrombie & Fitch when one of its stores refused to hire her, citing her hijab as counter to its "look policy" for employees. The Commission even fails to recognize religious liberty as the first and foremost of Americans' civil rights—the first freedom that appears in the Constitution's First Amendment. It simply dismissed both the concept and the practice of religious liberty as a cover for hatred.

For those conservatives who put the Court front and center in their 2016 decision-making, this sort of story is familiar, despite rarely being covered in the mainstream national press. Large swaths of grassroots America see a one-way ratchet that aims to make it more difficult for religious believers to think, speak, and act in accordance with their deepest beliefs—the core of religious liberty.

They watched in disbelief as the Obama administration dragged the Little Sisters of the Poor, an order of nuns dedicated to serving the homeless and elderly poor, to the Supreme Court for refusing to comply with a Health and Human Services Department mandate requiring employers to adopt insurance plans covering contraceptives and abortifacient drugs—both of which are prohibited by Catholic doctrine. A narrow exemption drawn up by HHS to ameliorate the situation was laughable: It did not apply to any religious employer that served people outside its own faith—which happens to be a big part of what many religious organizations do. As Daniel DiNardo, archbishop of Galveston-Houston, observed: "Jesus himself, or the Good Samaritan of his famous parable, would not qualify as 'religious enough' for the exemption, since they insisted on helping people who did not share their view of God." Pastor Rick Warren, the California megachurch pastor who had previously offered the invocation at President Obama's inauguration, stepped in to defend the Little Sisters and to warn that "religious liberty is going to be the civil rights issue of the next decade."

The Obama administration's treatment of the Little Sisters of the Poor was, to many Americans, only the highest-profile example of a broad effort to squeeze religious expression, and religious believers, out of the public square. Conservatives see these campaigns operating with particular zeal on college campuses, where sexual identity politics are bumping up against religious liberty. Earlier this year, Harvard placed the university's largest Christian student group,

Harvard College Faith and Action, on "administrative probation"
after the group requested that a member of its student leadership
step down after she decided to pursue a same-sex relationship—in
violation of the commitments required of club leaders. Last year, the
University of Iowa kicked the Business Leaders in Christ off campus
for requiring that the group's student leaders uphold its mission—including a commitment to abstain from certain sexual conduct. (The
dean of students informed the group that it could return provided it
"revise" its beliefs.) Similar episodes, often accompanied by appeals
to dubious "hate speech" restrictions, have recently occurred at the
University of North Carolina, Vanderbilt, Rutgers, and dozens of
other institutions.

It is obvious to most Americans that groups necessarily "discriminate" on the basis of belief and practice in leadership selections.
No one would mandate that the Black Student Union accept a white
supremacist as its president, or that the College Republicans accept
a Bernie Sanders Democrat to head their organization. But when it
comes to complex debates about sexual ethics, "tolerance" has sometimes come to look like a pretext for pushing religious believers to
the margins.

For our purposes here, though, the issue isn't which groups are
right or wrong in various disputes. The issue is whether dissenters
from campus majoritarian orthodoxy are getting a fair hearing—
and that's rarely the case, in the eyes of conservatives. The Commission on Civil Rights' report on religious liberty went almost entirely
unreported in the mainstream press. Reporting on the treatment of
Christian clubs on campus is restricted almost entirely to conservative outlets and religious broadcasting. The Little Sisters of the Poor
received press, by dint of their case reaching the high court, but the
nuns were generally treated as representatives of an anti-woman,
retrograde worldview, while HHS secretaries Kathleen Sebelius
and Sylvia Burwell were depicted as valiant defenders of women's
rights.

For many conservatives, the mainstream media time and again
fails to see the world from their point of view—and, what is more,
often shows little interest in trying.

Our Missing Serial Killer

Dr. Kermit Gosnell's name should elicit the same shock and repulsion as Jeffrey Dahmer's and Charles Manson's. Yet you probably haven't heard of him. The "why" of this story is instructive about the stories our national media fail to see—or choose not to see.

Gosnell was a Philadelphia abortionist who for more than a decade engaged in a pattern of cruel, sadistic behavior toward his patients, mostly poor, minority women and their unborn children. Among his habits was keeping severed babies' feet in jars as trophies. One witness reported seeing at least a hundred beheaded fetuses. Another recounted a child who survived a late-term abortion screaming in pain.

Gosnell's cruelty extended to the women seeking abortions. One woman, who changed her mind about getting an abortion, testified that Gosnell tied her up, beat her, and drugged her before performing an abortion against her will. LaToya Ransome's abortion went so badly that it left her disabled and in need of open heart surgery. Gosnell accidentally punctured the uterus of a 19-year-old patient but restrained her in his clinic, refusing to let her leave to seek adequate medical care; after several hours and extraordinary blood loss, she was forced into an emergency hysterectomy. Another patient suffered convulsions during her procedure, fell off the table, and hit her head—but Gosnell wouldn't let her leave and stopped her friend from calling an ambulance or leaving to find help. Forty-one-year-old Karnamaya Mongar died in 2009 after Gosnell ordered extra anesthetics under peculiar circumstances.

Gosnell was eventually convicted of murder. Many of his former employees came forward to tell tales about his systematic killing and his grotesque stockpiling of body parts.

Regardless of one's position on abortion, this should have attracted front-page, wall-to-wall attention from the start. But it didn't. Why not?

Because, as some reporters and editors later admitted, they were reluctant to cover any abortion-related story that might help the pro-life cause. Megan McArdle, an abortion-rights defender, thoughtfully and responsibly later reflected on her decision not to report the story—and she confessed that she should have: "The truth is that most of us tend to be less interested in sick-making stories—if the sick-making was done by 'our side.'" Jeffrey Goldberg, editor-in-chief of *The Atlantic*, agreed that the media collectively had made a mistake: The Gosnell "case touches on several national policy concerns, including regulation of abortion clinics and the morality of late-term abortions," he wrote. Such introspection is a credit to these individual writers, but it's the industry exception, not the norm. A *Washington Post* health policy reporter rejected criticism of the *Post*'s lack of coverage, dismissing Gosnell as a "local" crime story. (She later retracted the description, acknowledging Gosnell's crimes as "horrifying.") And even outlets that covered the story tended to sanitize Gosnell's carnage. The Associated Press, writing about courtroom testimony describing a hundred-plus fetal beheadings, titled its story: "Staffer Describes Chaos at PA Abortion Clinic." To understand how this headline appears to pro-life readers, imagine a school shooting reported under the headline: "Coach Disappointed over Premature End to Playoff Game." Or imagine a deadly mine explosion summarized as: "Maintenance Crew Frustrated at Inadequate Working Conditions."[13]

As *USA Today*'s Kirsten Powers noted, the proper word for Gosnell's activities is "infanticide." He was a bona fide serial killer. But it was only reporters like Powers and *The Federalist*'s Mollie Hemingway who managed to shame other news agencies into reporting on him.

The result of selection bias of this sort in decisions about what news is news has led tens of millions of Americans to divorce from the mainstream media, citing irreconcilable differences. Since the Gosnell story, I've met several Nebraska women who've told me that they'd been apolitical all their lives but had recently joined the GOP after concluding that the media refused to report on heinous crimes in order not to hurt the abortion-rights cause. Similarly, I've heard from women in churches who never considered themselves enthusiastic Republicans—and who vigorously object to Donald Trump's personal behavior—but now describe themselves as "reluctant Trump zealots." They explained that they feel antagonized and condescended to by the national press. Being approached by Nebraskans who want to explain their evolution from anti-press to pro-Trump is a common experience for me when I'm back home from D.C. on weekends.

I'm not writing this to inflame anyone on the subject of abortion. I'm simply trying to demonstrate why it is that millions of Americans have turned to Fox News, Rush Limbaugh, and other right-wing outlets for the news, to the exclusion of almost everything else. They've wearied of the uncomplicated, left-leaning picture of the world presented by the mainstream press for three decades. Too many anomalies piled up in the minds of right-leaning newsreaders—and they eventually chose a different model.

I readily acknowledge that there is a great deal of nuttiness in this alternative, right-leaning media (about which, more to come). But there is also far too little soul-searching by national political reporters about why the caricature of the "liberal elite" rings so true to so many of their fellow citizens.

Who Fact-Checks the Fact-Checkers?

A couple summers ago, I spoke at an event in Park City, Utah, just after Mitt Romney. Following my address, CNN anchor Wolf Blitzer approached and offered some kinds words about my speech. Along the way, he seemed to be congratulating me on my reasonableness. This was nice of him, but I was uncomfortable with some of his characterizations of my views. Like many others, he appeared to have mistaken my criticism of candidate Trump's unwillingness to acknowledge obvious and indisputable facts or the American creed of universal dignity as somehow an embrace of a progressive agenda.

"You do realize that I'm the second- or third-most conservative member of the Senate, right?" I asked.

He seemed nonplussed. "You know what I mean," he continued. "You're a part of the reasonable middle." He seemed to be saying: You're like me. I obviously don't know Blitzer's policy preferences or voting record, but I do know a number of places where we part ways:

for example, I'm not particularly fond of the relentless "Breaking News!" chyrons at CNN, which largely advertise items that are not news, let alone urgent news. I think hyperbole like this desensitizes viewers to what is really important and makes thoughtful political discussion more unlikely.

The conversation was very cordial, but I decided it might be beneficial to argue a bit more. So why not bring up CNN's treatment of Romney, since he had just spoken? "But you understand that I identify with the frustration people from Nebraska felt over the regularly dishonest way CNN covered the last [2012] election, right? They're still angry over what Candy Crowley did during the debate. She failed in her job as a journalist."

Blitzer looked at me, confused—which, in turn, confused me. It took some awkward stumbling around together for us to figure out where we were missing each other.

I was referring to Crowley's work moderating the second Obama-Romney debate in 2012. Apparently this had made so little impression on him that he couldn't recall it at first. I had to give him a few details before it returned to his mind.

In case you have the same reaction, let me summarize: Governor Romney was hammering President Obama for not acknowledging a 2012 "act of terror" in Benghazi that killed multiple Americans, including Ambassador Christopher Stevens, until two weeks after the attack on U.S. government facilities. As Romney pressed his argument, Crowley, the moderator, interrupted to "fact-check" the GOP nominee. "He did, in fact, sir," she said. She was claiming Romney's charge was false.

Romney was visibly confused. Crowley, supposedly a neutral third party, wasn't asking a question, and he wasn't out of time. He appeared not to know how to respond. Should he argue with her, the moderator?

Media fact-checkers later confirmed that Romney's criticism of the president was accurate—Crowley's "fact-check" was, in fact, wrong—but this was after the debate, and after almost all viewers had turned the channel. Crowley herself eventually agreed that Romney was "right in the main." But her interjection changed the momentum of the debate, gave Obama a respite, and took the sting out of Romney's attack. It made Romney look dishonest, even though he was fully accurate in his claim.

Republicans, even those not in love with Romney's candidacy, saw Crowley's intervention as representative of the press: not dispassionate arbiters, but open partisans. The story dominated conservative headlines for days after the debate and remains a lingering psychic wound.

Yet it apparently made so little impression at CNN that Wolf Blitzer didn't even remember it.

Again, to many Americans, Crowley's conduct fit a pattern. In the late 1990s, it was revealed that the *New Republic*'s Stephen Glass had simply made up whole-cloth several of his stories. The movie *Shattered Glass*, based on a *Vanity Fair* article by Buzz Bissinger, depicts how this serial liar cultivated a liberal appetite for his fabrications—namely, by playing to a certain worldview. One of his articles included lurid descriptions of sexual escapades and drug use among attendees at the 1997 Conservative Political Action Conference. Glass was fired when his tall tales were discovered, but one can ask why his editors weren't more skeptical. Could it have been confirmation bias?

In 2004, after forty-four years at CBS News, anchorman Dan Rather aired a story that George W. Bush went "absent without leave" when he was in the Texas Air National Guard. After an independent investigation of the story, CBS fired Rather, having learned that he failed to authenticate documents he had obtained and lied about doing so, and that his team had been in touch with John Kerry's campaign during the planning of the segment. But now, he's back working at MSNBC as an analyst—of journalistic quality. In 2015, it was revealed that NBC's Brian Williams had also badly exaggerated the turmoil he experienced overseas. Part of the newscaster's lore was that he was aboard a U.S. helicopter forced down by RPG fire during the Iraq War in 2003. The story had been repeated so often that no one thought to question it—until soldiers actually on the helicopter hit by rockets and small-arms fire revealed that Williams hadn't been with them in their Chinook. After being fired by

NBC, he too was hired by MSNBC, where he regularly offers commentary about alleged conservative hypocrisy.

I can't count how many times people have complained to me about the fact that Williams still has a platform. This is weird; my job is serving in the U.S. Senate. How did I become a therapist for Nebraskans' media laments? Because there is among many of my constituents a deep sense that the national media no longer represents them; that we are no longer in this together, that there is in fact no "we" at all. "It's like the media doesn't even try to appeal to truth," one rancher told me recently.

And so while my parents wanted us to watch the news to get an accurate sense of what's going on in the country, many among us on both sides of the aisle now demand not factual accuracy but partisan loyalty. It's us versus them, they think. It's Fox News versus MSNBC.

Alone in the Electronic Glow

"Don't make me doubt Fox," one lady responded when I debunked an inaccurate story. "They're the only channel I can trust." This is a common sentiment among people who have televisions—electronic hearths—going all day in their living rooms. It isn't an accident that Fox News recently changed its motto from "Fair and Balanced" to "America's Most Watched, Most Trusted" network.

In Chapter 1, we considered Robert Putnam's argument that in America, "Connections among individuals, social networks and the norms of reciprocity and trustworthiness that arise from them" have eroded dangerously. As recently as the early 1990s, it wasn't like this.

As a result, we have a country of increasingly disconnected people sitting around watching news that riles them up. We noted the unique loneliness that older men in the United States face. Not surprisingly, a paper from the *Proceedings of the National Academy of Sciences* shows polarization is growing faster among elderly Americans than among those under 40.[14]

Retired seniors now watch *fifty hours* of television per week. Fox News viewers are among the oldest—68 years old, compared to a median age of 60 among CNN and MSNBC viewers. In a society that has fewer and fewer groups to which we naturally belong, it's no wonder that lonely older folks take comfort in a substitute television family. People want to be in a group. They want to belong. This trope has appeared in every high school movie ever made—and probably in every high school building ever built. When the unpopular kid gets a chance to sit with the cool kids, it's not long before he's mocking the social outcasts whose ranks he just left. The pressure to belong, the desire to belong, makes people forget the Golden Rule. Empathy is hard work. Regrettably, when it comes to politics, we adults forget, too.

Our isolation has deprived us of healthy local tribes with whom we share values and goals and ways of life that uplift us, and so we fall into "anti-tribes," defined by what we're against rather than what we're for.

It's a sorry substitute for real belonging, but it's better than nothing. We might not have much in the way of community, but at least we aren't as ludicrous as those sanctimonious liberals on MSNBC, or as absurd as those blowhard conservatives on Fox. There's something comforting in joining people of a similar mind-set ("we") to denounce "them."

No one wants to sit alone.

And so, liberals and conservatives no longer believe the same things, we don't understand how our opponents believe what they believe, and we soothe our lonely souls with the balm of contempt.

Of course, where there is demand, supply will emerge. And it turns out that "contempt" is big business.

Post-truth: (adjective)

relating to or denoting circumstances in
which objective facts are less influential
in shaping public opinion than appeals to
emotion and personal belief.

—Oxford Dictionary,
2016 Word of the Year

4

THE POLARIZATION
BUSINESS MODEL

Newsflash: There Are Nutjobs Everywhere
The Need to Name Evil ❧ They Know What They're Doing
Everyone Is a Click-Baiter Now ❧ The Great Chicken Scare
From Common Experiences to Common Enemies
From Local to National to Niche Markets
Conservatism Doesn't Make Good Radio ❧ "It's Just a Game"
The President Plays the Fiddle ❧ It's Gonna Get Worse Before It Gets Better
Hope Beyond a Broken Business Model

SEAN HANNITY IS GOOD AT WHAT HE DOES. SO GOOD, IN FACT, that his daily cable news show is number one nationally, and his daily talk radio show is number two. TV and radio are very different media, but Hannity has mastered both. There's a reason he reportedly earns a ballpark $40 million annually. You might not like what he's doing, but it's definitely on purpose.

So what is it he's doing?

He explained the core objective of his two different programs to the *New York Times*. It's not to promote a particular conservative agenda, or to encourage American patriotism, or even to offer coherent arguments against liberalism. His core cause is to rage.

"I'm mad," he explained.[1]

That's the starting point. Each episode, on both formats, begins with something that makes him mad enough to emote, mad enough to let others participate in a collective experience of catharsis.

Most cable news and talk radio shows today—on both the right and the left—operate this way. The leading programs are orchestrated by executives and personalities who understand well that there's real money to be made in helping people keep their fears and hatreds aligned. Still, Hannity is without peer. He is careful not to claim that he's offering viewers accurate news from an unbiased perspective or giving due consideration to competing interpretations of complex events. Instead, he heaps up serving after serving of what one of my Senate colleagues calls his "Hey-can-you-believe-this-shit?!" messaging.

The storyline is simple: Liberals are evil, you're a victim, and you should be furious. Hannity tells a lot of angry, isolated people what they want to hear. And he has the delivery down to an art form.

We'd all be better off, as would our communities, if we understood the game he and his colleagues—on both sides of the spectrum—are playing.*

Newsflash: There Are Nutjobs Everywhere

We've all heard the phrase "cherry-picking," a form of selective reasoning where someone cites facts that support his preferred position while ignoring conflicting data. In modern America, though, cherry-picking looks like a sophisticated rhetorical device compared to the trend called nutpicking. (Not, mind you, "nitpicking," which is pointing out irrelevant details just to antagonize.) "Nutpicking" is when people scour the news to find a random person saying or doing

---

* The examples of media malpractice I detail in this chapter are predominantly from the right. As explained in the introduction, this is a function of my daily life experience of being a Republican and representing a state that has been overwhelmingly Republican for decades. I simply know the world of the right better. But it is readily apparent that very similar echo chambers exist on the left side of the political and media spectrum as well.

something really dumb, and then use that nutjob to disparage an entire group of people, as if the nut is representative.

The left does it. In the lead-up to the 2010 midterm elections, liberals tried desperately to find an ugly racist in the Tea Party. Nut-seeking camera crews were deployed to Tea Party rallies, but none of them ever secured the sought-after, tight racist soundbite. If they had, we'd all have seen the clip hundreds of times by now, with the words of the moronic racist burned in our ears and his face burned on our retinas—and the larger tax-cutting movement branded as having him as its supposed spokesman. (After a 30,000-person rally in Washington, D.C., where some prominent liberals claimed they heard racial slurs, Andrew Breitbart offered $100,000 to anyone who could produce video of the event from that day, but no one ever produced evidence to collect.) If you sign up for any Democratic fundraising email lists (which I have done, because I imprudently thought I should read some of the idiotic rhetoric not only from my "side" but from the other side too), you'll read about some redneck wearing a MAGA hat who made a YouTube video of himself kicking his dog. The subject line of the email will read something like: "Revealed! Trump Supporters Hate Animal Rights."

The right does it, too. Many conservative websites are thrilled to discover an adjunct professor at a community college who told his Accounting 101 class that he thinks Jesus of Nazareth was a black transsexual. On the homepage, the headline screams: "Propaganda U: Loony Liberal Professor Attacks Christian Students in Class!"

It's a popular exercise, because it's not hard. In a country of 320 million people, someone, somewhere, is doing or saying something asinine right this minute.

Hannity's coverage of last year's horrific mass shooting at a Las Vegas country music concert could serve as a "how-to" guide for nut-picking. On the evening of October 2, 2017, almost four million people tuned in to his show to help make sense of what had happened the previous night. Hannity began by summarizing the attack, then turned to a scathing condemnation of left-wing media figures' efforts to "politicize" the tragedy. He played a CNN segment in which correspondent Jeff Zeleny noted that "a lot of these country music supporters were likely Trump supporters." Then he read a Facebook comment from CBS attorney Hayley Geftman-Gold, who said she was "not even sympathetic" to the victims of the shooting, since "country-music fans often are Republican gun toters." (By the time of Hannity's broadcast, Geftman-Gold had already been fired by CBS.) Finally, Hannity cited a tweet from the account @TheResistANNce, apparently run by a self-identified progressive schoolteacher: "Oh, they're probably Trumptards," wrote the Twitter user, referring to the concert audience. "I hope only Trumptards were killed." "Where is your human soul to tweet that out?" asked Hannity.

Even Matthew Shaer, who penned a critical profile of Hannity for the *New York Times*, admitted that it was a masterly sleight of hand: "Ten seconds of decontextualized TV, one cruel Facebook comment and one tweet had been pressed into service as evidence of the moral malignancy of the left as a whole—of half of the entire country."[2]

Start watching for nutpicking, and it's amazing how much national "news" is devoted to turning a random social media account into a full-scale indictment of this or that group. That's because it's good business. Hosts, producers, and executives know that Americans are primed to despise each other—they just need a target. And anger is intoxicating. We'll keep coming back for more.

The Need to Name Evil

Most of us recognize that this state of affairs isn't healthy—for us as individuals, or for our country as a whole. Yet tens of millions of us continue to tune in, day in and day out. It's kind of like drinking too much. We know it's bad for us—but we need the buzz.

Sociologists who study the "psychology of enemies" have learned that having foes has real psychic value. Enemies help give life coherence. They give us someone to blame, and they help us know what to expect. In one study, researchers asked participants to imagine a powerful enemy—maybe ISIS. Afterward, people tended to perceive the world as *less* disordered and dangerous. Naming the enemy helped put limits, conceptually, on what the enemy was capable of. A version of this happens after events like car accidents or cancer diagnoses. Was the driver drinking? Is the patient a smoker? We appreciate being able to hang onto these concrete explanations, and we're troubled when they're not there.

Media coverage of the Las Vegas shooting showed precisely this dynamic at work. The shooter—a 64-year-old multimillionaire real-estate investor with no criminal record—didn't fit the normal profile. Struggling to make sense of the attack, Fox News personality Brian Kilmeade said something revealing: "With Bin Laden, we knew who to hate. With Sandy Hook, we had that mutant living in his basement. [But with the Las Vegas shooter] we don't even know enough about him to hate him yet." Bin Laden was a jihadi terrorist; the Sandy Hook shooter was deeply mentally ill; but why did the Las Vegas shooter do what he did? Kilmeade, like many of us, was searching for coherence. We need each particular horror to fit into some larger story with which we can make sense of the brokenness of the world.[3]

Sean Hannity's solution to this conundrum was to redirect the desire to blame someone to a concrete, and politically convenient, target: a left-wing CBS executive and the anti-Trump Twitter user.

As it happens, though, the Twitter user Hannity cited, @TheResistANNce, didn't exist. When reporters went to track down the schoolteacher supposedly behind the account, peculiarities emerged: the account had no archived tweets; the profile photo had mysteriously morphed from a middle-aged woman into a young man; there were discrepancies in the creation date of the account; and the actual tweet was only ever seen by two people. What Hannity aired, and what went viral online, was a screenshot. Although this was not of Hannity's doing, the infamous tweet was a hoax.

Journalists regularly make mistakes. It's not hard to get hoodwinked by counterfeit social media accounts. But Hannity never corrected the record so far as I have been able to find. Having given his millions of viewers the impression that Trump supporters were killed and that liberals cheered it, he moved on. It was a grotesque distortion of reality. It was, quite literally, fake news.

They Know What They're Doing

Media organizations are businesses, and many of them have finally learned the No. 1 rule of business: the customer is always right. The polititainment industry, in talk radio and on cable television, but especially on the internet, is constantly honing its abilities to measure consumer preferences and figuring out ways to tailor content to match the target audience. That is to say, they're not telling you what's news; you're telling them—usually without knowing it.

For the average news website, whether a blog in the fever swamps or a high-profile outlet, the bottom-line demand is simple: to get more readers to interact with articles, because advertisers will pay top dollar for an engaged readership. Analytical tools measure how long visitors stay on each article and if they will click to see additional content inside an article. People willing to sit through an ad are worth more, as are people who share articles. (Only 55 percent of Americans will spend more than fifteen seconds reading an article.) The pop-up polls at many sites are not measuring anything about what share of Americans believes X or Y; they are measuring whether or not you're a good mark for an ad. News sites, especially those you interact with frequently, know a good deal about you: your location, your sex, your approximate age, and, of course, the types of things you read and don't read. If you get a daily email from a news site, they know which emails you do and don't open—and future emails are tailored to those preferences. On the same day, two readers of the same publication will see two very different lists of "must-read" articles.

The business model is entirely short term: They want to keep you right there, right now, clicking for as long as possible. The web designers who are working behind the scenes with media executives to keep you constantly clicking and playing conceive of their work as being very similar to that of video game designers and engineers.

You can see the model compressed and crystallized on social media. Growing and keeping people interested in a political social media account, as professional social media managers will tell you, is not a glamorous business. It's simply a matter of capitalizing on the outrage feedback loop: spot something stupid an obscure liberal/ conservative said; use it to malign all liberals/conservatives; watch your profile rise as you become a hero to people on your side and a villain to people on the opposite side; rinse and repeat.

In our digital age, provocative social media is the only profitable social media. The incentive structure in the media complex rewards pushing the gas, not tapping the brakes—or qualifying a point. Celebrities, political big shots, and media outlets have junior staffers constantly tweeting and posting, giving readers new reasons to click—and the sharper-tongued the post, the better. (For the record, I'm personally responsible for all the tweets on @bensasse, for better or worse. No professional "ghost-posting"—although my teenage daughters do constantly pitch me on joke tweets. FYI: The lame ones were probably Corrie's.)

Clicks are cash, and social media managers know that pushing the envelope is the pathway to followers and profits.

Eventually the cycle grows old, and some of the political personalities or ghost-posters want to do something that is more useful for their neighbors and countrymen than simply riding another boring wave of outrage. But how do they escape a system whose primary fuel is indignation? I have interviewed some celebrities who have tried to break out of the vicious cycle of rage-inflammation by turning their attention to uplifting stories or by trying to introduce some nuance into outrage-of-the-day coverage. But guess what happens?

No one wants nuance. We want white hats and black hats. No one clicks, metrics plummet, and readers grumble that their knife-fighter went soft, lost her edge, "sold out."

Some people are okay with losing their notoriety—and the opportunities and wealth that frequently accompany it. But not many people. Most learn their lesson and throw themselves back into the outrage loop, now committed less to being the scourge of the opposition than to making sure they don't fall out of favor with the audience. There are a whole bunch of people I've heard from in the political media who despise their own song-and-dance routine—but are too in love with their fame, their influence, or their money to give it up. What else are they going to do? This has become their work.

The same logic increasingly drives cable news panels—the kind with several "talking heads" floating on the screen, arguing a topic. Professional commentators have learned that the camera cuts away from the person who sits silently and lets his opponent lay out an argument. "Respectful listening" doesn't make for good TV. Producers teach that movement attracts the eyes of the viewer, knowing that if someone's head isn't shaking "no" in disbelief, the viewer will be more tempted to change the channel. That's why pundits, desperate to make the drive to the studio worthwhile, and motivated to get invited back, constantly interrupt or theatrically disagree even when it's not logical—or even if they're actually polite people in real life. The goal is to create the most visually interesting segment possible—even if "interesting" doesn't align with reasonable, or fair, or useful to viewers.

Everyone Is a Click-Baiter Now

Okay, so some TV and internet programming is shady-used-car content—but there is still new Cadillac and Mercedes content too, right? There have been salacious scribblings since gladiators filled the Colosseum. Surely we can take comfort in the guardrails at serious, established journalistic entities.

But the truth is messier.

The *Washington Post*, after it was purchased by Amazon founder Jeff Bezos, began refining a new digital content assessment tool called "Bandito." Editors place two versions of an article online under different headlines. Then, in real time, the system determines which version is more popular with which readers, and eliminates the less attractive version where it is less effective. Because this is useful technology, many publications are experimenting with copycat versions of it. But there's an obvious problem with these tight-feedback-loop technologies: they rely heavily on the confirmation bias of readers and viewers. Readers are prone to click on more sensational headlines, and that means headlines are going to tilt in a more sensational direction—not only because of the technology, but as headline writers anticipate how to respond to consumer demands.

Note how almost every major news site in recent years has adopted, in some form, what has become known as "the *Buzzfeed* headline"—for example, "Canada's Response to Russia's Anti-LGBT Propaganda Law Is Totally Awesome." *Buzzfeed* understood the way people consume news online better, and earlier, than its competitors. Online readers, who move more quickly from one article to the next than readers of a traditional, in-the-hand newspaper, want headlines that not only tell them *what's happening*, but also *what to think* about what's happening—or, as *Buzzfeed* recognized, what to *feel* ("totally awesome").

This use of long, salacious headlines has only increased as "sharing" has become a more important part of every site's business model. You're worth more as a reader if you're consistently posting articles to your Facebook or Twitter accounts, or emailing them to your family and friends. Have you noticed that, on most news sites, the sharing buttons are at the top of articles, well above the content text? That's because web designers know that the overwhelming majority of people will not make it even to the third paragraph, let alone the bottom of the page. If most of us are only spending fifteen seconds (max) on any article, outlets have to convince you to share it quickly—and the best way to do that is by writing a headline that you'll agree with. The web designers understand that all the action has to happen at the top.

Of course, as news sites change to accommodate readers' flitting attention, they encourage those habits. And some readers seemingly share articles simply to signal their agreement with the headline ("Look at me! I am the kind of person who agrees with this statement!"), not because anything in the article is useful or insightful.

But—getting back to Bandito—at least the *Washington Post*'s experiment is primarily about headlines attached to stories already determined by editors to have journalistic value. What happens if the distribution and feedback algorithms begin to determine not just the headlines but also which articles get written in the first place? We presume that an article's existence is adequate proof of its importance. But what happens when articles are written not to increase understanding but simply to boost clicks?

The Great Chicken Scare

In April 2018, the *New Yorker* published an article by Dan Piepenbring about fast-food chain Chick-Fil-A, which had recently opened another Manhattan location on Fulton Street. Chick-Fil-A is one of the nation's largest chains, and it was recently ranked the most popular fast-food restaurant in the country, according to consumer satisfaction surveys. New Yorkers apparently like the restaurant too, with one store's line sometimes running out the door and around the corner. Another Manhattan location says it sells a chicken sandwich every six seconds.

What was Piepenbring's angle, though? "Chick-fil-A's Creepy Infiltration of New York City," the headline blared. The restaurant, wrote Piepenbring, "feels like an infiltration, in no small part because of its pervasive Christian traditionalism." According to Piepenbring, the Cathy family, which founded and owns the restaurant, peddle a conspiratorial, anti-gay agenda, their restaurant is a sort of megachurch, their advertising is "morbid," and their food is "palliative." Piepenbring even attacked the chain's trademark cows for their lousy spelling.

Since sneering tirades about chicken sandwiches are not the sort of content historically associated with the *New Yorker*, which in the same calendar year won a Pulitzer Prize for Ronan Farrow's series of important articles exposing decades of hushed-up sexual predation in Hollywood, a reasonable reader might be tempted to worry about the mental faculties of the magazine's editorial staff. Do literary Manhattanites genuinely fear a Great Chicken Crusade?

No. But an essay about the looming specter of Christian-supremacist poultry products is precisely the sort of thing to anger the rubes. Which is exactly what happened. Thousands upon thousands of shares and forwards and retweets later, one's stance on the *New Yorker*'s Chick-Fil-A screed was a convenient left-versus-right sorting mechanism, and the publishers were thrilled to have the clicks.

A senior producer at one of America's largest cable news networks once let me in on "rule one" of their segment selection: "We only do two kinds of stories," he told me—"those that make people who love us love us more, and those that make people who hate us hate us more." Following the *New Yorker*'s piece, I asked some publishing executives about this line. The responses were nearly uniform: the same logic is becoming the norm at print publications as well. I asked them to unpack this logic.

"There are no possible 70-percent-of-America audiences anymore," one executive explained. "All we can do is try to create 'stickiness' among the 1 percent of the readers we have a shot at. So that means getting attacked is almost as valuable as being loved."

Experts in media business models all emphasize the importance of cultivating a passionate core group of followers—an excitable 1 percent who love the content so much that they'll share it, talk about it, and make it go viral. This enthusiastic bunch is described as "sticky," meaning they'll come back week after week. But at least as important as the sticky in a media outlet's thinking is the angry. Getting people angry enough at you to share an article or clip is almost as valuable as getting them to endorse it. If you can gin up outrage, then cast yourself as the victim when attacked and rally supporters to you, the shares climb further.

For content providers, all clicks are good clicks.

From Common Experiences to Common Enemies

How did we get to this point—of angry, fractured hyper-partisans? How did anti-tribes replace genuine tribes?

In 1951, the television show *I Love Lucy* debuted—and more than two-thirds of Americans tuned in to watch. We had just been through a depression together, then won a world war together, and now the Baby Boom was on; seemingly everyone had a sister or aunt or daughter or granddaughter navigating the joys and pains of pregnancy. We had a lot in common. Obviously, grave social problems afflicted the country—*I Love Lucy* premiered to a nation where racial segregation was both legal and brutally enforced—and for many

Americans, "normal" life was a grim experience of second-class status. Nonetheless (as we explored in Chapter 1), there was optimism
across basically every group—and there remained an astonishingly
widespread sense of togetherness.

And part of that had to do with a common popular culture. For
the next few years, *every* American knew Lucille Ball and Desi Arnaz.
Almost every family across the land was buying or saving to buy a
TV, and whether in their own living room or in the living room of
their next-door neighbor, they were growing up with Lucy and Desi.
Everyone knew their history, their facial tics, their pet peeves, their
soft spots, and Desi's latest antics. Was this life-changing cultural
content? No. But it was *shared*. Lucy, Desi, and the evening news
were like a nightly national "homeroom."

For those of us who weren't alive at the time, it's almost impossible to imagine the degree of communal experience. In the last
decade-plus, the most watched serial program (as opposed to a onetime event like the Super Bowl) was when *Sunday Night Football*, for
a short run in 2014, claimed a 14 percent share of American households. By contrast, Lucy and Desi regularly captured almost 70 percent of America.*

This "common culture" continued into the 1960s, even as the
political scene began to roil. One-third of Americans tuned into
The Beverly Hillbillies on any given evening. As Charles Murray has
observed, there are structural reasons for this: "The explanation for
the ratings of 1963 is simple: There wasn't much choice. Most major
cities had only four channels (CBS, NBC, ABC, and a nonprofit
station of some sort) at most." Still, limited choices had an upside:
everyone tended to be watching the same things. Watercooler talk
was easier.

Even two decades later, in 1983, 125 million people—54 percent
of the country—tuned in for the finale of *M*A*S*H*, a long-running,
indirect exploration of the toll of the Vietnam War (via the artistic

---

* For a brilliant analysis of, among other things, what happens to any sense of shared experiences, shared meaning, and shared facts when most Americans have 500-plus channels and unlimited other options at their fingertips, I highly recommend Yuval Levin's
The Fractured Republic.

cover of a show set in the Korean War). So many New York City residents flushed their toilets immediately after the show's conclusion that it set a record for pressure on the city's sewage and water system. Some 1 million Gothamites held it during the last minutes of *M*A*S*H* in order not to miss Hawkeye's final monologue.

Why do New Yorkers' historic flush patterns matter? Only because they suggest the extent to which Americans once stocked their imaginations with the same things. Hawks and doves took very different positions about Alan Alda (who played the character Hawkeye) and his war skepticism, but *M*A*S*H* gave everyone some common ground for debate. Absent television-on-demand, broad cross-sections of different parts of America were still watching the same dramas unfold. By contrast, it was considered impressive when *Game of Thrones,* HBO's megahit fantasy series, drew almost 4 percent of Americans for its sixth-season finale.

To appreciate how narrowly tailored our political subcultures now are, consider that today's best cable news ratings look pitiful not just compared to *I Love Lucy*, but even to an average *Game of Thrones* episode. Fox News's *Hannity*, despite being the most popular cable news program, draws only about 1 percent of the country any given night—an average of around 3.2 million people. The second most popular show, MSNBC's *The Rachel Maddow Show*, averages 2.8 million people—well under 1 percent.

We sometimes use terms like "the public" or "the American imagination," as if these things still actually exist today. In reality, these monolithic terms fail to capture what's currently happening. The massive proliferation of choices means that we have not one town gym with everyone watching the same game and cheering for the same team, but rather one big train station platform with everyone listening to their own headphones—"alone together." The public square has been replaced by many squares, smaller and more private than ever.

Perhaps the one silver lining in all this is that very few of us are actually watching the most politically polarizing programming. Yet somehow, no one has escaped the gravitational pull of the 24/7 cable news model.

From Local to National to Niche Markets

The distribution of information used to be a fairly straightforward process—a simple matter of trying to deliver the maximum amount of content to the widest possible audience. Geography needed to be traversed. It's useful to think of American media in three phases. Phase One was when media was local. There was a good deal of yellow journalism and biased reporting, to be sure, but it was geographically constrained. Most stories that mattered were local or regional. Many municipalities fell prey to conspiracy theories about distant bankers—but these stories reflected real tensions between consolidated financial interests far away and competing parochial interests. There wasn't much of anything that counted as national media.

Phase Two began when technology allowed the development of a truly national market. Obviously, some newspapers had aspired to a national reach, but it was radio in the 1920s that really made possible one nationwide news audience, with the three broadcast television networks in the 1940s eventually solidifying viewers. With television news dominated by three outlets, a small group of powerful executives exercised enormous power over what families watched every night, what news they would receive, and how that news would be presented. Not accidentally, the high-water mark of the Big Three oligopoly was also the high-water mark of the sense of national unity. But just as technological developments created one national market for news in the middle of the twentieth century, so too did subsequent technological developments cause it to fracture. Technology gave rise to the television cartel—and then technology broke it up.

This unraveling was the beginning of Phase Three of American media, in which we are living today—albeit at warp speed, with instant feedback loops telling broadcasters and web publishers what we want more and less of, right now.

When cable television was invented, hardly anyone would've guessed the changes it would inaugurate. In 1948, cable brought mountain and other remote areas into the national conversation by transmitting to places too distant for broadcast signals. But in the 1960s and 1970s, as cable moved into cities and metro regions, its main effect wasn't to bring new people into the conversation but rather to enable more diverse programming—which had the effect of carving people *off* the one conversation.

To paraphrase Ken Burns, the great documentary filmmaker, America quickly became a place with a whole lot of "pluribus," and very little "unum." Today, 93 percent of Americans have access to more than 500 programming networks.

As cable expanded its reach, power shifted away from network execs and toward cable operators (who decided which channels were carried and promoted). But a much bigger disruption arrived with the internet, which almost completely removed the problem of distribution and significantly lowered barriers to entry for content creators. New, often free, blogging software allows anyone to become a publisher. YouTube allows anyone to become a filmmaker. If the characteristic experience of the mid-twentieth century was of "one-to-many" news media—one Walter Cronkite addressing many CBS viewers—the characteristic experience of the twenty-first century is many-to-many: everyone talking to (and over) everyone all the time. We have extraordinary liberty to watch, read, listen, and create—but the downside is a tsunami of information.

We have not figured out how to address the challenges this presents. We know that today every form of nuttiness can find validation, and any legitimate claim can be debunked. The internet is a place where chemtrails are real but the Moon landing is a hoax. It's a place tailor-made for confirmation bias. *There are how many sites dedicated to the benefits of cabbage-only diets? I'm sold!* (My Google search on it just yielded over five million results. That many people can't possibly be wrong, can they?)

I have a friend who believed as a kid that he could move paperclips by sheer force of mind. This was nuts, but he quickly learned this, so he turned out okay. After a bit of boasting, we demanded he demonstrate his skill. He failed, we roasted him, and everyone moved on to more important endeavors. But had my friend discerned his "powers" in 2018, he might not have told his real-world friends. Instead, he likely would've done an online search, found a digital support group, and spent years posting evidence of telekinesis on message boards devoted to paranormal activity under the screen name "Mind-Over-Matter Man." As "community" moves from family and friends—people who've seen you with bed head—to people who exist only as usernames, it becomes a lot easier to lose your hold on reality. Your older brother will put you in a headlock and noogie you until you stop acting like a goofball. "BadAzz1212" on Reddit won't.

Political media outlets have figured out how to exploit this trend. People more and more insulated from real people and the day-to-day concerns of real life are easier marks. They are the fanatics who tune in, click, and share, all day, every day. As their grip on reality gets weaker, the media's grip on them gets stronger.

Conservatism Doesn't Make Good Radio

When I was running for office in 2014, I had no in-my-belly anger about the state of American political media. I had always been a conservative, and there were some thinkers and writers I paid attention to, but because I had never been a political addict, I wasn't a heavy political news consumer. What I've described as polititainment—the Sean Hannity model of stoking outrage—was alien to me. But between 2014 and 2016, I got to know it intimately—coincidentally, because I got to know Sean Hannity.*

On the campaign trail in Nebraska, I was outspoken about my frustration not merely with Democrats but also with congressional Republicans. I regularly said that I didn't hear either party

---

* The conversations quoted in this section, with one exception, occurred before I ever thought of including them in these pages. The context was primarily either Fox News personalities or producers asking me about Donald Trump, or me asking why so many personalities I had previously thought were staunch conservatives were acting in such aggressively anti-conservative ways. Conservatism, in my view, begins with an understanding of the world as a broken place always at risk of spinning out of control. A conservative, then, is pleasantly surprised to find so much good in the world. He or she responds in profound gratitude for the gifts we've received and consequently aims to *conserve* or preserve those blessings, and to steward an order under which those blessings might be shared with even more people, all of whom are possessed of inexhaustible dignity and inalienable rights. Conservatism is, therefore, antithetical to an attitude that says to "burn it all down." Because conservatism is in part a disposition of gratitude, it is opposed to a culture of grievance or universal victimhood.

articulating a long-term vision for tackling the generational challenges we face—especially those surrounding the future of work, the future of war, and the broad erosion of support for the First Amendment. My stump speeches included many lines like: "We commit to celebrating the enduring American beliefs that unite us far more than the particular policy debates that sometimes divide us." Neither party seemed to have a plan for the future, so I ran against both of them.

Because I had gone after Republican leaders for lacking a long-term vision for the nation's challenges, my arguments resonated with critics of the establishment GOP. Hannity apparently heard things that he liked in my willingness to criticize not just opponents but my own side—and, after having me on his radio show, he announced that he was endorsing me. In one 2014 program, he said: "I think you will instantly, I predict, not only win your race, but I think you'll instantly become a leader of ideas and solutions in the Senate.... And I have the same admonition for Republicans as you do. I think they've been timid and weak and visionless. And unless they get their act together they're going to lose people like me." I was grateful for any and all support, but given his reach, his endorsement was particularly encouraging.

Surprises started when I was finally in D.C. "Hannity hasn't been a conservative for years," one Fox News personality said to me, shortly after my arrival. "He's smart, and he figured out long ago that teaching and defending conservatism is both harder and less effective than just hitting some crazy liberal. He's a broadcaster first, and it doesn't make great radio to defend a complicated idea in a consistent way. He's doing something that makes great radio. But it isn't conservative."

These comments obviously foreshadowed the battle between conservatism and populism in the 2016 Republican presidential primary, but they also brought to mind an old academic debate about whether the electorate is better understood on a "one-hump" or "two-hump" theory. A one-hump theory assumes that there are many voters in the middle, and a candidate succeeds by persuading more of these movable people to join his side rather than his opponent's. A two-hump theory assumes that there are very few undecided voters in the middle, so a candidate succeeds by stoking greater turnout among the voters already on his half of the political continuum. I had always been a one-hump guy—thinking of America as one community and believing that forward-looking solutions might appeal not just to 51 percent but even to 70 or 80 percent of the electorate. Because of my new experiences in Washington, however, I was beginning to wonder if I was wrong. I saw in government much more divisive nonsense than I'd anticipated—and it was pretty obvious that the divisiveness "worked." To my chagrin, I was in the process of coming to believe the two-hump theorists might be closer to an accurate reading of our situation.

Media types were way ahead of me. Obviously, most TV personalities are not trying to speak to any broad middle of the electorate but are rather competing only against others at roughly the same point on the ideological spectrum. The goal is to be seen as more "pure" and more combative—everyone wants a fighter. I didn't understand it at the time, but I've concluded that people like Hannity liked me because I gave them a competitive edge in their efforts to sell themselves to their audience as the "purer" conservative. By supporting me, Hannity burnished his anti-Establishment bona fides and built his audience's trust. He was strengthening his own million-strong anti-tribe.

"It's Just a Game"

Three years after endorsing me, Hannity went on the air to announce that he was rescinding his endorsement. He called supporting me "one of the biggest mistakes" of his career.

What had I done to justify Hannity's strident repudiation? Had I voted the wrong way on important legislation? Had I abandoned a core conservative principle of some sort? No. I had criticized President Trump's suggestion that media outlets should have their "licenses revoked" for covering him in a way he dislikes—a suggestion I suspect Hannity (rightly) would have throatily denounced had its source been President Hillary Clinton. In fact, I was making good on something I had promised Nebraska voters, and Hannity, in 2014: when I disagreed with the president on ideas or policies, I would say so, whether it was a Democrat or a Republican in the Oval Office. When I suggested to Hannity on Twitter that he was the one who had changed positions, not me, he called me "useless" and attacked me for not caring about American cybersecurity. This was a peculiar charge, given that I sit on the Senate Armed Services' Cybersecurity subcommittee and have made the issue a focus of my time in Washington; and given that Hannity had just months before aired a fawning interview with Julian Assange, whose WikiLeaks organization has published hundreds of thousands of pages of classified American intelligence. (Two months after Hannity's interview, WikiLeaks published nearly 9,000 pages of confidential material from the CIA, including sensitive information about covert Agency cyber tools.)

My experience with Hannity turned out to be unusually unpleasant, but what I learned was instructive. His model works—and other people are struggling desperately to replicate it. In my nearly four years in the Senate, I have had three of the top twelve conservative hosts in America sidle up to me in some informal setting after they'd shellacked me on the air. The context was the same in each case: I had defended some conservative principle against President Trump, so I'd gotten crosswise with part of their audience. The hosts knew that I'd been consistent in my positions, but many of their listeners—who now identify Trumpism with conservatism—wondered if I'd "gone liberal." The hosts couldn't afford to lose a quarter or a third of their audience, so they attacked any Republican who questioned President Trump. They wanted to know if I was angry at their spin.

"You get it, don't you?" one of them said, smiling at me. "You understand why I have to hit you?" I didn't. "Our audience lumps you into the RINOs [Republican In Name Only] now. You can't take it personally." In spite of the back-slapping assurances, I was incredulous. In Nebraska, you simply don't make up false charges against a person because those listening want to hear them get bashed. Trying not to sound moralistic, I said as much.

"Oh, come on!" the host replied. "You know how the game is played. You're a big boy, and it's just a game."

No, it's not—at least not to me.

I don't fly away from my wife and kids five days a week to be part of some high-stakes Harlem Globetrotters show. I actually believe that America is an exceptional nation and that the republic is worth struggling to preserve. I don't much care about their treatment of me, but I *am* disgusted by the way so many media personalities view our nation as their personal vending machine. In exchange for wild accusations and exaggerations, they get rich and famous—and we, their viewers and listeners, get a shallower, angrier, less workable America.

The President Plays the Fiddle

To many national commentators worried about polarization, the great divide in American life is between Fox and MSNBC—the rhetorical homes of the political right and left. Often they aren't even reporting the same stories. When they do, the coverage is so different that it's hard to believe they are describing the same set of facts. This is one of the reasons it's so difficult to have fruitful conversations—we can't even agree on what happened. I know some folks in Nebraska who, after a series of disputes over politics, decided to "trade primary news sources for a week." The conservative could watch only MSNBC and other progressive outlets; the Democrat could watch only Fox and listen to conservative talk radio. At the end of the week, each side felt like they understood their friends on the other side much better—and both sides resolved to start watching less cable news. A local stockbroker, one of the conservatives, reported: "It was amazing. It was like I took a trip abroad without leaving my living room."

This was a useful way for neighbors to try to listen to each other more sympathetically, but I think it obscures the larger problem—namely, that MSNBC and Fox are, at bottom, not all that different.

Obviously, the networks target different political audiences—but this is, in an important sense, a superficial distinction. Both channels put politics and power near the center of America. Both are impatient with the often ho-hum rhythm of ordinary life. Both want simple, good-versus-evil dramas. It's no accident that both networks covered Donald Trump (the quintessential showman) obsessively even in the weeks prior to the start of his campaign in the summer of 2015.

Indeed, contrary to so much hand-wringing and finger-pointing, the president did not create our polititainment problem. The incentives to gin up short-term outrage were already there. He's just exploited them better than anyone else has.

When Donald Trump fanned the flames of "birtherism"—the belief that President Obama was not a native-born American citizen—he knew that the wacky theory had, in fact, originated on the left. When he suggested that Ted Cruz's dad had a hand in the assassination of JFK, he recognized that media were already using "reporting on other reporting" as a backdoor way to allow titillating but unsubstantiated content into their "serious" news coverage.

Crazy has long had a constituency, including among "respectable" people. Candidate Trump's genius was simply to pull back the curtain. Consider this: In a 2007 Rasmussen poll, 61 percent of Democrats were open to the idea that George W. Bush had advance knowledge of the September 11, 2001, terrorist attacks—and among those open to the idea, half were *sure* that the Republican president knew the attacks were coming and did nothing to stop them. Similarly, the grassroots power of MoveOn.org succeeded in getting General David Petraeus rebranded as "General Betray Us" across large parts of America—then scrubbed its website of any reference to that campaign when President Obama subsequently tapped Petraeus to lead the war in Afghanistan. The mainstream media largely ignored this nuttiness.

Donald Trump created none of this—he simply plays the fiddle "better" than anyone has ever managed before. He figured out how to put the widely read tabloid material right on the front page. The president talks openly about the fact that he sometimes tweets outrageous things simply to watch the media hyperventilate. The topic could be the Kennedy assassination or 9/11 as an "inside job"; the source could be the *National Enquirer* or *InfoWars* (the conspiracy site the president thanked for helping him win the election). His goal is to provoke. He finds it entertaining.

And the media plays into his hand, every single time. By April 1, 2016, with a month still to go in the Republican primaries, Donald Trump had received the equivalent of $2 billion in free television coverage. All sixteen of his GOP opponents, by comparison, had received $1.2 billion *combined*. By the day of the November general election, Trump had earned just under $5 billion in free media— $1.75 billion more than Hillary Clinton.[4]

I believe the president's lack of interest in facts is disastrous for small-R republican government—in which dealing with day-to-day political responsibilities, as well as with major crises, depends on an informed citizenry that can make considered decisions. But it's absurd to pretend that Trump created this environment. He misspells words on purpose ("covfefe") and makes grammatical errors on Twitter because he can count on the media to blow it out of proportion—to his benefit. Media outlets need to keep the clicks coming, and Trump is always looking for attention. They attack one another relentlessly, but they're not really enemies; they're a perfect match in the new attention economy.

Democratic constituents regularly ask me if the president is racist. Race is (rightly) one of the most sensitive subjects in American life. Sadly, the president is obviously insensitive and seemingly indifferent to the racial horrors of the past and to the ongoing work to create a more perfect union for every American without regard to the color of his or her skin. But beyond that initial question, it's also important to recognize that something else is going on here as well: President Trump *uses* race to rally people *against the media*. Candidate Trump's horrible remarks, such as the ones about "the Mexican judge" (from Indiana) and David Duke (the notorious racist), typically originate at times when he is trying to switch from one media narrative to another, springboarding himself back to top billing in the news cycle.

This is reality TV provocation, pure and simple. He loves it when the chyrons scream, *Surely, surely, this is the thing that will take*

Trump down! He's finally gone too far! He wants the twenty-four-hour coverage obsessing over him and his double-downs, partial pivots, and salacious provocations.

And the media love the constant eyeballs on their sites.

It's good for everyone—except, of course, the rest of us.

It's Gonna Get Worse Before It Gets Better

It isn't just senators who wonder if they're wasting their lives. A senior network producer told me after a recent segment, "Sometimes the funhouse aspect of this whole thing seems to be winning the day. This isn't why I went into this business." It's a common lament. Over the past few years, I've heard multiple serious journalists wonder aloud whether facts will ever make a comeback. "I feel like I'm wasting my life," one worried.

They are saying something obvious: Most media business models—network or print—are broken. Some of this is a consequence of technology. But it's also the direct result of a decision to lean into certain consumer attitudes and preferences, and to prioritize certain values (e.g., entertainment) over others (e.g., genuine relevance). Perhaps consumers will eventually grow tired of this diet, and they'll find themselves willing to pay a premium for accuracy and balance. But perhaps not. It might be the case that marketing swallows the journalistic enterprise whole. A world where all news is tabloid news is a grim prospect. But a lot of good reporters, many of whom feel increasingly trapped by the new symbiosis between readers and content producers, think this is where things are headed.

Les Moonves, chief executive of CBS, summed up the attitude of many media execs when he said of Donald Trump's candidacy, in February 2016: "It may not be good for America, but it's damn good for CBS."

Some technology companies have been thinking about how to create a genuine "marketplace of ideas" where people with different views could wrestle through hard questions honestly and amicably. But everything about our new technologies seems to push us away from listening to our neighbor and toward shouting at him—that is, away from empathy and toward narcissism. More technology makes the world smaller, but that doesn't mean that when we're pressed together we'll hug.

Not long ago, Facebook announced that it was changing its algorithms to make sure users see the type of news they want in their feed. The result of this was that fake news and conspiracy theories gained more traction, as different communities isolated themselves from each other. Because no one saw anything they didn't want to see, they simply became more convinced of their own views—including the most dubious, idiosyncratic, or downright nutty of them. Facebook's response was to try to find ways to incorporate user feedback to police or grade content: X is a reliable source; Y isn't. But, to no one's surprise, liberals who saw pro-life content were likely to unfollow or block the source and to dispute the content of the posting. Conservatives responded the exact same way to content promoting gun control. Facebook's test ended up with a variety of important topics cordoned off as "hate speech."

Which is to say, there will not be an easy tech fix for our quandary. Moral dilemmas can't be resolved by a computer. More quantitative power doesn't inexorably solve fundamentally qualitative problems.

In a context where exactly 50 percent of America now believes that reporters simply make up stories about Donald Trump, it isn't surprising that only 17 percent of Republicans think journalists as a whole consistently tell the truth. It isn't just that living in ideological bubbles makes it harder to criticize one's own side; it's also that it actually becomes harder to *believe* credible charges against one's own tribe. It wasn't just that Republicans wouldn't criticize former Alabama Senate candidate Roy Moore's exploitation of underage girls; it was that many Republicans wouldn't believe the charges against Moore in the first place, because they were first reported by the *Washington Post* and CNN. As *The Atlantic*'s Julie Beck has written, we're building "pillow forts" of comfortable information around us and making it more and more difficult for anything we don't want to hear to penetrate.[5]

This trend is going to get worse. As the barriers to entering the national media market continue to crumble, and the distinction between sites that aspire to something like objectivity and those that don't collapses further, there is likely to be a surge of conspiracy theories and made-up news, of the sort that cropped up frequently during the 2016 election—not just chemtrails but Pizzagates. Politicians will exploit the connection between clicks and votes, and pander even more to audiences that want to see themselves as victims. And with so many voices endorsing our fears, larger shares of us will likely end up with persecution complexes, constantly offended and ready to fight.

In the final analysis, we have a very difficult chicken-and-egg problem on our hands. Freedom depends on an informed citizenry, and an informed citizenry depends on serious journalism that takes facts seriously and grapples with those facts honestly. But good journalism is less and less likely when there are fewer and fewer readers with an appetite for something more than titillation. Producers and consumers work in tandem—for better or for worse.

Right now, the pool of trust that once made that relationship constructive has all but dried up.

Hope Beyond a Broken Business Model

We are going through a civilization-warping crisis of public trust.

We have more information—and more complex and technical information—available to us than ever before, and from an array of sources. This is an odd problem that no society has ever before had to tackle. And because we also have less daily work and more leisure time than ever before, we are consuming more of this information. But quantity does not magically become quality. Our opinions aren't more thoughtful, or our characters more noble, simply because we have more data. We might know a lot, but we aren't necessarily becoming wiser.

The only conceivable way we can make sense of all this information would be by knowing who to *think with*, who to trust. That's just another way of saying that we need real, local, in-person communities. But our communities are in collapse.

If you feel hopeless, you're not alone. As mentioned above, even among the creators and distributors of the click-baity, outrage-of-the-day content, there is a widespread feeling that we are twittering while Rome burns.

The good news is that these vicious cycles really can be stopped. What some might regard as the bad news, though, is that these problems cannot be solved by legislation or by a more powerful executive. There is no silver-bullet way to restore a republic characterized by empathy and self-restraint except by the cultivation of healthy habits among its citizens.

What is wrong with us is exacerbated by technology, but it did not originate with technology. What is wrong is that we have let our habits corrode, and our affections warp. We have been willing to accept cheap, distant anti-tribes when, in reality, only hard-built tribes of blood, sweat, and tears can fulfill us.

National renewal will come only by a recovery of wisdom and empathy. Developing again the habits of a free people will require work, to be sure, but that's nothing new. Sustaining a republic—and the freedom it promises to every individual—has always required self-restraint, self-sacrifice, and love for our neighbor.

The next four chapters outline four of the steps we need to take to get there.

PART III

OUR TO-DO LIST

Ultimate danger to America "cannot come from abroad. If destruction be our lot, we must ourselves be its author and finisher. As a nation of freemen, we must live through all time, or die by suicide."

—Abraham Lincoln

5

BECOME AMERICANS AGAIN

One Nation, Precarious ❧ Civics 101
James Madison, Philosopher for the Twitter Age
The Emperor Who Wasn't ❧ The Spirit of Liberty
"We All Live on Campus Now" ❧ The Amoralization of America
Never Perfect, but Always "More Perfect" ❧ Know Your Blind Spots

THE CREATION OF THE UNITED STATES OF AMERICA IS A strange event in the sweep of world history—strange enough that it should probably be called something other than a "nation." "Country" doesn't quite work—too pastoral, too evocative of lazy summer landscapes for a people as industrious and adventurous as we are. So "nation" is a half-step better. But it's still not great. "Nation" comes from the Latin *natio*, meaning "birth," which rightly indicates that traditional nations are based on a shared birth—that is, shared bloodlines. Not so with us.

Hitler, ever obsessed with bloodlines, complained that the United States was "not a nation, but a hodgepodge." He was right on the fact—but wrong about it being a problem.

We Americans have long embraced our hodgepodge-ness. "Give me your tired, your poor, your huddled masses yearning to breathe free," the poem on the pedestal of the Statue of Liberty proclaims. "Send these, the homeless, tempest-tost to me, I lift my lamp . . . !" We don't discriminate against you because your dad's in jail and your clothes are in tatters. Lady Liberty beckons the gritty, the entrepreneurial, the bold—the people who would cross the entire ocean in pursuit of freedom.

Over the last year, I've had occasion to meet with a number of senior Chinese officials, and they're always quick to point out—as a kind of diplomatic trash talk—how *young* the United States is compared to China's forty-five centuries of history.

Fair enough. We're babes, historically. But (as long as we're trash talking) age is not always what it's cracked up to be. And, besides: doesn't this discussion miss the point? China is a nation in the classic sense. It is blood and soil. It's a great wall, a fascinating people, an extraordinarily long-lived culture.

But America is something different. America is an *idea*—it is a creed.

The American idea is a commitment to the universal dignity of persons everywhere.

That's what America is. The millions of people who've braved dangers of every sort to come to our shores: they believed in that idea of universal human dignity. That's why they're Americans.

The history of America is the history of trying to realize this idea. For our purposes, think of U.S. history as divided into two major phases. Phase One was the eleven-year period from the declaration of American independence in July 1776 to the composition of the Constitution at Philadelphia in 1787. The men who participated in the Second Continental Congress and in the Constitutional Convention articulated the ideals toward which the young country would aspire: "to establish justice," "to promote the general welfare," "to secure the blessings of liberty," and so much more. They set down what America meant. Phase Two has continued ever since. It is the struggle for a "more perfect" union, the attempt to live up to the ideals of universal dignity, justice, and freedom laid down by the Framers. By working to secure for each of our countrymen and women the *freedom from* coercive power, we help to secure for every American the *freedom to* live lives of love, worshipping as we see fit, serving our neighbors, and pursuing happiness and friendship.

This is why Abraham Lincoln and Martin Luther King Jr. are essential American "Founders," even though their great labors—in the 1860s and 1960s, respectively—were four score and a-century-and-four-score years after the "miracle" at Constitution Hall. When Lincoln freed millions of slaves from their shackles, and when King loosened the bonds of segregation and inequality, they were lifting America up—toward those ideals it has always held forth but not always lived up to. The Founders set down what America meant, but because of their own brokenness, and because of the economic power of slaveholders, they did not achieve the idea of America. Lincoln and King appear not to reject but to carry forward the Founders' dream: to more perfectly realize the marvelous American idea of liberty and justice for all. This, and nothing less, is what America means.

Over the next four chapters, we will explore ways to better live out the American idea against the forces that, in recent years, have weakened it. As we've seen, cultural fragmentation, technological developments, and economic upheaval have undermined the feeling of togetherness that Americans shared just a few short decades ago. For most Americans, these processes have caused social capital to evaporate from under their feet, leaving them feeling helpless in the face of bigger and more complicated social and economic challenges. As natural, healthy tribes—family, friends, workplace, and neighborhood—have crumbled, we've turned to anti-tribes: an us-versus-them politics and a rage-fueled media complex that exploits our divisions for clicks. Reclaiming the American idea against all this means returning to the beginning: to our basic commitment to the inexhaustible, inviolable dignity of every person, and to our recognition that an effective and enduring politics can only be built atop this fundamental conviction.

One Nation, Precarious

Ask someone to describe our country, and they'll begin to tick off symbols: John Wayne, pickup trucks, fireworks, Walmart, saying "y'all," cheap beer—or Joni Mitchell, Tesla, Whole Foods. But what do these things have to do with America? I happen to like NASCAR, and my kids and I belt out Toby Keith lyrics while fishing—including his post-9/11, anti–bin Laden ballad lines like, "We'll put a boot in your ass / It's the American way"—but I'm aware that none of this is uniquely "the American way." There are people who appreciate NASCAR but not Toby Keith, and there are people who like party songs but not auto racing, and there are people who despise both.

But you know what? None of those things has much to do with what America is.

A lot of people, including (and perhaps especially) sophisticated political folk, show a tendency to reduce America to certain consumer choices: America is just wimps in Priuses! America is just yokels with "truck nuts"! But that's wrong, in both directions. America isn't your preferences about how to spend your day off ("Muddin'!" "The Met!"). America isn't your fashion choices ("Camo pants!" "Yoga pants!"). America isn't your cultural signaling ("They're called freedom fries!" "I wouldn't be caught dead in a Cracker Barrel!"). And America surely isn't about your skin pigment or your ethnic identity.

America is an idea.

Well, America is an idea—*until it ceases to be.* That is, America is an idea until we let it devolve into something less. And that's what we're flirting with right now. The threat to the American idea is real in our time.

We have a bunch of Americans today who want to destroy America. They want to burn it all down. Some of these pretend that they are "right" and others that they are "left," but they're neither. Honest advocates from the right and from the left acknowledge that the things that make us American supersede—that is, they come before, and take priority over—the policy issues that can be arrayed across a right-to-left spectrum. As we saw in the last chapter, many of the loudest voices are actually just hucksters aiming to make a buck. Yelling, "Damn straight! Screw you!" at our opponents will not make us feel less lonely. Cursing the other political party will not draw us together as friends in pursuit of common goals.

In addition to the professional rage-peddlers, we have another, even larger group of Americans who just don't care enough about any of this to be bothered. America might be going to hell, but as long as there's another show to bingewatch on Netflix . . .

We've come to assume that the American idea can be neglected year after year after year and nonetheless endure. It can't. It's an idea—and as such, it needs to be taught and learned. It needs to be passed on and lived out.

But for fifty years now—basically since our late-1960s bender mellowed into our 1970s hangover—we've been raising children who simply haven't been asked to internalize our shared values. As polling data regularly confirms, they simply don't know who we are. Their parents and teachers—the generations before them—have failed to transmit the essential lessons. And we've come to a point where widespread ignorance of who we are and what we believe threatens our future.

There is no law of nature that says the United States must always exist, although we often seem to think so. That's partly because we've been lucky. We haven't had much experience in the kinds of catastrophes that overwhelm societies. No foreign power has invaded our soil since the British in the War of 1812. Even at the height of the Cold War, when the Soviet Union's nuclear capabilities meant homemade basement shelters, bomb drills (multiple times each year for us at Trinity Lutheran Elementary), and constant anxiety, Americans still lived their day-to-day lives basically in peace. We've overcome the ravages of plagues and natural disasters. We recovered from a devastating civil war.

Still, the assumption that America will carry on no matter what is new. Throughout our history, our wisest statesmen have warned that America's greatest risk has never been attack from abroad but rot from within. The question has always been whether the Republic could long endure if the house was divided internally. Way back in 1787, Benjamin Franklin was stopped as he left Constitution Hall by a woman wanting to know what kind of government the Convention had established. "A republic," he replied, "if *you* can keep it."

Civics 101

How to keep it? Things are more precarious than most people realize. "Freedom is never more than one generation from extinction," Ronald Reagan warned. It cannot simply be mechanically transmitted to our kids "in the bloodstream." Instead, it "must be fought for, protected, and handed on, for them to do the same."[1]

But caught up for decades in shinier technologies and glitzy creature comforts, we haven't stopped to discuss with our children who we are as a people. We don't have a shared understanding of our underlying inheritance, and our ignorance is tearing us apart at the seams.

The terrible 2016 election did not cause our disunion; it was just a painful symptom of the bigger disease—which is our growing disinterest in the meaning of America. We have not worked to pass on the great American idea. Our unsatisfying politics is not the cause of our deformed discourse; the ugliness of our public square is only one more effect of our civic neglect.

A government of, by, and for the people puts extra pressure on *the people* to live in a manner consistent with self-government— crucially, even when we vigorously disagree on matters of mere policy. Policy fights are important, but not nearly as important as agreeing about our fundamental civic principles.

Where should we start? The two indispensable insights of the American experiment are inextricably linked: each and every individual is created with dignity—and therefore government, because it is not the source of our rights, is just a tool.

When Jefferson wrote: "We hold these truths to be self-evident, that all men are created equal . . ." he was affirming a common understanding: Human dignity is intrinsic, not conferred on us by any man-made power. Government exists to do the work of securing our preexisting rights. Government—that is, power—cannot be absolute; it is only an instrument we use to secure the freedom necessary for the most important pursuits.

If we're going to preserve that freedom, we need to reflect carefully on our limitations. The Founders would be proud if we took more seriously, and taught our children more deliberately, at least these four core truths about human nature and government:

- We're flawed—and naturally inclined to fight.
- Those who wield government power shouldn't be trusted to resolve many fights or to declare many winners and losers.
- Politicians shouldn't confuse their temporary roles with ultimate meaning.
- Citizens in a republic must cultivate humility—or the experiment will inevitably collapse.

This is why, at the heart of America's constitutional structure, is a commitment to *anti-majoritarianism*. America believes in big and grand things about human nature and human potential. America believes in poetry. But the only way to preserve sufficient space for true community and for meaningful, beautiful human relationships is to have a *political* philosophy that emphasizes constraint—constraint that applies as much to ourselves, with our tendency toward absolute certainty and self-righteousness, as to the government.

James Madison, Philosopher for the Twitter Age

I'm glad that visitors to the nation's capital are able to see our Constitution, which, completed over 230 years ago, is now safely preserved under glass at the National Archives at Seventh Street and Pennsylvania Avenue. But even more than seeing the paper, I wish that visitors could hear a reenactment of the full-throated debates of the various drafts that were drawn up en route to that final document. The U.S. Constitution is one of the most important documents in human history, but it was not handed down by God on Mount Sinai.

It is the product of fifty-five very flawed men who wrestled long and hard about human nature and the proper uses of government.

We all remember that our Founders had strong views about freedom and equality and about how government depended on the consent of the governed. But we tend to forget that our system rests on an even greater core conviction: human beings are fundamentally fallen, selfish, and inclined to let our passions run roughshod over our reason. Simply put, the Founders believed that we're very broken.

Today's pop psychology and talk show hosts, with their *listen-to-your-heart* and *be-true-to-yourself* approaches to life, would baffle eighteenth-century Americans, who were wary of moral intuition. Colonists taught their children that imperfect human beings could see the world only imperfectly, through unreliably self-centered lenses. Children learning their alphabet from the *New England Primer*, the most important and most widely read textbook in seventeenth- and eighteenth-century North America, began with human fallibility from the letter "A": "In Adam's fall, we sinned all."

James Madison, our fourth president, knew the rhyme and the worldview. We remember him chiefly as "the father of the Constitution," but this preindustrial thinker is also, counterintuitively, a practical philosopher for our digital age. The @SageOfMontpelier would not be the least bit surprised by the vitriol spewed on Twitter, because he believed rabid partisanship (what he called "faction") was inevitable. The "latent causes of faction," he wrote in *Federalist* No. 10, are "sown in the nature of man."

In other words, Twitter, Instagram, Facebook, and Snapchat didn't create our darker impulses; they simply revealed them. Madison explained that a "zeal for different opinions concerning religion, concerning government, and many other points" has always "divided mankind into parties, inflamed them with mutual animosity, and rendered them much more disposed to vex and oppress each other than to cooperate for their common good." We've always been imperfect, passionate people living in community arguing in overheated ways with other imperfect, passionate people.

Madison, grasping our inadequacies, went on to describe the basis for every angry social media post ever written: "As long as the reason of man continues fallible, and he is at liberty to exercise it, different opinions will be formed," he wrote. "As long as the connection subsists between his reason and his self-love, his opinions and his passions will have a reciprocal influence on each other; and the former will be objects to which the latter will attach themselves." Yep—Madison knew we would have selfish and angry opinions; he just didn't know we would have smartphones.

We might expect Madison to follow this up by taking the colonists to task, hectoring them for their endless sniping. But he doesn't. Madison resists any naïve expectations about humanity's ability to overcome pettiness and self-absorption. Instead, he looks for structural solutions that can temper and contain our selfishness. Since "causes of faction cannot be removed," he wrote, "relief is only to be sought in the means of controlling its effects."

The key, then, is creating and preserving the right kind of government: a government that can constrain people who try to deprive us of our rights, but a government that is, itself, constrained, so that it doesn't deprive us of our rights, either. Madison was no fool. "If men were angels, no government would be necessary. If angels were to govern men, neither external nor internal controls on government would be necessary." But that's not our situation. So, "in framing a government which is to be administered by men over men, the great difficulty lies in this: you must first enable the government to control the governed; and in the next place oblige it to control itself." Determining and sustaining the proper role of government requires serious thought, in each new generation, about who we are, and where we go wrong. As Madison says: "What is government itself, but the greatest of all reflections on human nature?"

And so our Founders, starting from their keen-eyed view of human nature, created a system that had "checks and balances," so that power was dispersed among many groups and interests, and no one faction could seize the entire system. The Founders recognized that the best solution was *pluralism*.

Madison encouraged everyone to conceive of themselves as *creedal minorities.*

Assume that if you believe anything important or hold anything dear, it will not always align with majority opinion. Wise republicans (small-"r" republicans)—by which he meant all citizens of this new experiment in liberty, who had just observed a century-plus of religious war in Europe—should be aiming to preserve space for peaceful argument and thoughtful dissent. Government isn't in the business of setting down ultimate truths. It doesn't decide who's saved and who's damned. Government is merely a tool to preserve order, to preserve space for free minds to wrestle with the big questions. Government is not the center of life but the framework that enables rich lives to be lived in the true centers of freedom and love: homes and communities.

Our Founders built democratic government as a new alternative to monarchy, but they also intentionally built an *anti-majoritarian* government because the worst form of democracy—mob rule—is always a danger against which we must be on guard. If we fail to preserve our anti-majoritarian guardrails against the mob, we will end up subjected to the capricious will of a populist, self-certain, unreflective majority. Do you believe the Twitter mob will never come for you? The Founders urge us to do the hard work of protecting ourselves and our vulnerable neighbors against the majority that says might makes right. That work requires keeping the majority humble—not allowing them to impose compulsory, one-size-fits-all solutions on the big riddles of life. It also requires constantly renewing our commitment, in every sphere of life, to the dignity of every person. In those ways, we strive "not only to guard the society against the oppression of its rulers, but to guard one part of the society against the injustice of the other part."

The Emperor Who Wasn't

"Humility" is not a word much associated with modern politics, but it's a value with deep roots in the political tradition we've inherited. George Washington thought it essential that his descendants understand it, so he labored, in word and deed, to teach the early American republicans. This teaching—more than serving for eight years as president—was probably what he conceived of as his life's most important work.

General Washington's first truly great lesson for our people was not winning the Revolutionary War (against, we tend to forget, some very distracted English and very disengaged German mercenary soldiers). Instead, it was resigning his commission as head of the Continental Army when the war was over: "Having now finished the work assigned me, I retire from the great theatre of Action; and bidding an Affectionate farewell to this August body under whose orders I have so long acted, I here offer my Commission, and take my leave of all the employments of public life." If we understood this moment better, Washington's words would set off fireworks in our hearts, because what happened here was an astonishing act of self-restraint.

Washington, having just risked his life for his countrymen, has won the battle and become indisputably the most popular man in America. The people don't really know what comes next, but they want leadership—and they would surely have made him king had he wanted the position. But instead, he comes to a meeting of the Continental Congress—which represents the rule of the common man, rather than the rule of the rich or well-born—and he relinquishes control of the army. He lays down power. He could have been an American Julius Caesar, holding sway over a new North American empire. But he refuses. He doesn't seek power over his neighbors; instead, he seeks to teach them that they should look for their happiness and fulfillment in their families and in their communities, not in the halls of power or in the ranks of military might.

This is not abstract history. Each of our lives has been shaped by this noble act. It helped not just to promote the creation of a specific limited government, but it also infused our political culture with a skepticism of power-seekers.

Washington had long admired Cincinnatus (519–430 BC), an ancient Roman politician and military leader who had been called out of retirement to defend Rome against an invasion. Cincinnatus won the war in just fifteen days—and then shocked all of Rome by returning home. He laid down power. Washington, and many of his contemporaries, believed Cincinnatus embodied the indispensable civic virtues of humility and self-restraint. Power is for a purpose, and that purpose is not to elevate those who wield it.

Washington and his friends were well read in the great Roman historians—Livy and Tacitus and Plutarch—and to them history showed that a republic could not survive without these virtues. So, Washington refused to accept a salary for leading the Continental Army and subordinated himself to the will of Congress, hoping that others would follow suit. After he resigned, he joined an association of former military officers who cared for fallen soldiers, widows, and children. They called themselves the Society of the Cincinnati, a plural form of the name Cincinnatus, to indicate their commitment to humble service.

Washington didn't want to leave the domestic bliss of Mount Vernon in 1787—he had, he thought, finished with public life for good—but he reluctantly accepted the call to chair the Constitutional Convention. A year later, he was elected by acclamation to serve as the first president of the United States, at a time when there were no term limits. The new position—more powerful than the executive position under the ineffective Articles of Confederation, America's first, short-lived governing document—gave him the chance to accumulate power. But he chose, again, to model the limits of power and the importance of humility. He chose to embody the understanding, articulated by Madison, that government is a reflection of human nature, and that since both the governors and the governed are flawed, the system needs people who demonstrate modesty. Washington would not wear his military garb as president. He rejected honorific titles, instead preferring to be called "Mr." Washington, and so on.

In his second inaugural address, delivered in the early spring of 1793, Washington reminded his fellow citizens that they should not bow before him, that they were his peers, and that they even had the power to impeach him: "[I]f it shall be found during my administration of the Government I have in any instance violated willingly or knowingly the injunctions thereof, I may (besides incurring constitutional punishment) be subject to the upbraidings of all who are now witnesses of the present solemn ceremony."

Translation: There will be no kings here. There should be no permanent political class. The people will rule. And that means the people, too, must concern themselves with self-restraint.

Washington wasn't done teaching. In his Farewell Address in the fall of 1796, as the nation prepared to elect his successor, he had a warning for his fellow citizens. Anything he said would have carried great weight; he was doing something unthinkable to most foreign onlookers: voluntarily surrendering the highest office in the land. So what did he choose to discuss? The departing president urged his fellow countrymen—"in the most solemn manner"—not to descend into partisan acrimony. He said that the abandonment of shared principles would be the most likely way America would come apart.

In other words, he was previewing Abraham Lincoln by three generations: if America is going to die, it won't be because we lose a military battle; it will be by suicide.

Elections are not to be understood as a competition to see which side can impose its will on the other. "The alternate domination of one faction over another, sharpened by the spirit of revenge natural to party dissension," Washington warned, "is itself a frightful despotism." He was writing to us. If he were penning an op-ed on our elections today, I suspect this would be his exact warning. The goal of an election, he thought, is not to secure power to be used as a bludgeon. Rather, the goal of an election is to determine who will best steward this experiment in self-government for the next short while—before returning to the farm or suburb or small business or Rotary Club. The winners aren't the Good Guys, and the electoral losers aren't the Villains who need to be crushed.

Historians estimate that the Farewell Address was the most published American document in the first half-century of the new republic. It provided the model for how young Americans should think about our government, its limits, and the necessity of modesty and humility from both leaders and the citizenry. It was more studied in schools than the Declaration of Independence.

Today, too few Americans know Washington's parting address, but Congress still has it read aloud once a year. (When I was privileged to deliver the 2017 version of the forty-six-minute address to the Senate, I considered wearing a throwback powdered wig. My wife vetoed the plan.) Surprisingly but happily, Lin-Manuel Miranda's attempt to recover this essential American reticence about wielding political power—which the Broadway hit *Hamilton* suggests with the song "One Last Time"—has reintroduced something of Washington's spirit into the American bloodstream. Miranda's Washington announces to Hamilton, who's holding the pen, that "We're gonna teach 'em to say goodbye." (In real life, Madison was the scribe of the address.) The retiring president wants "to warn against partisan fighting," which will weaken the nation. Hamilton protests that people will charge that he is the one who is weak; he must be strong, he must fight on! But Washington is wiser, and his focus is on the long-term health of the Republic:

> If I say goodbye, the nation learns to move on.
> It outlives me when I'm gone.
> Like the scripture says:
> "Everyone shall sit under their own vine and fig tree
> And no one shall make them afraid."

We don't appreciate what Washington did because it was so successful that we tend to think about it as the way the world should work. But in fact, it's still rare in the world. Power is no different from money (which is just power stored in a bank) in this regard, and nobody walks away from a pile of money. Well—some people do, by giving it away, and that's the point. Washington gave it away. How wildly strange it was for Washington to do this—and how wonderful for us that we are the recipients of his gift.

The Spirit of Liberty

Washington's warning not to regard power as the center of life—his call to humility and its sister virtue, empathy—is not just for the handful of folks who hold office. His example is not just for our "public servants," who are to understand that part of their service is, after fulfilling their responsibilities, to head home to the fig trees of their own Mount Vernons. No, humility is a universal American calling. In a nation that believes in the dignity of each individual, it is necessary to create a culture that gives leeway to everyone to believe and to live as their conscience dictates. The "we" who must cultivate humility is not just "we, the senators" but—far more importantly—"we, the people."

"The spirit of liberty is the spirit which is not too sure that it is right," said one of the most prominent jurists of the twentieth century, Judge Learned Hand. "The spirit of liberty is the spirit which seeks to understand the minds of other men and women; the spirit of liberty is the spirit which weighs their interest alongside its own without bias." Judge Hand is not making the mistake of asserting that nothing is true, or that the truth is impossible to know. After all, when Hand gave this famous speech, World War II was raging. The American people thankfully recognized that we were right about the evils of Nazism, and we resolved to defeat it. Yet, even amid our triumph over Hitler and the Axis powers, President Roosevelt was ordering the mass-internment of Japanese-Americans on bigoted suspicions that they might spy for Imperial Japan, and Jim Crow laws were being ruthlessly enforced across the South. Even in victory, we demonstrated our failures. No, the judge was pointing to the great Washingtonian virtue: humility.[2]

It's a difficult thing to maintain Hand's spirit of liberty. Our vices—our arrogance and ignorance and self-absorption—conspire against it. Nonetheless, we (small-"r") republicans have the responsibility to affirm the dignity of our fellows. A republic acknowledges that its citizens have souls, and healthy citizens of a republic likewise acknowledge the souls of fellow citizens—whether we're well disposed toward them at the moment or not. Personal humility in our political culture flows from the awareness of *both* our neighbor's capacity for good, and our own capacity for error.

Russian writer Aleksandr Solzhenitsyn, a convert from Communism, notes the risks of zealous self-certainty: "In the intoxication of youthful successes [as a Communist organizer], I had felt myself to be infallible, and I was therefore cruel." He wrote, in *The Gulag Archipelago*, "In my most evil moments I was convinced that I was doing good, and I was well supplied with systematic arguments." Motivated reasoning was everywhere.

He insisted that the "line dividing good and evil cuts through the heart of every human being, and who is willing to destroy a piece of his own heart?" That principle, although the product of a Russian novelist reflecting on his time in a Soviet prison camp, powerfully captures the humility necessary to undergird our system of government. America is not a place for those so convinced of the rightness of their every cause that they are always ready to use force to vanquish their opponents. Rather, America is a place for those who believe that fallen humanity—including me and you—is so often in error that we are reticent to use force. We would prefer to extend the debate, and try to argue and persuade another day.

Our government's ineffectiveness, so often on display, is therefore not only the product of modern failures of execution; gridlock is also an intentional design feature of our system. The Founders wanted it to be difficult for fallible people to wield too much power, especially when it comes to the most important things—curtailing the freedom of speech and the free exercise of religion, the rights of assembly and press and protest. If the people who run the government get to decide what speech is permissible, or which religion is true, we're in a world of trouble. It's not just that they might be wrong (and—let's steady ourselves for some big news—government officials are often wrong, about a whole lot of things). It's that even if they're right, no one can be compelled to believe something. No one's mind can be changed with a billy club.

Part of what it means to be a human being is to have a soul that exists beyond the reach of government. And that means that the big questions are forever above government's pay grade. Our system is explicitly designed to bow to the dignity of each individual—and though we've failed grotesquely at times, the genius of the American experiment is its capacity for self-correction and improvement. By acknowledging that government is necessary because men are not angels, and that checks on government are necessary because governors are not angels either, we prepare ourselves for errors and create structures that move us toward a fuller realization of our animating principles.

Too often our debates about the degree of government intervention in the economy—once the best way to distinguish Republicans from Democrats—swallow up our ability to remember and reaffirm what the term "limited government" actually means. *Limited* government is not the same concept as *small* government. (I'm in favor of both, by the way, but limited government is infinitely more important than small government.) "Limited government" is not a Republican position; it is an American position. It refers simply to our belief that individual rights exist prior to government, and that government exists to preserve and protect those rights—the rights that you have by virtue of your dignity as a human being. You do not have rights because the government decided to be generous to you; you have your rights because you are created with dignity.

The Founders established this system of limited government— that is, they imposed constraints on government coercion—in order to give every citizen the space to follow his or her conscience. Communities of love and hospitality flourish only when people freely affirm them. Government cannot do that for anyone. Politicians must stand back and stand down. Or, as the First Amendment puts it: "Congress shall make no law respecting an establishment of religion, or prohibiting the free exercise thereof; or abridging the freedom of speech, or of the press; or the right of the people peaceably to assemble, and to petition the Government for a redress of grievances."

The idea of putting two religion clauses in this amendment— both an anti-establishment clause and a pro-liberty clause—was not intuitive. Before Philadelphia in 1787, most people assumed that government needed to define true religion. Across most of Europe, religious and cultural unity was enforced by the state. An important debate throughout much of Europe and in colonial America was whether you were allowed to dissent from the official state church— that is, whether minority religious positions would be tolerated. The Framers' view, our view, is different: We begin by announcing that religion is so important that the central government doesn't get to be in the business of religion at all. Our citizens are free to follow their beliefs, to exercise them, and to assemble with coreligionists—and the central government cannot interfere with that free exercise, or let any majority use the tools of the state to establish one denomination or prohibit another.

In America, we are all minorities. And so we should all be nervous about any temporary majority and the powers it seeks.

The other four freedoms of the first amendment—speech, press, assembly, and protest—flow from our anti-majoritarian bias. We believe in the free consciences of free souls. We protect dissenters, no matter how unpopular they might be. Our five First Amendment freedoms aren't broken into separate amendments because they are intimately connected—and, ultimately, rely on one another. Freedom of religion would not be worth much if the state could prohibit your assembly. Your freedom of speech would be constrained if you could not publish what you discussed. Your freedom of the press would be constrained if it did not include the right to protest what the government was doing wrong. And so on.

We can see how important this has been, simply as a practical matter: In places where vigorous argument about big ideas (religious and otherwise) has been prohibited—for example, in seventeenth-century Europe, with its tax-supported state churches—diversity of opinion regularly flared into violence. But our experience has been different. When we can wrestle freely and forthrightly—in person and in the press—we have safety valves that depressurize tense situations. People will inevitably battle; the challenge is how to successfully channel these conflicts into words rather than swords.

Vigorous debate and real understanding are the only long-term antidotes to violence in any large nation. A healthy republic requires not just the legal freedom to debate, but a culture that welcomes debate and is open to understanding the perspectives of disenfranchised groups. That culture depends on habits of charity and empathy and respect. We'll never understand why our opponents act the way they do if we refuse to listen—really listen—to their arguments. We have to live and breathe Judge Hand's spirit of liberty.

"We All Live on Campus Now"

But this is not happening in America right now. You know that while you're here, reading this book, someone is screaming down his political opponents on your Facebook page. It's always been difficult to argue our positions dispassionately, but it's getting harder the more we organize our fellow Americans into Good Guys and Bad Guys even before the "conversations" begin. In the digital age, it's easy to repudiate the spirit of liberty with the swipe of a button. All of us are susceptible to the mindless self-righteousness of the Twitter mob, absolutely certain that we're on the "right side of history" on every issue, no matter how small.

But, of course, the problem is not only online or on cable news. Perhaps the most dramatic suppression is happening on our campuses—ironically, the place most closely associated with freedom of thought, where generations of young men and women have come into their own, sharpening their minds through wide reading and vigorous debate. On American campuses we now see the roots of several large-scale changes in our political culture, and they are all unhealthy: the suppression of speech, the amoralization of our politics, and the rise of "hate speech" as a legal bludgeon.

On November 6, 2015, I delivered the Buckley Lecture at a conference on free speech at Yale University. The event fell just a few days after an unexpectedly intense campus controversy over—of all things—Halloween costumes.

Administrators, who wanted to avoid hurting the feelings of minority students, had issued instructions not to wear "culturally insensitive" costumes like feathered headdresses, turbans, and sombreros. One professor, Erika Christakis, objected to the heavy-handed bureaucratic intervention. She sent an open email (received by approximately 8 percent of Yale undergraduates) suggesting an alternative way to handle potential conflicts. Acknowledging the good intentions of administrators, she nonetheless suggested that there was no need for higher-ups to police their students' attire. Surely, the students were mature enough to handle the matter. "[I]f you don't like a costume someone is wearing . . . tell them you are offended. Talk to each other," she wrote. "Free speech and the ability to tolerate offense are the hallmarks of a free and open society."[3]

A firestorm ensued. Students demanded that both she and her husband, sociology professor Nicholas Christakis, be removed from their posts. An angry student mob surrounded Nicholas as he tried to get in his car, berating him for two hours. A video of the episode shows students calling him "disgusting," ordering him to be quiet in the face of the screaming. He was accused of being "racist." No one, least of all the Christakises, had defended insensitive Halloween costumes; Erika had simply suggested that college students were not so fragile as to be unable to work out these matters without bureaucratic regulation.[4]

It didn't matter. Eventually, after persistent accusations of "institutional racism" and of facilitating "violence" against vulnerable students, Erika resigned her position. Nicholas took a sabbatical, and they left town.

The episode vested the free speech conference with an unexpected sense of urgency. My speech was uneventful, but the level of animosity on campus toward "them"—however defined—was markedly greater than when I had taught at Yale as a graduate student fifteen years earlier.

This is not an isolated incident but rather a brush-fire sweeping across the country. Social scientist and *New York Times* bestselling author Charles Murray was shouted down at Middlebury College by a combination of students and so-called anti-fascists (Antifa) who accused him of racism, and a protester pulled the hair of Allison Stanger, a liberal professor at the event, ultimately putting her in a neck brace. She doesn't agree with Murray; her offense was simply inviting him to campus for a debate in the first place. Brown University students called for the cancellation of a College Republican event featuring conservative commentator Guy Benson, citing an "inextricable connection between Benson's ideologies—fiscal conservatism and free market ideology—and real, tangible, state violence against marginalized communities." His beliefs, they claimed, are sometimes used to enable white supremacy and fascism. Note that the claim was not that Benson believes in or in any way enables white supremacy, but that someone might misuse his ideas about economics—so he must be silenced.[5]

Barack Obama has publicly worried about this drift away from open debate. He disagrees with the view that "students at colleges have to be coddled and protected from different points of view." At a 2015 town hall with Iowa high schoolers, the president lamented that "some college campuses . . . don't want to have a guest speaker who is too conservative, or they don't want to read a book if it had language that is offensive to African Americans or somehow sends a demeaning signal towards women." He rightly explained that "that's not the way we learn." When you encounter someone with whom you disagree, "you should have an argument with them," he encouraged. "But you shouldn't silence them by saying, you can't come because I'm too sensitive to hear what you have to say."

Unfortunately, not many young people seem inclined to heed Obama's advice. Few campuses have seen violence yet, but more and more colleges are inculcating their students with the idea that they are entitled to live without offense, without encountering ideas that they don't already embrace. But if that's the case, what's the point of the university? Education requires encountering ideas you didn't already know or hold. But many colleges are instead creating "safe spaces" and cry rooms, areas where students can self-segregate to protect themselves from ideological challenges—physical quarantine zones to accompany things like "trigger warnings." This sort of activism is un-American in the deepest sense: It says we can only live with people who are exactly like us. This is a direct assault on our commitment to universal dignity, and a big national step backward.

Actual debate that touches on deep, closely held beliefs is hard—partly because we know we might be wrong, even about some of our strongest convictions. But it's also difficult because we're typically not very good at seeing perceived opponents as real people. Doing so requires struggling against our instinct to impose our will on others. "What alarmed me most . . . was what I saw in the eyes of the crowd," Dr. Stanger wrote in an opinion piece about the violence at Middlebury. "Those who wanted the event to take place made eye contact with me. Those intent on disrupting it steadfastly refused to do so. They couldn't look at me directly, because if they had, they would have seen another human being." The protesters who attacked Stanger, or who tried to cancel Benson's speech, believe bad ideas are tantamount to acts of violence, and might require violent suppression. It's easy to argue that position in an essay or on social media; it's harder when your opponent is standing in front of you.[6]

But that's precisely what is so troubling about the current antidebate movement on campus: The context isn't online; it's in person, face to face. Of course, it's also shocking because suppressing dissenting or minority views is fundamentally antithetical to the American idea.

Some observers think that this is just a product of the university bubble; they're confident that entry into the "real world" will jolt students out of their radicalism. But it's a mistake to think this trend is automatically self-correcting. "When elite universities shift their entire worldview away from liberal education as we have long known it toward the imperatives of an identity-based 'social justice' movement, the broader culture is in danger of drifting away from liberal democracy as well," Andrew Sullivan writes in his thoughtful essay "We All Live on Campus Now":

> If elites believe that the core truth of our society is a system of interlocking and oppressive power structures based around immutable characteristics like race or sex or sexual orientation . . . this will be reflected in our culture at large. What matters most of all in these colleges—your membership in a group that is embedded in a hierarchy of oppression—will soon enough be what matters in the society as a whole.

The fact that college campuses, once the cornerstone of free expression and open debate, are now among the most intellectually intolerant spaces in America should concern us deeply.

Is there such a thing as institutional racism and does it exist in America today? Yes, and of course. So what should be done? One option is to debate openly and honestly the data and different perspectives; another is to try to win only by force. The former might win some converts; the latter likely leads only to backlash.

The former is American; the latter is factionalism, the very embodiment of what Washington and Lincoln feared most.

The Amoralization of America

When one half of the nation demonizes the other half, tendrils of resentment reach out and strangle whatever charitable impulses remain in us. Eventually, this tempts even judicious people to start defending the indefensible.

I have a soft spot for many college Republicans, who risk social alienation by voicing unpopular political opinions on frequently far-left campuses. Some of the most thoughtfully energetic people in America are these young conservatives who are willing to defend life and liberty despite enormous social pressure to conform to campus orthodoxies. Often, they're mocked and maligned. That's tolerable for a while. But over time, this treatment has a profound effect. When the progressives dominant on campus refuse to engage—or, worse, knowingly tar conservatives as "fascists" and "neo-Nazis"— many people resort to circling the wagons. Absent real conversation, antagonism can masquerade as a pretty satisfying alternative.

This is partly why so many formerly principled groups have started to invite ridiculous speakers like former Breitbart editor Milo Yiannopoulos to campuses across the country. Yiannopoulos might say some things that tickle the ears of those sick of political correctness—but he is anything but conservative. He's a provocateur, open to doing whatever helps build his "brand"—including cozying up to white nationalists. But since it happens to drive progressives up the wall, some young Republicans have been happy to welcome him to campus. With his flair for self-promotion, Yiannopoulos branded his series of college visits beginning in late 2015 "The Dangerous Faggot Tour."

Anyone familiar with Yiannopoulos's long history of self-promoting outrage knew that his views were repulsive—but many people nonetheless backed him because of who turned out *against* him. On February 1, 2017, the date of Yiannopoulos's scheduled appearance at the University of California, Berkeley, black-clad thugs showed up with weapons, bats, and Molotov cocktails. Some 1,500 protesters descended on Sproul Plaza, setting fires and physically assaulting bystanders. They caused $100,000 in damages to facilities, and succeeded in getting Yiannopoulos's event canceled by local law enforcement. There were no "good guys" in this clash; neither Yiannopoulos nor his opponents are much interested in meaningful debate, let alone recognizing the dignity of those with whom they disagree. Still, many people watching the episode at home found themselves willing to cheer the white nationalist sympathizer over the masked vandals.[7]

There is a deep and corrosive tribal impulse to act as if "the enemy of my enemy is my friend."

But sometimes the enemy of your enemy is just a jackass.

Of course, this tendency to overlook the flaws of those supposedly "in the tribe" doesn't afflict just college students. I saw it up close—or rather, heard it up close—from little old ladies who were absolutely furious with me for refusing to support Alabama Senate candidate Roy Moore. It's rare for people in Nebraska to become emotionally invested in a faraway Senate race—but then this was no normal Senate race. Judge Moore, former chief justice of the Alabama Supreme Court (twice removed from that position), wore a cowboy hat, rode to the polling booth on a horse, and pulled out a gun during a campaign rally (to show that he *really, really* supported the Second Amendment—or something). He also was a credibly accused sexual predator; several women came forward and said a then-thirty-something-year-old Moore had pursued inappropriate relationships with them when they were still teenagers.

This was not enough to erode his political support among some Republicans. When the Republican National Committee, which had initially opposed him, reversed course and decided to give money to his Senate campaign, I criticized the decision. I also made clear that if the National Republican Senate Committee (NRSC), of which I am a member, spent any money on Moore's behalf, I would no longer raise money for it or donate to it.

That's when the little ladies in a couple of churches erupted. They weren't mad at Moore; they were mad at me for opposing him. "If you aren't for Moore, you're for the Democrat," they asserted. No, I wasn't, I explained. (I was—and am—for better long-term choices than what this race offered.) "But don't you know that you're just playing into the hands of the liberal media?" one asked. I replied that I simply believe the women, so I can't be for Moore. But "if the accusations [against Moore] were true," they pressed, "why are they just now coming out?" (I expect these women had no trouble believing the decades-old accusations against Bill Clinton.) Though they wouldn't have let Moore babysit their granddaughters, they were willing to overlook the ever-growing body of evidence against him and give him the political benefit of the doubt. The *Washington Post* was rolling out the accusations only after the Republican primary was over for reasons that should be apparent to me, they argued. They were hardened against the possibility that the *Washington Post* might simply have uncovered some inconvenient facts. Moore was "one of us," so he got a pass from these ladies.

In anti-waste, small-government circles in D.C., many conservative political activists—who built entire careers criticizing Obama administration agencies' gratuitous spending—now hesitate to acknowledge questionable spending decisions by the current administration, especially when the waste is uncovered by mainstream media outlets. "I don't want to be a tool of the left," one of them told me. But isn't the goal to reduce wasteful spending? To Republican activists who think they've been slighted for decades by a biased media, the first-order problem is team loyalty. When asked about a Republican official who appeared to have acted unethically (repeatedly), one Tea Party activist responded simply: "Well, I know that if the *New York Times* is saying he's corrupt, he probably isn't."

This is untenable. Many of the same conservatives who vigorously oppose allowing bureaucrats in D.C. to dictate policy allow the D.C. media to dictate their political positions: If the *Times* or the *Post* wants X, then they're for Y. We shouldn't pretend that an election is going to change any of this.

We need to have the courage to admit that sometimes both options stink. But we're increasingly beholden to an us-versus-them paradigm. We need to see that there's a better way.

Never Perfect, but Always "More Perfect"

In the early 1990s, so-called hate speech rules proliferated across American universities. Today, about 40 percent of colleges surveyed "maintain severely restrictive, 'red light' speech codes that clearly and substantially prohibit constitutionally protected speech," according to the Foundation for Individual Rights in Education. A similar share of Americans under age 35—just over 40 percent—tell pollsters that they think the government should restrict offensive speech. They worry that freedom of speech will allow people to say something that might hurt someone else's feelings.[8]

The impulse to call in the feds (or the administration, or whatever other governing authority) is troubling. Rude or offensive people should face social consequences and loving rebukes from their friends, not the heavy hand of government. I wouldn't cross the street to hear anything Milo Yiannopoulos has to say, and I would challenge my friends who wasted their time with his provocations, but the politics of a speaker have nothing to do with whether or not they are allowed to exercise their Constitutional rights.

As a former college president, I believe deeply in the kind of character development that can result from people living in close proximity while freely exchanging ideas and pursuing truth together. But that happens precisely *because* people are engaged, not coerced. Cultures are changed for the better only when individuals are persuaded and transformed, not beaten into silence. "I don't doubt the good intentions of the new identity politics—to expand the opportunities for people previously excluded," Andrew Sullivan writes. "But what we have now is far more than the liberal project of integrating minorities. It comes close to an attack on the liberal project itself. Marxism with a patina of liberalism on top is still

Marxism—and it's as hostile to the idea of a free society as white nationalism is."[9]

Ultimately, our experiment in liberty has advanced toward a "more perfect union" when we have tried to build on universal dignity by engaging ideological opponents, not when we've merely run them over. We must win them, not beat them. Abraham Lincoln, while arguing in 1859 that America was not living up to her ideals, did not begin by rejecting Thomas Jefferson because of the gulf between his principles and his practices. Instead, he called the nation to align its practices with the third president's stated principles. At a time when the North was fomenting against slavery, Lincoln had—by today's Twitter standards—a ripe chance to energize his followers, ramp up his retweet counts, and impale Jefferson on his own hypocrisy. This would have allowed him to discard Jefferson's ideas and make up his own rule book. Under 2018 rules of engagement, everyone would do this. But Lincoln took a different road: Acknowledging the limitations of an experiment dependent upon flawed human beings, Lincoln nonetheless lauded Jefferson for having anchored the Declaration in "abstract truth, applicable to all men and all times . . . that to-day, and in all coming days, it shall be a rebuke and a stumbling-block to the very harbingers of . . . oppression." He was seeking to persuade—he aimed to grow the movement, not merely deepen the stickiness of the already converted.[10]

There is no more malignant apostasy from the principles of the Founding than the institution of slavery. Our colonial period and most of the first century of the Republic were blighted by this grave evil. But the exceptional thing about America is not that we indulged slavery—slavery has been a feature of human societies since the beginning of time—but that we abolished it, and precisely because it was unreconcilable with our principles. Jonah Goldberg explains well in his recent book, *Suicide of the West*, that abolition, not slavery, was the unprecedented thing. Lincoln recognized that the republican project in liberty could not truly flourish until the "hodgepodge" was bound together in a creedal commitment to freedom for everyone, regardless of color. The history of injustice in America does not invalidate our core principles; no, our resolve *against* injustice is an affirmation of the living force of those principles. Eventually the spirit of liberty prevailed, and the Thirteenth, Fourteenth, and Fifteenth Amendments at the close of the Civil War codified our dramatic step forward.

That has been true, too, in the long struggle for racial equality that has been ongoing ever since. War freed the slave, but military might could not change the hearts of men. The establishment of Jim Crow and the rise of the Ku Klux Klan made clear that racism was a cancer far from eradicated.

It was the civil rights movement that carried forward the American idea. "There are to-day no truer exponents of the pure human spirit of the Declaration of Independence than the American Negroes," began W.E.B. DuBois, the first black American to earn a Harvard doctorate, in his 1903 book, *The Souls of Black Folk*. Earlier, in essays in *The Atlantic*, he had outlined the long-term struggle for civil rights, which he called the "concrete test of the underlying principles of the great republic."[11]

Two generations later, Martin Luther King Jr. and his allies would shape a struggle anchored in Gandhi's theory of nonviolence. Reaffirming all five foundational rights of the First Amendment (religion, speech, press, assembly, and protest), the civil rights movement took its spiritual nourishment from churches and published invitations to rallies and boycotts. What resulted—at the March on Washington, for instance—were some of the greatest assemblies and acts of protest in American history. The heart of the march was the Reverend King's immortal words of petition—and hope. All five First Amendment freedoms were in full view, their importance made manifest.

King's genius, and the key not just to his success as a midcentury civil rights leader but as a latter-day American Founder, was his unwavering respect for every man. His famous "Letter from Birmingham Jail" aims not merely to secure the rights of African-Americans but also to change the hearts of his opponents, whom he resisted—vigorously—but never hated. "All segregation statutes are unjust because segregation distorts the soul and damages the personality."

King had no tolerance for violence: "We must not allow our creative protest to degenerate into physical violence," he proclaimed from the steps of the Lincoln Memorial during the March on Washington. "Again and again we must rise to the majestic heights of meeting physical force with soul force." The "new militarism which has engulfed the Negro community must not lead us to a distrust of all white people, for many of our white brothers have evidenced by their presence here today that they have come to realize that their destiny is part of our destiny."

King was dedicated to the American "we."

Reverend King knew that the path to success could not be zerosum—our side wins and your side loses. We now know from our own history that the way forward had to go via love of neighbor, even though in many of the darkest moments, it surely seemed that all roads led only to greater ugliness. Nonviolence was better than violence; love was better than hate. Americans didn't embrace civil rights as a legal matter first but rather as a right and proper way to respect the dignity of other individuals, of moms and dads and sons and daughters. Images of extraordinary endurance and hope, from places like Birmingham and Selma, accompanied the lyrics that rang in Americans' ears:

> *We shall overcome*
> *We shall overcome some day*
> *Oh, deep in my heart, I do believe*
> *We shall overcome some day*
> *We'll walk hand in hand, some day*
> *Oh, deep in my heart, I do believe . . .*
> *We shall live in peace.*

Throughout his letters, speeches, and sermons, King consistently emphasizes not merely securing civil rights but pursuing the goal in the right way—in an American way. He rebuked white pastors who refused to speak up in favor of the civil rights effort, contrasting them unfavorably to the early Christians who were willing "to suffer for what they believed." "In those days the church was not merely a thermometer that recorded the ideas and principles of popular opinion; it was a thermostat that transformed the mores of society," he wrote. And so it would be for the civil rights movement under his leadership, by means of persuasion and civil disobedience, not insurgency and force.[12]

Deep, enduring change does not come through legislation or elections. Meaningful change comes as lots and lots of individual minds are persuaded and hearts changed. Deep change allows people to change their minds without needing, first, to "eat crow." It tolerates provisional and partial agreements. It's the logic of neighbors who live side by side. It's the logic of the long-term, which respects the dignity and agency of debate partners. Warriors view the present moment as make-or-break for all time—but neighbors do not. Neighbors see today's conversation not as the last discussion we'll ever have, but as a precursor to tomorrow's. We can and will visit again. We can continue talking, and listening. We can be open to future persuasion—and to being persuaded. We need not win everything by force, and we need not win everything right now.

Nicholas Christakis, I believe, knows this. While being berated in the Yale courtyard, he talked civilly and looked students in the eyes. And when the viral video made the Yale students look like bullies, Christakis tweeted, "No one, especially no students exercising right to speech, should be judged just on the basis of a short video clip." In the coming days, he and his wife invited students who disagreed with them to join them for brunch at their home.

Brunch. We can break bread with people with whom we don't already agree on everything. That's the spirit of liberty in action.

Know Your Blind Spots

Talking begins with recognizing our blind spots. Arnold Kling, author of *The Three Languages of Politics*, suggests that each of the three major American political persuasions filters the world through a particular lens:

- Progressives see the world as a battle between victims and oppressors;

- Conservatives see the world as a battle between civilization and barbarism;
- Libertarians see the world as a battle between freedom and coercion.

Each group interprets events differently and comes to different conclusions in no small part because it starts from a different guiding premise. Still, we can see that all three lenses spot different facets of reality—even if each has its own blind spots.

Russ Roberts of the Hoover Institution, following Kling, shows what each group misses. Progressives, "in their eagerness to empathize with the victim . . . can turn the victim into an object rather than an independent actor. Poor people are so oppressed in the liberal view, they don't just have limited agency to choose and live life in meaningful ways." Conservatives, on the other hand, "in their zeal to preserve civilization and the American way of life," often "demonize those that they see as a threat to civilization. They can forget that most immigrants are hard-working individuals who want a better life for their children." Finally, libertarians—how Roberts himself identifies—"often romanticize the power of economic freedom. We struggle to imagine that some people are poorly served by markets, that some transactions involve exploitation of ignorance and that the self-regulation of markets can fail." He confesses that libertarians, in their "zeal to de-romanticize government," often just "ignore the good that government does, especially in cases where freedom might perform badly."[13]

When we understand these different starting points, it's easier to empathize with political opponents, even if we still passionately disagree with their policy preferences. Understanding each other better doesn't mean that we stop debating and join hands around the campfire—but it does help us to talk, having dispensed with the self-deceptive assumption that our opponents simply hate and want to crush us. When we start from the assumption that our opponents are like us—decent folks who want what's best but who start from a different place—we are more likely to be respectful and to have a conversation that's productive. We can treat our opponents as individuals rather than as representatives of some malevolent bloc.

CPAC, the American Conservative Union's annual megaconference, has long been among the most important annual events for the nation's most energetic conservative activists. It's always been a little eccentric—attendees are more than a little likely to be donning tricorn hats and carrying "Don't Tread on Me!" flags—but nonetheless full of enthusiastic, patriotic people. In 2018, however, when a speaker noted that illegal immigrants tend to have far more conservative values than one might expect, the audience erupted into loud booing. Wondering if perhaps the booing was directed not at his statement but at the act of illegally crossing the border, the speaker, radio host and *Forbes* writer Rick Ungar, pivoted from illegal to legal immigration. He began to describe the glories of a naturalization ceremony at a county courthouse.

If you've ever attended or participated in one of these ceremonies, as I have been fortunate to do, you know how they can make the heart soar. The swearing-in of new citizens—new Americans affirming *our shared creed*—is the culmination of years of work and dedication. The new citizens had to get green cards, learn English, and pass a civics test (that a huge share of native-born Americans cannot pass, according to recent surveys).[14] After reams of paperwork and years of waiting, they raise their right hands, they take an oath of allegiance to our Constitution, and each new citizen pledges to "absolutely and entirely renounce and abjure all allegiance and fidelity to any foreign prince, potentate, state, or sovereignty, of whom or which I have heretofore been a subject or citizen."

Everyone sings "America the Beautiful" or the national anthem. People weep. It's an extraordinary experience.

But as Ungar described the naturalization ceremony, and as he encouraged young conservatives to "open their arms" to these (legal) immigrants, he was booed again. To many CPAC attendees, Ungar sounded too much like the "other side."

That's a tragedy. And there are many similar examples we can point to from both the left and the right. Political opponents are now on the prowl for opportunities to mock or silence their opponents—as if the really important dividing line in life is between Republicans and Democrats.

So, is there any good news to be found? Yes. The good news is that most Americans have no interest in "conservatives" who boo naturalization ceremonies or "liberals" who cheer Antifa thugs. Similarly, most Americans know that neither the Democratic nor the Republican Party really has a long-term vision for the challenges we face. I could cite recent polling on this question, which shows that less than 30 percent of the public identifies with either major party—but just do an impromptu survey yourself: How many of your friends at the coffee shop have confidence in either of these parties to lead us to a healthy future?

We need something different.

That can start by recognizing what binds us together. It's not our consumer choices—Denny's vs. Le Diplomate. What binds us together as Americans is our unwavering conviction that, in spite of all our differences—some insignificant, like food preferences; some important, like theological beliefs—we share a belief in freedom for all. We believe that every American should be permitted to follow her conscience, speak her mind, exercise her deepest beliefs.

If we make a habit of reaching out and loving our neighbor, over time we prove, without realizing it, what we've inherited from our beginnings in eighteenth-century Philadelphia: Our people, and all people everywhere, are imbued with inexhaustible, inviolable dignity. They're endowed by God with inalienable human rights. Government is our shared project to secure those rights. America is the idea of freedom and justice that we all embrace and pursue in common.

Day by day, what you choose,

what you think, and what you do

is who you become.

—Heraclitus

6

SET TECH LIMITS

The Good Stuff Will Be Irresistible 🐾 Living to Age 200
The Robots Are Coming 🐾 I'm John, and I'm a Digi-holic
What We're Giving Up 🐾 Sex Without People
Texting by Night, Sleepwalking All Day
Transcending Our Bodies? 🐾 Losing Our Place in Time
Aspiring to Be God 🐾 More Family Meetings at Dinner
Find Some Tech-Skeptical Friends
Redeem the Time 🐾 Don't Get Implants Yet

STEVE JOBS, THE FOUNDER OF APPLE, REFUSED TO ALLOW HIS children to have an iPad: "We limit how much technology our kids use," he told the *New York Times*. "We think it's too dangerous for them."[1]

Last year, I started asking tech billionaires and other Silicon Valley entrepreneurs if they allow their kids unfettered access to smartphones. "Hell, no," one responded. "We know how powerful those things are."

The paradox here is painful: As Americans are increasingly tempted to buy into the idea that more tech saturation is a cost-free escape from the boredom and inconveniences of life, the creators of these new technologies are themselves increasingly guarding against letting technological devices cut them off from those essential parts of life. If we are going to successfully rebuild community in the digital age—if we are going to be happy—we are going to need to realize anew that humans shouldn't aim to be "free from" real people and real places, but aim rather to be "free to" grow roots into those people and places.

"Technology" is just a fancy word for really, really big tools. We've always had it—the wheel, the fork, the steam engine—but it's nonetheless true that what is happening now is radically different from past explosions of innovation: Our combination of mobile computers and exponentially larger algorithms has put us in the middle of a wave of innovation that promises to enhance the capabilities of our minds, not just our bodies. As we'll see in this chapter, technology enthusiasts have begun talking about "uploading our memory" to the cloud, and "merging" men and machines. We're on the cusp of enormous challenges not just to our powers of control, but to our entire idea of what it means to be *human*. But we seem to be moving forward on autopilot. One of the great challenges of the twenty-first century is to pause and think carefully about the technology that promises (or is it threatens?) to transform the ways we live—and the ways we understand ourselves.

Because the consequences of not looking before we leap are likely to be very scary.

The Good Stuff Will Be Irresistible

Let's start with the obvious: We like technology. It's novel, and eye-popping, and useful. If it didn't serve our purposes, we wouldn't use it. And we're just getting started—there's lots of extraordinary technology coming our way.

Scientists in Japan are developing a headset that can read and translate people's thoughts into audible language. Initial tests at Toyohashi University of Technology in 2018 found that a prototype has a 90 percent success rate recognizing numbers from zero to nine, and has a 61 percent success rate recognizing single syllables in Japanese. The device will be exponentially more effective within five years. It could prove a lifeline to people with severe disabilities,

including paralysis. People suffering from "locked-in syndrome"—
a condition that sometimes afflicts stroke victims by paralyzing the
body and facial muscles but leaving the consciousness unaffected—
could use the brainwave-reading device to communicate normally.
In the same vein, SpaceX founder Elon Musk launched Neuralink
in 2017, a company tasked with developing technology that can connect human brains to computers. He thinks that "neural lace" systems will successfully implant "tiny brain electrodes that may one
day upload and download thoughts."[2]

There are many engineering and technical riddles yet to be
solved, but many of the tools our futurists envision are now constrained only by processing power and battery life limitations. Algorithms are getting better all the time, and the stunning advances in
artificial intelligence over the last two decades will likely accelerate
going forward.

To evaluate the possible pace of coming changes, consider the
case of AlphaGo, an artificial intelligence designed by DeepMind, a
subsidiary of Google. AlphaGo is currently learning to play the ancient Chinese board game Go. Go is sometimes compared to chess—
but it's far more challenging. Because Go's board is a 19x19 grid, the
number of legal moves is estimated at 2×10^{170}—which is greater
than the number of atoms in the universe. When I first started reading about AlphaGo, I assumed that it must be like Deep Blue, the
IBM machine that in 1997 defeated Garry Kasparov, perhaps the
greatest chess player in history. But AlphaGo and Deep Blue are very
different. Deep Blue was built to play chess. It used its massive processing power to map millions of possible moves. AlphaGo is something altogether unique.

Because Go has exponentially more iterations than chess, it presents a challenge to traditional AI methods—for example, the "brute-
force" method used by many chess computers, in which at each turn
the program calculates every possible move and selects the best one.
But in Go, there are simply too many possibilities. What AlphaGo
does, instead, is play game after game of Go, "learning" from its wins
and losses what moves are best in a given situation. (AlphaGo began
with an inbuilt record of 30 million moves, taken from actual games

played by people, and learned from that foundation. A more recent version, AlphaGo Zero, which defeated its predecessor, learned the game *from scratch*.) In March 2016, when AlphaGo played Lee Sedol, the world's leading Go player, machine beat man four games to one, for the first time ever. But that's not what's mind-boggling.

AlphaGo is only getting started. It is just learning how to learn. DeepMind lead developer David Silver explains: Humans "have a limitation in terms of the actual number of Go games that they're able to process in a lifetime. A human can perhaps play a thousand games a year; AlphaGo can play through millions of games every single day." It isn't sufficient to think of AlphaGo in terms of brute-force calculation, because it has been programmed to use its powers for abstract learning; technologist and author Adam Greenfield describes AlphaGo as "a stack of multiple kinds of neural networks and learning algorithms laminated together." As time goes on, artificial intelligence programs will get better and better at pattern recognition and reproduction, "even those seemingly dependent on soulful improvisation." Already AI programs have produced remarkable emulations of Rembrandt paintings and Bach compositions.[3]

CereProc, a Scottish company, is developing technology that would allow people who have lost their voices to use a program that would convert the text they type into the unique sounds of their original voices. Gone would be the relatively crude, robotic tones people remember from the late Stephen Hawking. As a demonstration project, CereProc's developers reproduced John F. Kennedy's "lost speech"—the speech the thirty-fifth president would have delivered in Dallas on November 22, 1963, had he not been struck down by an assassin's bullet. The company used audio and text from 831 of Kennedy's recorded speeches and was able to reproduce almost seamlessly all 2,590 words of the twenty-minute remarks he was supposed to give later that day. It's a remarkable composition, blending thousands of fragments of audio using cutting-edge computer technology. "We use machine learning and artificial intelligence techniques just to try and figure out how he moves his pitch and the duration of his sounds through his sentences," engineer Chris Pidcock told Radio Scotland. "We took his existing speeches and material, and we cut it up into tiny pieces and stitched it back together into a new speech. JFK had a really unique speaking style, and getting his intonation correct was something that we had to spend some time on."[4]

Brookings scholar Darrell West has been studying technology companies that are developing sophisticated tools for diagnosing hard-to-detect cancers. Merantix, a German medical device company, has a new application for medical imaging that has made it cheaper to detect cancerous lesions on the lymph nodes. Humans could hypothetically complete the same series of analysis, but since a radiologist is "able to carefully read only four images an hour," reading 10,000 images would be "prohibitively expensive if done by humans," says West—over $250,000 per procedure. Soon the machine will be able to perform the task for only a few dollars. "What deep learning can do in this situation," West maintains, "is train computers on data sets to learn what a normal-looking versus an irregular-appearing lymph node is." What is prohibitively expensive today could become a regular part of checkups in the near future.[5]

Researchers are applying the same concepts to many other cancers. Colorectal cancer is the third-leading cause of cancer death in the United States, but it's treatable if detected early. Japanese researchers recently demonstrated a new diagnostic tool that takes less than a second and is 86 percent accurate. That success rate will improve with time as the machine draws from a wider range of data. The researchers at Showa University believe they can create an automated system that requires no extensive training to operate, putting the tool into the hands of minimally trained medical technicians.

Technology is going to keep substituting for labor, and it is going to deliver both higher quality and lower cost results.

Living to Age 200

A number of Silicon Valley engineers, biotech researchers, and—maybe most important today—venture capitalists believe we're within two decades of an "inflection point" when breakthroughs in computing and nanotechnology will extend human life expectancy, first by years and then by decades. The more ambitious (you might say utopian) among them speak of potentially adding more than a year of life expectancy *every year.*

You read that right—they believe natural death might be effectively "paused" for a while.

Forty years ago, engineer and entrepreneur Eric Drexler first conceived the idea of building microscopic robots to do . . . well, just about anything. Long before the word "nanotechnology" had entered popular parlance, Drexler predicted a coming era when devices "the size of viruses" would begin to cure disease. "Our ability to arrange atoms," he wrote in his seminal book, *Engines of Creation*, "lies at the foundation of technology."

For centuries futurists and science fiction writers have been speculating on a world where man becomes immortal, but in recent decades some of these speculative visions have started to connect to actual innovations in the lab. Initially, the breakthroughs seemed more like nerdy games than real-life tools. In 1989, researchers at IBM used a highly specialized scanning microscope to manipulate thirty-five xenon atoms to spell out "IBM." Now, however, geneticists and biochemical engineers have used that technology to develop medicines and therapies based on patients' DNA and RNA, with more advanced treatments coming all the time. Thousands of carbon-based fullerene molecules can be strung together to produce nanotubes that, according to *Wired* magazine, are "100 times stronger than steel and more electrically conductive than any other substance known." Nanotubes are already being used in pharmaceuticals, including vaccines and gene therapies, but researchers expect that they will soon become useful for tissue regeneration. Rice University chemist and Nobel Laureate Richard Smalley, who discovered the underlying molecule in 1985, predicts that nanotube wires will eventually "be so efficient that they might 'easily replace every high-voltage cable in the world.'" Subhasish Mitra, an electrical engineer at Stanford, thinks we're on the verge of seeing an exponential leap forward in battery life that will make it possible for advanced, tailored technologies to become regular parts of our everyday environment. Think pacemakers that last 500 years, not ten years. How these various technologies will converge is hard to envision, but the likelihood of dramatically different lives is not.[6]

Many futurists see a world where microscopic computers will be swimming around in our bloodstream repairing cancers before we even know we've been diagnosed. Some talk of "eliminating" cancer and of curing all the major diseases that routinely cut life short: heart disease, stroke, diabetes, and more. Others have their sights trained on surmounting the breakdown of the body that comes "naturally" with age. Instead of organ *transplants*, they speculate about organ *regeneration*. Imagine no more dementia, no more muscle atrophy.

Imagine living to be 200 years old. Some of these scientists and investors think we should already be dreaming of living to 2,000.

The Robots Are Coming

In a broken world, there are many unmet needs—but people are finding new ways to use machines to address them. It won't be only the abstract diagnostic or interventional-surgical tasks that our AI robotic "doctors" will perform; they will include some of the more personal and emotional tasks, too. Primitive "nursebots" have been around for more than a decade, reminding patients to take their pills or helping them in and out of the bath. But they are likely, soon, to become involved in more common, quasi-social support tasks, too.

Sherry Turkle, an MIT professor who studies technology and society (and whose popular work every mom and dad in America should be reading), took her students to visit assisted-living facilities and nursing homes. They wanted to understand how lonely and declining older folks would interact with a robot doll called My Real Baby, which simulates the sounds and movements of an infant. In almost every instance, the patient was at first repelled by the doll. But soon men and women alike were caring for the doll as if it were a real baby, even as they insisted it was just a "mechanical thing" or an "inanimate object." A woman named Edna ignored her visiting real-life great-granddaughter to continue doting on her doll, while simultaneously telling Turkle's students that she felt no connection to it.[7]

We're going to have a hard time resisting the allure of next-generation machines. Although we'll know that they are machines, the interfaces are going to get progressively better, and we'll marvel at how "lifelike" they feel. They'll likely be programmed to generate simulated emotions—cries for attention, for example—and respond to human "input."

Turkle and other researchers have already found ample evidence that adult sons and daughters find it much easier to "walk out that door" of the nursing home when they know Mom or Dad has a "companion," even if the companion is battery-operated. We can imagine robot hospice nurses keeping the dementia sufferer occupied and offering succor to the dying. It takes no great leap to imagine people likewise accepting sophisticated robots as babysitters for children.

Before we scoff, we should pause to reflect on our own relationships with our smartphones. We tell ourselves we're in control, but is that true? Whether we're playing with a sophisticated doll or scrolling through social media, the feedback we receive from our technology—the ways that it tickles our dopamine receptors—makes us feel better somehow. In Edna's case, Turkle writes, "My Real Baby's demands seem to suit her better than those of her great-granddaughter." Actual kids, it turns out, can be fussy, demanding, and unpredictable. My Real Baby gave Edna "confidence that she is in a landscape where she can get things right." She knows that the robot cannot develop feelings for her, that its "emotions" are fake, but Edna gets to "care" for the robot—and the robot mimics emotions in ways that allow Edna to choose to feel that the relationship is reciprocal.

Turkle contends we're in a robotic moment, where people are forming "intimacies" in solitude with machines. Many will argue that a sociable robot is better than nothing. But throughout her important book, *Alone Together*, Turkle tells heartrending stories of people—children, the disabled and infirm, the elderly—who find it easier to relate to machines than to other people. That's by design. "Digital connections and the social robot may offer the illusion of companionship without the demands of friendship."

I'm John, and I'm a Digi-holic

When we contemplate massive technological change, it's tempting to project the problems and threats into the future—a future we won't have to bother with. But this isn't a debate about a *future* technological moment about which *other people* will need to make big decisions. This is about the habits that we ourselves are already internalizing, right now.

New York University business and marketing professor Adam Alter has been studying addictive technologies and the people who build them. "A well-designed game," he writes, "fuels behavioral addiction." It's no accident that so many titans of Silicon Valley have been so scrupulous about limiting their own children's exposure to the technology they sell. According to Alter, it's "as if the people producing tech products were following the cardinal rule of drug dealing: never get high on your own supply."[8]

The old adage, traceable to the Greeks, that "too much of anything is bad" is mostly right—but it's hard to become too addicted to the rhythm of eating well, sleeping right, and loving to work out. The key here is the rhythm, the pacing. What the Greek philosophers were really teaching was moderation in all good things. Develop an addiction—but choose the right addictions. That is, choose to form the right habits. Recognize that overindulgence turns us into slaves.

Have Americans become slavishly addicted to their screens? Without a doubt. The Pew Research Center in March 2018 found that 26 percent of us admit to being "almost constantly" online, up from 21 percent just three years before. Nearly 40 percent of Americans ages 18 to 29 are online virtually every minute they're awake.[9] The median American checks "our smartphones every 4.3 minutes," says Tony Reinke, a journalist in the tradition of legendary media theorist Marshall McLuhan. Reinke's description of his phone habits will sound familiar to many readers: "Since I got my first iPhone, a smartphone has been within my reach 24/7." Reinke uses his phone

> to wake me in the morning, to deejay my music library,
> to entertain me with videos, movies and live television, to

capture my life in digital pictures and video, to allow me to play the latest video game, to guide me down foreign streets, to broadcast my social media, and to reassure me every night that it will wake me again. . . . I use my phone for just about everything (except phone calls, it seems). And my phone goes with me wherever I go: the bedroom, the office, vacation, and, yes, the bathroom.[10]

We pretend that our screens serve us, but most of us will admit—when we're being honest—that our screens are dictating the relationship.

And perhaps the screens themselves will vanish. We're already bringing home the first generation of voice-activated digital assistants like Amazon's Alexa, Google Home, and Apple's Siri, to whom we're unwittingly confiding our secrets. (Earlier this year, an Oregon family's Alexa eerily recorded an entire conversation and sent a copy to a friend in their address book, apparently having interpreted background noise as a series of commands.) Wearable technologies such as the new Apple Watch and a host of smart augmented reality (AR) glasses are coming online. Google Glass, a relatively cumbersome set of computer-enhanced spectacles, failed to find a niche (its $1,500 price tag didn't help)—but some "heads-up display" that integrates real-time information into a wearer's visual field is likely to break through within the next few years. People who work in digital advertising think that smartphones and tablets will eventually be superseded by interfaces tailored to our bodies. "I think it's an inevitability . . . [that] screens are going to be gone," says Chris Neff, senior director of innovation for a Miami-based global advertising agency.

We're collectively pretending that having more tools is always a good thing and that the only constraints that matter are the technical ones.

But this isn't right. We should also be talking about the "demand side"—that is, about us. What do we need? What do we want? What end or purpose should technology serve? We should be talking about what it means to live well.

What We're Giving Up

Please don't misunderstand: I'm no Luddite. I'm actually Christmas-morning giddy about lots of these new technologies. But I don't think we've reflected adequately on the downsides—not just of what's coming but of what we've already embraced.

Seventy years ago, before DARPA's investment in the proto-internet at a handful of universities assisting the U.S. military's Cold War efforts, all of the computing power on Earth was barely what you have in your apartment today. By the 1980s, it was possible for middle-class American families to buy a pretty impressive desktop computer. A decade later, those same families were swapping emails over AOL. Another decade later, in 2007, the iPhone appeared. So, decade by decade, we leapt from no computing power to computing power to home computers to computers in our pocket. Now we have wearable computers, and soon we'll have implantable computers. Now is the time to pause for a national family meeting—and lots more individual family meetings—to discuss what we want from these coming technologies, before they make the decision for us.

When I got into the shower this morning after my workout, the only thing I had with me was my wedding ring. It's one little piece of gold—and it's a pretty decent summary of who I am: union of body and soul, nothing else. We are our physical beings, our learnings and memories, and our word—or our commitments and oaths. It's good to be reminded of that. It's a tonic against the feeling that I'm—how often do we say this?—"naked" without my phone.

I might be a little bit addicted to my devices (okay, I have three phones, so maybe I'm more than a little bit addicted)—but I can leave them behind for long periods of time. It isn't just during the shower. We turn them off and box them up for big portions of Sundays at our house. It's a bit disorienting, because we've oriented so much of our lives around these supercomputers in our pockets, but we still have the power today to say no to the temptation of the machine. I am still me without it.

But what happens if I start to saturate my life with technology that I wear—or technology inside my body?

Tech companies have been imagining "augmented human be-ings" for decades. In 2004, the U.S. Patent Office awarded Microsoft patent no. 6,754,472 for a "method and apparatus for transmitting power and data using the human body." In effect, Microsoft found a rudimentary way to use our skin to transmit information to the internet. In the eyes of some analysts, Microsoft isn't that far from "linking portable devices such as watches, keyboards, displays, and speakers using the conductivity of 'a body of a living creature.'"[11]

Put me down as someone who thinks we should talk a bit before we do this.

We should level with each other about the rafts of emerging data that suggest that we're losing something important as we become more attached to our screens. We're more anxious, more distracted, more depressed, and more downright exhausted.

We're losing our ability to read closely and think carefully (about which more momentarily). We're losing the ability to focus deeply on important work. We're likelier to spend our time seeking valida-tion from digital "friends" than to spend time with flesh-and-flood friends. We insulate ourselves behind filtered Instagram photos. And all the time we become *lonelier*, parched for genuine community.

We've become addicted to distraction.

It isn't accidental that lots of formerly utopian technologists have become more pessimistic about what technology will bring next. Both our anecdotal experiences and larger formal studies point in the same direction: We're increasingly bonding with our machines, and these virtual relationships aren't satisfying. As Professor Turkle puts it: "The ties we form through the Internet are not, in the end, the ties that bind." They are merely "the ties that preoccupy."[12]

Sex Without People

Sex is pretty great. It's not perfect, but it's pretty close. Want to know how to make it lousy? Make it free. No flirtation, no foreplay. No actual relationship, no commitment.

Tech can do this for you. Lots of studies are demonstrating that we are deforming one of the most basic, good things on earth.

Survey data suggest that there has been significantly less real sex in the United States since 2007, when the introduction of the iPhone and higher download speeds ramped up easy access to online pornography. Among 18- to 39-year-olds, almost half (46 percent) admit to having looked at pornography as recently as "yesterday," and "deepfake" technology has made it possible for users to create tailored pornography that seamlessly superimposes the faces of celebrities—or friends, exes, or Facebook connections—onto the bodies of porn performers. According to *Time* magazine, experts believe young men's "sexual responses have been sabotaged because their brains were virtually marinated in porn when they were adolescents. Their generation has consumed explicit content in quantities and varieties never before possible, on devices designed to deliver content swiftly and privately, all at an age when their brains were more plastic—more prone to permanent change—than in later life." We don't yet know how many, but there's a wave of young men suffering from porn-induced erectile dysfunction (PIED), a condition in which they can only become aroused watching porn; a real woman in the flesh is not enough.[13]

This is all, furthermore, before the widespread introduction of sex robots—which are already available from select manufacturers, albeit for $5,000, minimum. Still, it's a market niche entrepreneurs are eager to fill. What will happen when men can satisfy their sexual needs without the burdens of an actual human relationship? This isn't the place to unpack all of the data from demographer Nicholas Eberstadt's *Men Without Work: America's Invisible Crisis*, but partnerless sex is among the complex web of factors that has contributed to a massive increase in recent years in the number of 18- to 55-year-olds who have opted out of the labor force.

No one benefits from the degradation of romance that is taking place. Other than sports, I basically stopped watching television when *Seinfeld* went off the air. But it was impossible to ignore the cultural conversation surrounding the HBO series *Girls*, starring Lena Dunham. In an NPR interview, Dunham explained how she and her co-writers fashioned the show's uncomfortable sex scenes to depict what it's like for women to have sex with guys who grew up on a steady diet of pornography. Their sexual appetites are unusual and extreme, and, according to Dunham, there is pressure for women to go along. "For young women sex is about sex—but sex is also about wanting to be liked and wanting to be appreciated. And the fear, when you say no, is that someone will go, OK, well, then see you later. Like, that you will, you know, lose your loving audience." I have not seen these episodes—my wife uses the great phrase, "guarding your mental suitcase," that is, being careful about what mental possessions you haul into the future with you—but the sex scenes in the show are reportedly difficult to watch. One character urges his sexual partner to pretend to be an "11-year-old prostitute." Other scenes have come close, in the eyes of some protesting viewers, to rape.

In Chapter 2, we explored how loneliness has become a cultural epidemic. Sexual technologies are promoting the belief that we can get all the benefits of genuine intimacy without committing to a real person. That's a poisonous lie. We only flourish together, "in touch" with each other. Instead, we're undermining the most basic form of bonding—the act that is the seal of love between two people and the seed of family life.

Texting by Night, Sleepwalking All Day

Next to great sex, one of the best things in life is good sleep. But our digital tools are messing with this too. Technology disrupts our body's clock by removing us from our natural orientation toward time. Most of us sleep with our phones within arm's reach. We use them to help us fall asleep—like older generations used novels or *Letterman*—and we use them as our alarm clock.

But we're stealing our own sleep. Our eyes perceive light in various wavelengths, which have different color sensations, which in turn cause our brains to wind our internal clock. "Red light"— which is common at dusk—signals that it's time to go to sleep. "Blue light," which arrives naturally in the morning, signals to your body that it's time to face the day. Smartphones, tablets, laptops, and even e-readers emit blue light—which means they're acting like roosters at every swipe. We think we're winding down by catching up on the news and checking Facebook one last time, but we're actually undermining our body's ability to rest. Harvard researchers examined what happened to people who were exposed to 6.5 hours of blue light compared to the same amount and intensity of non-blue light. The blue light shifted sleep schedules by three hours, compared to only an hour and a half for non-blue light. Of course, this sort of sleep interruption doesn't even account for the various pings and dings and beeps and buzzes that occur when phones aren't in sleep mode.[14]

Teenagers need much more sleep than adults. Their bodies are changing and their brains are in a critical phase of development. Lack of sleep has a profound effect. The American Academy of Pediatrics now recommends up to twelve hours of sleep a night for teens. Instead, millions of our teens are up late into the night, bonding with their robot-friend. Naomi Schaefer Riley in her 2018 book, *Be the Parent, Please: Stop Banning Seesaws and Start Banning Snapchat*, believes many parents have allowed themselves to be sidelined from something fundamental—the basic decisions about "how their children are going to interact with the rest of the world." In her view, sleep deprivation is a consequence of a much larger abandonment of natural and social rhythms. She urges parents to think about the negative physical, psychological, and social effects of ubiquitous screens, pointing out that, by allowing them to permeate more of our children's lives, "we are likely to be changing not only the information they can access but also their habits, their personalities, and their tastes."

Sherry Turkle, the MIT professor, was once something of a tech-utopian, but has since turned in a more pessimistic direction, driven largely by her observations of generations raised in technology-saturated environments. It isn't only how our teens sleep; it's how we've taught them to live. Turkle first noticed in the 1980s that personal computers had excessive "holding power" on students at MIT, where technology became pervasive earlier than at most institutions. Her worries grew with the advent of the World Wide Web and the enormous popularity of services such as America Online. As connections to the internet went mobile, "the network was with us, on us, all the time," and we convinced ourselves—falsely—that digital connectivity was the same thing as being engaged.

According to Turkle, real life has been supplanted by "second life." Now, "insecure in our relationships and anxious about intimacy, we look to technology for ways to be in relationships and protect ourselves from them at the same time," she writes. "We bend to the inanimate with a new solicitude. We fear the risks and disappointments of relationships with our fellow humans. [So we come to] expect more from technology and less from each other."

A mother recently told me about wrestling with her kids about smartphones. She didn't want her teenage son to have one, but he explained that he "needed" one, because when he and his friends hang out, there always comes a time when everyone "escapes" into their phones. If he doesn't have a phone, he feels as if he's the only one in the room "who doesn't have a friend." Interesting word choice, no?

Hiding behind phones is a familiar experience for adults, too. We use phones to look busy at uncomfortable parties or in awkward social moments. Some of you who've dated in the modern world have dumped someone via text—or been dumped—in order to avoid a bumbling, emotional confrontation. Phones are social prophylactics, protecting us from the unwanted negative effects of face-to-face interaction.

Even at home, we're scared of real intimacy. As both the size of our residences and the distance between houses increase, people are physically more isolated. Strolls around the neighborhood and time on the stoop fade away. Many families, although still sharing the same address, are actually living "postfamilial" lives, to use Turkle's word. The frequency of shared meals has been progressively collapsing for half a century. Individual members of a family are regularly, as Turkle describes it, "alone together, each in their own rooms, each on a networked computer or mobile device. We go online because we are busy but end up spending more time with technology and less time with each other." We seek connectivity as "a way to be close, even as we effectively hide from each other."[15]

We're missing big aspects of being human here. In the real world, in good times and bad, for better and for worse, we communicate emotions largely through nonverbal exchanges. Neuroscientist Katri Saarikivi explained in an influential TED Talk that just seeing a happy expression causes our smile muscles to respond in kind. Conversely, when we see someone in pain, it stimulates the same parts of our brains as when we're physically suffering.

Our ability to know and feel partly depends on our bodies—on seeing and being near each other. This is where empathy begins. Recognizing our limitations—and therefore the necessity of physical presence—helps us live more fully human lives.

Transcending Our Bodies?

Not everyone agrees with me. Ray Kurzweil, whose groundbreaking work in optical character recognition technology enabled scanners that can read and translate text in virtually every language, is an unapologetic utopian. As he sees it, greater integration of technology and daily life is simply inevitable. Just as we "didn't stay in the caves, [and] we didn't stay on the planet," so too we are inevitably "not going to stay with the limitations of our biology."

Kurzweil predicts a moment, "the singularity," at which human beings and machines will merge; human beings will become more than human.

Elon Musk is also in favor of a man-and-machine synthesis, although for darker reasons: If, in the future, an AI machine has a goal and humans present an obstacle, "it will destroy humanity as a matter of course, without even thinking about it," he writes. "The least scary future I can think of is one where we have at least democratized AI, because if one company or small group of people manages to develop godlike digital super-intelligence, they could take over the world." Cheery stuff.[16]

But whether you follow Kurzweil's optimism or Musk's pessimism, the end result points in the same direction: A human being combined with computer intelligence wouldn't be quite *human* anymore. These thinkers are contemplating the outer limits of what's become known as *transhumanism*—although perhaps it's more accurate to call it *posthumanism*. In any case, it's worth thinking about the impulse—not because we're all going to become Iron Man next week, but because we can already see how humans are becoming molded to technology.

A decade ago, journalist Nicholas Carr wrote a famous article for *The Atlantic* that asked, "Is Google Making Us Stupid?" His answer, in so many words, was "yes"—but with a few caveats. Technology has always shaped our thinking. The advent of writing six thousand years ago led to incalculable advances in culture, literature, and science. But it also annihilated the oral traditions that had sustained societies for thousands of years. Writing led to a decline in memorization, because remembering on your own—that is, without the aid of a book—was no longer the only way to preserve a fact or story.

Now, the internet is changing our brains—that is, just as the introduction of writing changed our neural circuitry, the internet, too, is changing the wiring inside our heads. Carr described the "uncomfortable sense that someone, or something, has been tinkering with my brain, remapping the neural circuitry, reprogramming the memory." He wasn't losing his mind. But he could sense that his mind was changing. He wasn't thinking the same way he once did. In the past, "[my] mind would get caught up in the narrative or the turns of the argument, and I'd spend hours strolling through long stretches of prose. That's rarely the case anymore. Now my concentration often starts to drift after two or three pages. I get fidgety, lose the thread, begin looking for something else to do."

Carr's attention span, focus, and work habits had changed as he spent more and more time online. As a writer, he acknowledged that the "Web has been a godsend." Research that used to take hours or days could be done in seconds or minutes. But even when he wasn't working, Carr said, he was "as likely as not to be foraging in the Web's info-thickets, reading and writing e-mails, scanning headlines and blog posts, watching videos and listening to podcasts, or just tripping from link to link to link."

Carr's experience is familiar to me, and I suspect you'll be able to relate, too. I discovered the Google search engine in 1999, and it changed my life as a history graduate student. It made it easier to find obscure information quickly. But I suspect that I retained less of what I read during that period than I would have otherwise. I trusted a lot more to digital "memory"—as have most of us.

People don't read the same way in the internet age. We skim. That's especially true of the content we see on screens, but it's true of reading habits more generally, even when holding a traditional paper book with no hyperlink-rabbit-trail possibilities. Researchers have known this for more than twenty years. Most Americans are reading more words per year today than we did forty years ago, when television was the distraction of choice—but by "read," we just mean that our eyes pass over words, like skipping stones.

"Neuroscientists and psychologists have discovered that, even as adults, our brains are very plastic," Carr explains in his book on the subject, *The Shallows*. "They're very malleable, they adapt at the cellular level to whatever we happen to be doing. And so the more time we spend surfing, and skimming, and scanning . . . the more adept we become at that mode of thinking." The good news is that we can also retrain ourselves at other "slower" or "deeper" modes of thinking. But this retraining requires work, particularly periods of prolonged concentration and focus. This requires more than will; it requires reconfiguring our daily media and technology ecosystem, since online time essentially "crowds out" time for activities that require longer cycles.

Once upon a time, most of us thought of our character and personality as a product of two discrete inputs: nature and nurture. Few neurobiologists conceive of it precisely this way anymore, because the deep cleavage between the two implied that our "nature" was conclusively settled at the moment of conception. In reality, while there are firm biological limits on what we can become, big pieces of our nature—from our height to our vision to certain elements of brain structure—are significantly influenced by the nurture we receive early in life and by the ways we exercise our minds. The frontal lobe of teenagers, for instance, is not "completed" until years past puberty. This is partly why a 13-year-old can learn a new language much less painfully than a 33-year-old.

Why does all of this matter? Because new research suggests that our smartphones—or, more precisely, our obsessive use of smartphones—are rewiring our brains, too, particularly the brains of our children. No responsible parent would willingly hook her child on heroin. No careful mom and dad would let their kids eat nothing but cake and candy. But there's compelling evidence that many of the apps on our tablets are as addictive as heroin and as unhealthy as an uninterrupted diet of sweets—and by design. We know the harms of drugs and sugary foods.

The new digital addictions are at least as dangerous.

Losing Our Place in Time

Technology enthusiasts like Kurzweil often talk as if the only meaningful obstacle to their project is the cumbersome interface between AI and the human mind. But that's not the real problem. The problem with their utopian vision is that it denies the fundamental reality that humans are situated in time and space. And ignoring this existential truth brings loads of misery.

We're already seeing this in the way we use our phones. We regularly use our phones to escape the inconveniences and doldrums of our own lives, here and now.

Psychologists talk about dissociation, which is when people separate the details of an event from their awareness of it. It's common with trauma victims. But it's a condition that characterizes a lot of Americans—not because we're traumatized but because we're bored.

We mentioned earlier the significant quantity of research demonstrating that smartphones and social media are making us considerably lonelier and, consequently, less happy. It turns out that "lives are always more spectacular on the other side of the filter. . . . We found that the more you use Facebook over time, the more likely you are to experience negative physical health, negative mental health, and negative life satisfaction," writes Holly Shakya, a professor at the University of California, San Diego. Similarly, the more time one spends on social media, "the greater the association with anxiety symptoms and the greater likelihood of an anxiety disorder," says Anna Vannucci, coauthor of another study that examined the anxiety levels of 18- to 22-year-old social media users.[17]

It's easy to see that children and teenagers will be particularly susceptible to social media's siren song. Middle and high schools are the most ruthlessly status-conscious places on Earth, and social media brings the competition home. People of a certain age will remember the early social media network MySpace's "Top 8" feature, where users identified their top eight online friends; fights over virtual friendship strained more than a few real-life friendships.

But it's easy for anyone to be seduced. How many lives do you peek in on regularly on Facebook or Instagram? The average person has somewhere around 330 Facebook friends. That's 330 people who (seem to) travel more than you do, who (seem to) have a bigger house and a nicer car than you do, whose kids (seem to) behave better than yours. Social media accounts are exercises in selection bias—no one posts photos of themselves cleaning up the cat's puke—but we don't pause to remember that. We see a couple on the beach in Santorini, and seeing is believing. And because we'd rather not contemplate our dull lives, we keep scrolling, looking to escape—into precisely the glossy, airbrushed world that's responsible for this mess.

This spiral, which app designers are eager to prolong and intensify, is tearing us away from our here and now—which is maybe not the "perfect" life we imagine in our Walter Mitty moments but which is the only life that has any chance of fulfilling us. Here's the immutable reality that neither today's scrolling nor tomorrow's neural lace links will fix: We can't be in two places at once. We can't be on the beach in Cancun and also courtside with the kids at practice in Paducah. We have to choose. And having flown more than a million miles over the past few years, let me say: Skype can take a bit of the sting out of missing another Little League game, but there's no substitute for a place and a people to call home. As we've seen, the growing body of happiness literature is teaching us more definitively every year that a central component to a contented life is "rootedness"—having a sense of community.

Yet we undermine these roots every day by scrolling through feeds, trying to throw ourselves into a different time and place, because maybe things are better there. We're like the dog with the bone who sees his reflection below the bridge. "Look at that bone!" he barks, full of desire, and ends up losing the real bone in his mouth because he wants to chase an image that turns out to be nothing at all.

Tragically, Americans are losing their real families while chasing images on smartphones that often turn out to be nothing at all. We abandon real places and neglect real people—and for what? The undermining of local tribes never ends up being worth it, as the substitute virtual tribes we eventually join are generally much better at being *against* things than being *for* things. The end result is aching loneliness.

Aspiring to Be God

I've never thought of Adam Sandler movies as prophetic. But in 2006, a year before the iPhone and the faster download speeds it ushered in, Sandler starred in *Click*. His character, an ambitious architect, husband, and father named Michael Newman, goes to Bed Bath & Beyond to replace his home's lost universal remote. After meandering through the bed and bath sections, he finds an area called "Beyond," and another called "Way Beyond." There, he meets an eccentric named Morty (played by Christopher Walken), who gives him a remote that, Morty says, does, in fact, control the universe. Using it, Michael can fast-forward through the boring parts of life. When he fast-forwards, he's essentially on cruise control; his mind can advance while his body performs the rote tasks of life.

Obviously, Michael experiments. When his dog won't stop barking, he turns down the volume. When he gets a cold, he skips ahead to health. When he wants to have sex, he fast-forwards through the obligatory back massage. When he can't afford to buy bikes for his kids, he leaps to the next pay raise at work.

That's when he discovers, to his shock, that he's missed a year of life: his dog has died, his marriage is in trouble, and his kids have grown into people he doesn't really know. Alarmed, he tries to get rid of the remote, but it keeps reappearing in his hand. He wants to destroy it, but he can't. Worse, the remote starts automatically fast-forwarding based on his previous preferences. Even if he wanted to slow down and enjoy the small moments of life, his remote is now programming his patterns. He's become enslaved to his preferences.

At Michael's father's funeral, Morty reappears and apologizes to Michael for his loss. "I didn't want to take him," he said.

"What?" Michael asks, confused. Morty had appeared throughout his life, giving tips about how to navigate the remote—but this seems like a different role.

"I'm an angel," Morty reveals.

"I thought angels were supposed to protect people," Michael puzzles.

"I'm the Angel of Death."

Our devices are invaluable when they allow us to become more expedient and productive. They're splendid as a means to give us more time to invest passionately in our families and our communities. They are great as *tools*. But they can become angels of death if we allow it. And isn't that what we do when we start scrolling during a boring conversation with a family member? When we check Twitter during church? (Full disclosure: I once cynically live-tweeted a children's piano recital, and I refuse to apologize. The live-tweeting was incredible.)

Like us, Sandler never made one grand, once-and-for-all decision to escape his time and place. But with a little tool in his hand, he ended up making lots of individual decisions that collectively put his life on autopilot.

Sandler is Everyman as he tries to fast-forward through the boring parts of life to get to the stand-alone parts that he thinks will fulfill him. But in real life, much of what you end up appreciating about the hard-to-attain moments is the work required to get there. While he thinks he's been given a gift—cleanliness without showers, promotion without work, orgasm without foreplay—it was all actually a distraction while his life was being stolen. You can't just vault to the good parts of life.

That's the lesson of *Click*. (That, and that Christopher Walken is always hilarious, even as the bad guy.)

More Family Meetings at Dinner

The big problem we face is not that our technological interfaces are not yet good enough, but that we have not been thinking enough, and together, about what technology is and isn't good for. We don't primarily lack technology, we primarily lack wisdom. We lack habits for navigating this digital revolution. Healthy people will figure out a way to be rooted even amid the proliferation of tools allowing us to be rootless.

In my day job, I spend a lot of time in rooms known as Secure Compartmented Information Facilities, or SCIFs. It's a special room used for classified intelligence briefings—built to be spy-proof. When I go into one of these rooms, I'm not allowed to bring in anything with a battery. Not a phone, laptop, or tablet. Not even a Fitbit. When I first started disappearing in there for hours on end in 2015, it felt odd to be that unplugged. But then it started to feel good. I started to enjoy the undistracted focus during those meetings.

Recently, after hearing me voice some of the worries I've outlined here, one of my friends suggested that maybe the SCIF concept could be transplanted into homes. The idea of a family SCIF sounds a bit extreme—few people are going to build or modify rooms in their houses where electronics are forbidden or won't work. But maybe it's an idea worth considering over the coming decade. My family has started taking a "digital Sabbath" for a big chunk of Sundays—and like my time in a SCIF, it's liberating.

There are hints of innovators looking to use technology to help us limit technology, at least a bit. Graham Dugoni created Yondr, a pouch that locks, using a device similar to the anti-theft security tags you find in department stores. Over the last two years, nearly a thousand schools across the United States have adopted the Yondr system. Every morning, school officials collect students' smartphones and put them in the pouches, which the students carry with them. Then every afternoon at dismissal, a radio-frequency ID transmitter unlocks the pouches, releasing the phones back to their owners.

Yondr forces students to go cold turkey. The pouches enable them to redirect their attention back to what counts—whether that's the teacher giving a lesson at the front of the room or the friend sitting across the lunch table. "I don't reach for my phone as much," said one Boston-area student. "If you don't feed into the habit, the habit eventually slows down." Students report a sense of loss at first, but increasingly a sense of freedom—to be where they actually are, instead of feeling compelled to flee somewhere else.[18]

I've learned that many parents have lower-tech versions of the same strategy. After my last book on the challenges of our ever-fuzzier line between adolescence and adulthood, random parents at airports and across Nebraska began approaching to tell me how they've made their homes their neighborhood's "smartphone-free sanctuary." When their kids' friends arrive at their house, mom or dad greets them at the front door, smiling, with a basket into which all phones are deposited. It's forward-leaning parenting, to be sure, but here's what is surprising: The neighborhood kids are now choosing to congregate at that house. It took time, but many kids now prefer it. They *want* the constraint. These phone-free houses are actual *places*; when people are there, they're actually there.

Adults are getting in on the experience, too. Chris Rock, Alicia Keys, Ariana Grande, and many other performers regularly require concertgoers to hand over their phones before taking their seats. Yondr's Dugoni told NPR that more and more fans are expressing an interest in being *free from* their phones so they can be *free to* enjoy the event that they're physically at.[19]

Cal Newport, a computer scientist at Georgetown University, has become famous for insights seemingly at odds with his day job. High-achieving students and efficiency-addicted modern workers have turned him into a multi-time best-selling author for his advice about staying farther away from computers. To be clear, Professor Newport isn't anti-technology—he is a leading professor in a technology field. But he's skeptical of technology as an answer to bigger questions of meaning.

A few years ago, playing off Deep Blue and DeepMind, he coined the term "deep work." In his best-selling books, Newport helps people who want to live well think about how to overcome distraction.

One of his most controversial tips is to "quit social media." (Not, mind you, "quit the internet"—which besides being effectively impossible would almost certainly be disadvantageous.) As he points out, deep down most of us know that "network tools" like Facebook, Twitter, and Instagram, and "infotainment sites" like *Buzzfeed*, are more distraction than asset. They rarely aid productivity; instead, they reduce the ability to concentrate. "To master the art of deep work, you must take back control of your time and attention from the many diversions that attempt to steal them."[20]

Newport doesn't claim Facebook and Twitter are evil. He allows that "some of them might be quite vital to your success and happiness." But he argues that the vast majority of us, the vast majority of the time, are pretending we are using them as tools when we're really using them as distractions. "The threshold for allowing a site regular access to your time and attention (not to mention personal data) should be much more stringent," he suggests.

There is no disputing that specific technologies improve some people's quality of life in definable ways. But when every new tool has the potential to be used for good or for ill, we should think harder about each trade-off.

What precisely do you want out of social media? What are your objectives? Then compare those goals with the goals you've set for yourself in your personal and professional life more broadly. Newport suggests we ask: How does the use of a network tool fit in with those main goals? How does it advance or detract from where you want to go, what you want to do, and which communities you're trying to strengthen? "Keep using this tool," he advises, "only if you conclude that it has substantial positive impacts and that these outweigh the negative impacts." He wagers that if people think carefully about the pros and cons of their social media usage, they will conclude that it's more of a distraction than an aid to what they really want to do and be in life. "If you give your mind something meaningful to do throughout all your waking hours," he writes, "you'll end the day more fulfilled, and begin the next one more relaxed, than if you instead allow your mind to bathe for hours in semiconscious and unstructured Web surfing."

Technology changes our habits, our thoughts, our relationships, our loves. Anything that can cause us to hand over our time inevitably shapes who we are. We should be asking questions about happiness and purpose first, and about tools and technology second. Decide ends before means. Purpose before pathway.

It is possible to harness technology in ways that benefit our lives without letting it take over our entire lives. However, we can only achieve this if we decide where we're headed first.

Find Some Tech-Skeptical Friends

Living in a rural place, our girls need to drive to help our family with various tasks (rural folks can get a driver's license at 14 in Nebraska). We thus drifted, unthinking, into getting them smartphones for GPS navigation purposes. We could have met our needs with the combination of a Garmin and a 1990s flip phone—but we didn't pause to think about it. After a few months—as we observed the desperate phone-clutching and started reading the literature on neuroplasticity and brain development—Melissa and I began asking ourselves: What are we doing? How did we fall into this?

Our remediation began with having the girls read Cal Newport's book *Deep Work*—at which point they, too, became more wary of digital addiction. We decided we needed not more tech but, chiefly, more tech skeptics in our lives. Neil Postman, though now long dead, remains a key influence in our lives, and his prophetic book, *Amusing Ourselves to Death: Public Discourse in the Age of Show Business*, is a gift we continue to hand out to friends.

Another book we enthusiastically endorse is Andy Crouch's 2017 *The Tech-Wise Family: Everyday Steps for Putting Technology in Its Proper Place*. Crouch, the executive editor of *Christianity Today* and a father, encourages people to consider adopting "almost Amish"—or, more realistically, "*almost* almost Amish"—lives when it comes to technology outside the workplace. The basic approach is to embrace new tools when they advance specific ends—that is, goal-definable work—but to adopt a skeptical posture otherwise, so that digital tools are not permitted to remake daily life, social life, and family life. Do you really want technology to transform your affections and the way you interact with nature? If not, you need to take concrete steps to resist these go-with-the-flow outcomes.

Crouch and his wife didn't let their kids use screens until they were ten. Their family didn't have television until the kids were teenagers. They set stringent rules about how much screen-time the kids could have, including where and when. Everything in the Crouch home had its "proper place." Technology, Crouch says, is in its proper place "when it helps us bond with real people we have been given to love" and "when it starts great conversations." Conversely, technology is out of place when "we end up bonding with people at a distance, like celebrities," and "when it prevents us from talking with and listening to one another."

We've not been this intentional in our home, but we appreciate the Crouch family's decision to develop "ten tech-wise commitments" (not "commandments," Crouch emphasizes—we need prudential flexibility). The first is that the Crouches will "develop wisdom and courage as a family." To be explicit and transparent in front of other people about how you're struggling to become wiser requires a level of vulnerability that is painful—but eminently worthwhile. (Most of the commitments are like this: easy to understand, difficult to implement in a culture shaped by technology and consumerism.) The second is, "We want to create more than we consume. So we fill the center of our home with things that reward skill and active engagement." (Two chapters of my last book, *The Vanishing American Adult*, wrestle with a related challenge: How do we structure our children's lives to limit consumption and maximize work opportunities in a world where, despite the fact that working satisfies us more than consuming, consumption is easier and easier and meaningful work is rarer and rarer?)

The Crouch family pledged to "wake up before our devices do, and make them 'go to bed' before we do." How many of us use our phones as our alarm clock? (Don't. Buy a $4 alarm clock, and get your phone out of the bedroom.) For many people, checking email is the last thing they do before nodding off at night. A simple shift in our habits, by maybe thirty minutes a day, can make a big difference.

One of their most important commitments is simply to keep regularly in mind that: "We are designed for a rhythm of work and rest. So one hour a day, one day a week, and one week a year, we turn off our devices and worship, feast, play, and rest together." That "one day a week" many people will recognize as a Sabbath. As I've mentioned, in my house, we go to church on Sundays and switch off our phones for most of the day. It's my favorite day of the week.

Everyone is busy—but when our phones are on, we feel even busier than we're required to be. We need to create space. Happily, when we let go of the need to be constantly connected, we find the time to become meaningfully connected—to the people around us.

Redeem the Time

I suspect historians will look back at the early twenty-first century and wonder why humans were so willing, often to the point of desperation, to confide our deepest secrets, desires, and fears to machines and inanimate objects, while retreating from actual flesh-and-blood people. Why are so many of us so willing to give so much of our precious time to social media?

We don't want to say it out loud, but most of us know deep down that it's a kind of drug. It's a way of escape. It's an addiction.

On December 22, 2017, I decided to take my habitual Sunday "Twitter fast" and extend it through the Christmas weekend. But when Monday became Tuesday, and Tuesday became Wednesday, I hadn't gone back—and I felt freer. I felt like a burden was lifted. I've noticed how often my phone seemed to draw my focus away from an important moment toward some less important task. I've resented it, even when I've done nothing about it. Most of the important things in life—whether a burdensome work task or playing catch with my kid in the driveway—require focus. But the phone is a ready-made distraction machine.

Some years ago, I met a psychology professor from Oxford who told me that most people misunderstand what stress is. We typically think that it is having a lot to do. He thinks that's wrong. When someone has a lot to do, but they're making consistent progress on the most important thing, they're not stressed. They're satisfied. They often find themselves feeling that they're in a productive "zone." On the other hand, if there is something important that they ought to be doing but on which they're not making progress, that's when stress peaks.

The smartphone, with its endless apps, is designed to whisper to you that the thing you are doing is not the thing you ought to be doing. The phone isn't encouraging your progress; it's causing you stress. Want to know what hostile AI looks like? You're holding it.

I ended up taking a six-month "sabbath" from social media. We thought long and hard at my house before I went back—and when I did, I returned with rules. I use it only at certain times, for certain purposes, and—critically important—with specific audiences primarily in mind.

If I were forced to choose between having too much and too little digital input in my life and in my kids' lives, there is no doubt about my answer: Unplug. Life worked just fine before social media, and lots of neurobiological research makes clear that lives saturated by distracting technology are less happy. Digital addictions harm your mind, your body, and your soul.

But you don't have to choose all-or-nothing. There is a middle way. But only if we build guardrails against technology's tendency to swallow everything.

Some of the rules or guardrails are relatively obvious: Turn off most notifications and alerts. Stop checking in on retweet counts and likes. Read the comments on your posts only at a predetermined time (or just don't read them). Unfollow the politics addicts. Have places your phone is never allowed—such as at the dinner table. Take regular social media fasts—times of the day and days of the week where you don't open the apps. Constantly ask yourself: Two weeks from now, will I wish I had spent the ten minutes I'm about to spend on Twitter reading five pages of the book I'm carrying around instead (and oh, this plan requires constantly carrying a book around)? One of my most important rules is that I never allow any long chunk of work time to be interrupted by social media. Instead, I look at it primarily only in small, hard-to-use, backend-constrained chunks of time—boarding a flight or at the end of a workout.

These kinds of rules help restore sanity. But they're not the whole picture. The big leap forward for our family was recognizing that living well requires the right *audience*. When I was writing my dissertation, I got some great advice from Harry ("Skip") Stout, one of Yale's award-winning historians: "Have a specific reader in mind. Pretend that he or she is sitting next to your desk, and you're reading aloud to an audience of one. Pretend your audience is smarter than you are, but knows absolutely nothing about the topic." I set up an 8x10 photo of one of my aunts from the farm—and I wrote my dissertation to her.

In everyday life, thinking about audience means asking: Who's on my mind as I go about my day? Who am I putting in front of me? When we're constantly online, it means that the people who are literally, physically, in front of us—our spouse, our kids, our coworkers—are being sidelined in favor of people who are far away (some of whom we've probably never even met). One of my wife's friends looked at our life and commented: "Someone somewhere is always dying. Does that mean you should never actually fish with your kids? Should you never throw a ball with your son, because there is a crisis somewhere that could demand a political comment?" Her honesty hit me hard. When we prioritize "news" from afar, we're saying that our distant-but-shallow communities are more important than our small-but-deep flesh-and-blood ones. That shouldn't be the case. The other people in the comments section don't love you and never will; your spouse and kids do and always will. But often we let technology convince us that the people we should put in front of us are the people retweeting us and liking our statuses. We live richer, more fulfilled lives when we're directing ourselves to the right people.

When our family decided that we would go back to social media—chiefly Twitter for the adults, but there is some Instagram for the teenagers—we resolved to go back for definable purposes and with specific audiences in mind. I have a group of buddies from college and my early twenties that I keep up with (more on them in Chapter 8)—and we treat our social media mainly like a spring-board for an email chain. When I was a professor, one of the great things about a seminar was all of the side conversations it sparked during breaks or after class about other readings, topics, and ideas worth pursuing. In our house, Twitter is focused primarily on these definable relationships. When I use Twitter, I have the audience of those friends in my mind.

The danger of the digital world is when it supplants rather than supplements real relationships with real people in real places. Social media is always tapping us on the shoulder whispering false priori-ties. "NOW!" it warns. "You're missing out! This is the most impor-tant moment of all time—more urgent than the pledges you made yesterday, or than the investment you could be making in tomor-row!" Social media demands that you submit to the feeling that you should act only for NOW!

But it's not true.

If the ancient Greeks were to anthropomorphize social media as a deity, it would come as the temptress Immediacy. Not nature, patience, or generosity. Not oath, duty, or character. Not service, em-pathy, or love of neighbor. And definitely not wisdom, self-control, or deferred gratification. Only NOW! Immediacy.

At our house, after a healthy wrestling match about the danger-ous ways social media tries to pull us away from the communities we care about the most, we put a list of 16 truths up on our refrigerator. It's neither complete nor fancy, but our growing list is a way for our family, together, to make progress thinking about the duties we do and don't have to digital communities versus real ones. I am includ-ing it here in the hope that it might help your family, too.

Don't Get Implants Yet

In-home robots and widespread wearables are already here, and sales guys are going to be pitching you on implantables very soon.

We should go slow. Resist the ubiquitous cloud. We need to de-velop habits that will keep our families *grounded*. Some of the tools that are coming will be not just powerful but dangerous. We're going

DIGITAL TIME, REAL FRIENDS, &
WHAT WE CARE ABOUT . . .

1. Your thousandth social media friend won't make you any happier. Your fourth real friend will.
2. Uninterrupted time is life's most valuable limited resource.
3. Most news isn't news.
4. Envy isn't good therapy. Rage isn't good therapy. Working out is good therapy.
5. Do something now you'll want to talk about at the dinner table tonight.
6. Political addicts are weird. (And there aren't that many of them. They're just loud.)
7A. I'd rather be with the people I'm with right now than with the people I'm not with.
7B. If #7A isn't true, then spend more time with the right people.
8. Develop the right addictions. (Another word for addictions is habits. Habits determine character.)
9. Not every bad thing in the world requires a response from you.
10. Not every mean thing said to you requires you to acknowledge it.
11. You're not omniscient. Don't assume your bubble of information is the whole story.
12. You're not omnipotent. Taking in bad news you can't do anything about doesn't help anyone.
13. Sports Twitter is infinitely better than political Twitter.
14. Lots more social media is fake bots than social media companies admit.
15. The little old lady on your block probably has an important unmet need today.
16. Social media isn't great for deep stuff. It's great for humor. Let's be known as a family that laughs hard.

to need a national family meeting about how we will eventually impose limits on some of these. But in preparation, we need a lot more actual families holding family meetings about how to define the good life—and what tools help or hinder that quest. We should be excited about the potential of the tools that are coming our way—but we shouldn't pretend that none of those tools will have downsides.

Socrates never had an iPhone, but he was right about this regardless: "Beware the barrenness of a busy life."

Home is the nicest word there is.

—Laura Ingalls Wilder

7

BUY A CEMETERY PLOT

The Rooted Few 🐦 "That He Might Take Away the Body"
Chocolate Ice Cream Is Enough 🐦 Answering the Call
Contentment Is a Condition of the Soul
Tree-Planting and the End of the World

DEATH IS A WICKED THIEF. SO I TEND TO FIDGET WHEN PEO-
ple pretend it's normal—a corpse "looks so peaceful," or some other
pabulum. No, he doesn't, I want to protest. He's a father of three
with a dry wit. He got a pilot's license at 50 years old. He brewed IPA
for us last July fourth. He's supposed to be smiling and laughing and
setting off fireworks with us next week. Lifeless isn't "natural."

But at this particular funeral, I confess to having felt some relief. Jo was the mother of one of my closest buddies, and she'd been
suffering badly. Twelve years earlier, she'd had her first debilitating
stroke and shortly after became "locked in." It's a rare neurological
condition. Being locked in means that you're mentally all there or
almost all there, but you can't speak. And Jo lacked the muscle control to write out what she was thinking or feeling. For twelve years,
this woman had been a captive of her own body. It made me ache to
think about it.

"For all the saints, who from their labors rest," the congregation
sang. "We feebly struggle; they in glory shine."

It's a meaty hymn. No whitewash of the suffering we'd been watching for a decade. Then, in verses five and six, it doubles down on the contrast between this dark age and the hope of the age to come:

> *And when the fight is fierce, the warfare long,*
> *Steals on the ear the distant triumph song,*
> *And hearts are brave again, and arms are strong . . .*
> *But lo, there breaks a yet more glorious day;*
> *The saints—triumphant—rise in bright array . . .*

Jo hadn't known strong arms for years.

Because of my friendship with her son, I had hugged that woman for twenty-four years. I loved her. I was indebted to her. She was like an aunt to me. But life had separated us. By the time of her strokes, I was living two time zones away, so when she started to decline, I'd not been able to visit as much as I wanted. I swallowed the emotion as the congregation arrived at the last lines: "Soon, soon, to faithful warriors cometh rest. / Sweet is the calm of Paradise the blest."

As the organ faded out, a small, elderly man shuffled his way up to the pulpit. I didn't know him. He was an immigrant who'd come to the United States from the Netherlands in middle age and settled in that little town. He'd gotten to know Jo. His accent was thick. I didn't catch every word. But in passing he mentioned that he'd gone to Jo's nursing home multiple days a week for ten straight years. He sat next to her bed and had his devotional time in her room, aloud. He explained that he did this—instead of reading it silently to himself—so that the words of hope he found in Scripture could give her life, too.

She couldn't speak, but he would make sure she wasn't alone in the silence.

I lost it.

I cried, hard and ugly. This man—I felt I owed him a massive debt. His gift was simple, but he'd given it again and again. All I could manage was to be with Jo in spirit; Mr. Van Dee showed up in person, day in and day out, Bible in hand.

I had to fight the urge to run up and throw my arms around him. That would surely have confused him, as we'd never met—but to me, it was like he'd done this thing *for me*.

The Rooted Few

This book is not about theology. It's about community. But, like many Americans, some of the most important communities in my life are founded on shared theology. Therefore, since I need to touch on it a bit in this chapter, I hope you'll indulge me. The goal here is not to persuade you of anything theological, but because this chapter will be proceeding with an argument directly influenced by my Christian worldview, it seems respectful to explicitly acknowledge this.

We are limited by our bodies.

For thousands of years, philosophers have argued about the nature of the soul and the body—and how they relate. Christians believe that God created both the body and soul, and that one day Jesus will redeem both. The Apostle's Creed, the statement of the Christian faith recited around the globe weekly for seventeen centuries, puts it this way: "I believe in . . . the forgiveness of sins, the resurrection of the body, and the life everlasting. Amen." What's crucial here, at least for our purposes, is that God cares not only about immaterial souls but also about the material world. We're not spirits, zipping about. We're bodies, too. And that whole complex—body plus soul—is always in a particular place, at a particular time. We're right here, right now.

Place matters.

How often do we pause to take stock of that?

Look around you, right now. What's there? I see two dogs dozing at my feet, and I hear a third one whining from the girls' room to join me out here on the deck. The sun is not up yet, but I can see dawn light on the horizon. A bird is chirping—four notes, pause, the same four notes; a little morning chime. If I go back inside, I'll hear my children snoring. One of them needs to leave for cross-country practice in an hour (it's going to be hot). Another has managed to leave a trail of junk from the garage all the way down the hall. My son appears to have put two dozen minnows into a ring of coffee mugs around the kitchen sink. (Oxygen deprivation looks to be taking its toll.) The hook for car keys is down a set—that will cause a problem in sixty-three-ish minutes. All around me is the familiar detritus of life, waiting to be picked up again and tossed about in the whirlwind of the day. The house is quiet, but everything hums with meaning and anticipation. It's like the moment right before the orchestra starts. (Although, once the fights over shower time-slotting start, our mornings are often more cacophony than symphony.)

What you see and hear will be different, of course. But here's the important question: Are your surroundings familiar—or strange? Inviting—or alienating? Filled with people who love you—or isolated and lonely?

We mentioned Richard Florida in Chapter 2. Recall that Florida, an urban studies theorist, insightfully classifies modern Americans into three groups: the mobile, the rooted, and the stuck. The mobile glide from place to place, happily surfing the wave of the digital revolution. Flexible and adaptable, they are the big winners of the new economic upheaval.

The stuck, by contrast, not only reside in a less-than-ideal place, but they also lack the money or the inclination—or, more broadly, the social capital—to search out a better life. Although they might change physical addresses, they aren't able to build a network of healthy relationships. Despite our tendency to think that the rise of the mobile economy means that Americans in general are becoming more mobile, the stuck are the fastest-growing class in American life. (Tyler Cowen's astute book, *The Complacent Class*, helps explain this paradox.)

Between the mobile and the stuck are the rooted—the shrinking number of people who can choose to embrace the joys of thick community in a particular place. They recognize the advantages of settling in one place and of walking into the corner store—or the Elks Club, or the dentist's office, or the school auditorium—and having people know them by name. They enjoy many, if not all, of the economic benefits of the revolution, but without the frenzy of being constantly on the move.

The problem, as analysts of America's fastest-growing counties have shown, is that there's no longer an obvious way to join the rooted. Many people find themselves on the horns of a dilemma: If you want economic opportunity, then you have to resign yourself to never settling down. But if you're unwilling, or unable, to commit to being constantly on the move, then you have to resign yourself to being left behind—to being stuck. The unsatisfying choice is between opportunity but no place to call home, or a home in a place where you'll struggle to pay the bills.

The widespread loneliness we're seeing today is in a way the product of this squeeze. Mobility breeds rootlessness, and our rootlessness results not in improved communities but in more isolation. Robert Putnam, whose work we discussed extensively in Chapter 1, suggests what he calls *the repotting hypothesis*: "Mobility, like frequent repotting of plants, tends to disrupt root systems, and it takes time for an uprooted individual to put down new roots." After having done this multiple times, though, many people decide—in the interests of preserving energy, both physical and emotional—to stop even making an attempt to put down roots. Building community takes time and energy and emotional risk, and so it's often easier to guard our heart than to invest. After all, we aren't sure how long we'll be around.

Obviously, this is a problem for the mobile person, who cuts himself off from the nourishment of his community. But it's also a problem for the stuck. When the mobile—who can be mobile because they have the social capital to support themselves, in the form of family and friends back home and a college degree (or several)— fail to invest, they deprive the stuck of access to their social-capital surplus. When the consultant goes to a new city and doesn't "plug in" to any social networks, no one benefits from what he has to offer—for example, his wealth, which he might be willing to give to a local charity; his time, which he might be willing to volunteer; or his skills, which might be in need somewhere. It's not just the consultant who loses something; it's everyone else who would have connected with him.

It's people like Jo, who needed Mr. Van Dee to say: "I choose to be here for you."

Our instincts on why we should delay "rootedness" are all wrong. I'll invest once I'm where I'm supposed to be! I'll have more time in a year! Once I move into a better neighborhood, I'll . . . No. The perfect will always be the enemy of the good. In the real world, the only real community is where you are.

We're an embodied people, and we're meant to connect to our specific place and time. The current time and place might be inconvenient or unappealing—or just plain boring. But if this nation is going to successfully navigate the rootlessness of the digital revolution, it will require us to figure out how to build habits of neighborliness—each in his own spot.

A Dutch immigrant taught me that.

"That He Might Take Away the Body"

In Lincoln, Nebraska, there's a homeless shelter at which I've had the chance to volunteer. The People's City Mission (PCM) is blessed with some extraordinary staff and good Samaritans who tend to their neighbors, helping people get back on the road to employment or to recovery from addiction. I've seen this good and important work firsthand, but I didn't expect any grand philosophical insights when I asked one of the employees there last fall about changes at PCM in the last couple years.

"The community [of homeless we serve] really, really, really loves the new cemetery," he announced.

What?

He nodded. "One of the biggest things the homeless in Lincoln used to fear was that they'd die, and no one would notice. No one would care. They had no idea what would happen to their bodies. They assumed no one else would know, and no one would ever come visit them."

I had never connected funeral arrangements to social capital—but there it was. The homeless in Lincoln, with no roots, no money,

BUY A CEMETERY PLOT 209

and no family, figured this out—and they were frightened. What would happen to them? PCM resolved to build a burial place, a spot that the men and women they served could know in advance. They created a beautiful memorial garden, where the names of the deceased are etched into the redbrick wall.

The message is clear: You are not forgotten. You may have been homeless in life, but we won't let you be homeless in death.

Mobile types, I've found, are not nearly as interested in this final resting place question. In fact, the idea of a "final resting place" seems uncomfortable to a society increasingly opposed both to permanence and to rest. Melissa and I realized this over lunch with my parents a few years ago.

Mom casually mentioned that they'd purchased cemetery plots adjacent to St. Paul's Lutheran Church in Arlington, Nebraska, up the road: "You guys should get plots next to ours," she suggested.

We looked at her blankly. It made sense to be buried in the St. Paul's graveyard near my parents, near the bluff overlooking the Elkhorn River. Our house is out in the country along a different river fifteen miles away, but this congregation has been connected to our family for generations. Mom's grandfather carved the altarpiece that's still in use at St. Paul's today. But we were young, and I'd just returned home to take over as president of the local college. Melissa and I had been on the move for fifteen years. Finding cemetery plots wasn't among the top 1,000 items on our to-do list.

"We don't really know if we'll stay here," Melissa finally mumbled. We'd paid taxes and rent in a dozen states. Which one would be our permanent home?

A few years ago I found myself chatting with a guy who'd worked at Los Angeles World Airports, the municipal organization that operates Los Angeles International (LAX) and Van Nuys (travelers served annually: upward of 75 million). "You'll find this interesting," he said. "Our baggage department at LAX has to manage a lot of the bodies."

He knew I'd advised some airline leadership teams back in the 1990s, so we were talking about all things airlines-related. But this was new. "'Manage the bodies'?"

"People die sometimes away from home, right?" he asked. Sure. "In a car wreck or of old age. Well, the bodies need to go back to where they're from, or to wherever they want to be buried."

He was right. I did find this interesting.

"What's crazy about California is there are a lot of people here, but no one thinks of themselves as *from here*," he continued. "Eight times more bodies left LAX than entered LAX last month." He shook his head. "This state is beautiful, and it's a magnet for many. But many people don't really think of this as 'home.'"

Chocolate Ice Cream Is Enough

Contrary to what our consumer culture tells us, there are significant costs to having so many choices. Every person reading this book is fantastically rich by historical standards. And new research is showing that—surprisingly—having too many options actually diminishes happiness, instead of promoting it.

Psychologist Barry Schwartz explains why this is true: "As the number of options increases, the costs, in time and effort, of gathering the information needed to make a good choice also increase," he says. "The level of certainty people have about their choice decreases. And the anticipation that they will regret their choice increases."[1]

For example, if you give people a choice between an ice cream parlor that has 400 flavors and one that serves only three flavors, almost everyone will choose the shop with more options. But studies show that customers with 400 choices end up feeling significantly less happy afterward than the ones who went to the store with just three flavors. Three is enough. You might think you want to eat caramel balsamic swirl, but chances are you'd be just as happy—or even happier—with chocolate. People faced with more flavor options experience decision anxiety and regret. They're afraid of not getting it right.

Researchers describe people who want to exhaustively evaluate their options as "maximizers." Tim Herrera, the editor of the *New York Times*' "Smarter Living" section, explains the danger: "Though maximizers tend to make better decisions, they are less satisfied with those decisions than are people who make quicker ones based on less research (those people are called *satisficers*). And the ultimate goal of maximizing is impossible: You'll never be able to examine every possible option before making a decision." It turns out that making the best possible decision at the cost of time and ease is often a worse overall experience than making a good-enough decision with less handwringing. There's much to recommend prioritizing faster and easier.[2]

Herrera suggests learning how to make "Mostly Fine Decisions," or MFDs. Some folks will see this as "settling," but that's true only if time is a) limitless and b) free, which of course it isn't. He believes more of us would benefit from understanding "the minimum outcome you're willing to accept for a decision. It's the outcome you'd be *fine* with, even if it's not the absolute best possibility." The chocolate ice cream is more than the MFD. It's good. You'll like it. Order it now. Let's get on with some happy, ice cream–enhanced conversation.

Relationships could use a little MFD. In Chapter 6, we hinted at how digital images of airbrushed women denigrate the actual women in our lives—who have stretch marks from giving birth, furrowed brows from the trials of life, laugh lines from the joys. But when it really comes down to it, the "real women" are the ones you want. You want someone who'll stick by you, someone you can work alongside, someone you can dream with, someone with whom you can share life's inevitable suffering. You want a flesh-and-blood friend, not an internet fabrication.

The desire for short-term satisfaction tempts us to think that the woman from the porn might be appealing. But she's not real. And after the short-term lust is satisfied, the loneliness seeps back in. What is real, and what gives me a strange and inexplicable and enduring joy, is the woman alongside whom I cleaned up a 7-year-old's puke at three o'clock in the morning two weeks ago. Was rushing a smelly, deeply unhappy child to the bathtub sexy? Was carrying dripping sheets to the washing machine blissful? Definitely not. But how extraordinary it was (is!) to have someone by my side for that— to have a partner and a friend. We did it together. She was my ally in battle.

It wasn't Instagram-worthy. But who cares? What is really worth having is someone who wants to work on a relationship, who wants to build together, and who recognizes that suffering—though still painful—is easier to manage when the one who falls down has someone to help him back up again.

Marriage offers the opportunity to experience genuine, deep friendship. But that takes work. So much love, sweat, and tears go into building a family. You're constantly learning what it means to "die to self." But it's so much better than any two-dimensional counterfeit.

We're tempted to pass on the hard work of community-building for similar reasons. Community can be difficult. It can be messy. It doesn't fall into place, like on the sitcoms. But—in community, unlike on Netflix, you can put down the roots that will help to give life meaning and richness.

As my friend the singer Drew Holcomb puts it:

> *You spend your whole life*
> *fightin' for a guarantee,*
> *when all you really need is a friend . . .*
> *You got lost in the chaos;*
> *You got lost in the ashes and dust,*
> *what you needed was someone to trust.*[3]

Answering the Call

As a child, Melissa lived in Birmingham, Alabama, next door to a Mr. and Mrs. Killian. Old Mr. Killian was a gardener, and he enjoyed teaching Melissa how to care for plants and soil. She was a good student. A few years into their relationship, Mrs. Killian developed Alzheimer's disease, so Melissa began to help them out around the house. Mrs. Killian declined. By the time Melissa was leaving for college, the old lady's memory was largely gone. Shortly before she left for school, Melissa asked Mr. Killian why he didn't put his wife in a nursing home. He was frail. Caring for Mrs. Killian was a 24/7 responsibility. "She has no idea who you are. The burden of caring for her is too much," she said, gently. "Why not put her in a home and get some rest?"

He nodded. "Most of the time, it's very hard," he said. "But she often wakes up in the middle of the night and asks for water, or she'll need help to the bathroom. And for ten minutes, perhaps two or three times a month, she'll know who I am again. I could never miss those moments." He paused, and then added: "I can't *not* be there for her, for that."

That conversation—that relationship—affected my future bride deeply. In fact, when I was getting to know Melissa in the early 1990s, one of the things that attracted me to her was that she visited the residents of the nursing home across from her apartment building in Cambridge, Massachusetts. Even now, she takes our kids to read to the blind, she takes food to shut-ins, she counsels underprivileged kids on college and career planning, and she is currently considering how she and some friends might start a prison ministry. That's who she is. She works to love her neighbors. As Mr. Killian might have said: She couldn't *not* serve those around her.

What I've witnessed in Melissa over the years is someone at-tuned—maybe not consciously, maybe just in her bones, but tuned in nonetheless—to the unique calling that each particular time and particular place makes on us. They're vocations.

Melissa didn't live in Alabama forever, but the Killians didn't live forever either. She was called to serve them at a particular mo-ment, during a particular stage in her life (and theirs), and she re-sponded. The same is true of the widows and widowers she's serving in the town we're in now.

When we look for reasons to avoid investing our time or energy or resources in a particular place or at a particular moment, what we're really doing is trying to dodge the call that it might make on us. We're trying to avoid the hard work of digging in. *But the hospital makes volunteers jump through so many hoops! But the Boys & Girls Club is all the way across town! But the widows I've met around here are mean!*

The only community that exists is this one, here and now. But we have to choose to embrace it.

Contentment Is a Condition of the Soul

Josh Gibbs is a high school teacher in Richmond, Virginia, who has been thinking and writing about the Book of Ecclesiastes for years. It turns out that this ancient "wisdom text" has a lot to say to adolescents—especially adolescents adrift in our consumer-oriented culture. His 2017 commencement address to his students at Veritas School is applicable to our discussion of rootlessness:

> A human life contains many seasons, many stages, and no matter what stage you are in, there will always come the temptation to believe that the next stage is the one where the good life begins. Just a little more power, a little more freedom, a little more money, and you could be happy.
>
> Junior high students cannot wait until they are old enough to drive, drivers can't wait to date, daters can't wait to graduate, graduates can't wait to move out of the house. Courting couples can't wait to set a date, engaged couples can't wait to tie the knot, newlyweds can't wait until they're not broke. Once you're not broke, you have kids, then you're broke again. You start in a career and can't wait until you're recognized for your achievements. You're recognized for your achievements and you become impatient for a raise.
>
> The next stage of life is always the one where you achieve the perfect amount of autonomy, freedom, and money. You're not greedy, but just a little more and you could be content. And so many people pass their entire lives like the mythic figure Tantalus, for whom the boughs of sweet fruit always receded just beyond his fingers when he reached for them.[4]

Many of us don't really invest in our communities or our relationships, because we're always anticipating what's around the corner. Who's about to walk in the door? But "the Devil preys upon those who believe happiness is just out of reach," Gibbs warns. "As with

Eve, he tempts us to believe that those in authority are selfishly hoarding the good things."

What we need is to let go of illusions and see where happiness actually can be found:

> While more money and more freedom can provide you with more pleasure, they cannot provide you with more *contentment*. The world is crowded with people whose lives abound in pleasure, but are miserable and dissatisfied nonetheless.
>
> Contentment is a condition of the soul, and it does not come with getting what you want, but in giving thanks to God for what you have been given.
>
> Any man who believes he cannot be content unless he has more time or freedom has made an idol of these things, for he believes that earthly things can grant spiritual virtue.
>
> A little more money and a little more freedom will grant a little more pleasure . . . for a while, but once a man has fallen into this cycle of thought, he realizes that if a little more freedom brought a little more pleasure, then a lot more freedom would provide a lot more pleasure—and then he becomes frustrated once again with his place in the world.

By now, even those unfamiliar with the Bible can hear the beat of Ecclesiastes approaching. There is a "time to be born and a time to die, a time to plant and a time to uproot . . . a time to tear down and a time to build, a time to weep and a time to laugh, a time to mourn and a time to dance."

The wise man learns how to grow where he is planted. He chooses joy.

He embraces the time and season, these people and this place.

In the literature of Judaism and Christianity, the longing for home is a constant theme. When we were created, we were placed in a home. But now we're in exile, stranded east of Eden, and we want to get back across the Jordan to Canaan. We want to see the Promised Land. We want to see the "wolf dwell with the lamb." We want to see the "blooms in the deserts." Our hearts are restless, waiting for the restoration of home.

Tree-Planting and the End of the World

British medievalist and novelist C. S. Lewis believed that our pain and discomfort in this world point to the fact that something is amiss—that there must be more to come. "A man's physical hunger does not prove that man *will* get any bread; he may die of starvation on a raft in the Atlantic," he wrote. "But surely a man's hunger does prove that he comes of a race which repairs its body by eating and inhabits a world where eatable substances exist." He makes a romantic analogy: "A man may love a woman and not win her; but it would be very odd if the phenomenon called 'falling in love' occurred in a sexless world." In other words, our desire for food points to the fact that nourishment exists; our yearning for reciprocal love highlights the existence of loving unions. And our aching for a better home suggests that we were built to find shalom, even if we can't quite reach it yet.[5]

That nagging feeling that we don't quite fit in here is much of the reason why people spend so much time decorating their homes, "nesting," and watching shows on HGTV. Every house is just a reflection of the good homes and communities we were designed to have but lost.

That's why the name of this chapter alludes to death. Nothing here on earth will be fully satisfying. But to the degree that we're going to find anything that satisfies on this side of the afterlife, it's going to be in the relationships with the people with whom we share work, experiences, suffering, and love.

That's not to say that people shouldn't move or that we have to stay in less-than-ideal situations. Sometimes change is good, and sometimes change is necessary. But the changes we pursue should be oriented toward the goal of finding a place to stay and to serve. Though my wife and I did eventually get plots at the St. Paul's graveyard on the hill north of Arlington, we really have no idea if we'll end up there. Our daughters might marry and start families and end up living two blocks from each other in Nashville or Austin. I doubt that we'd be able to resist the pull of moving near to them and to our grandkids. Who knows what the future holds?

When his disciples asked for help in learning how to pray, Jesus's response was disarmingly simple. We're to focus on wanting what God wants—may His Name be hallowed, not mine; His Will be advanced, not mine—and when it comes to asking for anything for ourselves, we should ask for . . . bread, for today. Not stable housing a year out, not steady employment into the next decade. Just a loaf of bread. And just for today.

But I want the whole future to be solved, now, put to bed! No, Jesus says. Ask simply to live more faithfully in the here and now.

There's a possibly apocryphal quote attributed to Martin Luther: "If I believed the world were to end tomorrow, I would still plant a tree today." Whether or not he said it, I like the idea of investing in a future that isn't guaranteed. Even if we might not enjoy the shade of the tree, we still know that this little act of creation is good. Likewise, we can love our neighbor, today, even if we don't know what the whole future holds.

I don't actually know where Melissa and my physical bodies will end up, when all is said and done—but I stopped trying to predict the future eight or nine years ago. For now, we're making a bet, investing where we are, and working harder at living in the moment. Buy the cemetery plot, and live in this place. Sure, the people around you are annoying, but the people in the next, "better" place are annoying, too. People everywhere are annoying. Community is hard. So what?

Commit anyway, and act as if your body is going to end up in the place where you are.

Eventually, you'll be right.

If you want to go fast, go alone.

If you want to go far, go together.

—AFRICAN PROVERB

8

BE A SMARTER NOMAD

Perpetual Homesickness 🪶 The Wild West Always Comes First
New Community for a Semi-Nomadic Age
We Overlook the Earliest Innovations
The Blessing of Smaller Backpacks: Go More, but Come Back
Keeping a Few Friends for a Lifetime 🪶 Through a Stranger's Eyes

IN A RECENT NATIONAL SURVEY, TWO-THIRDS OF AMERICAN homeowners said they don't expect to sell their current home—ever.

Most of them will end up surprised. It's difficult to say precisely how long the average homeowner is holding onto her home today because of the jolt of the 2008 financial downturn, but for many years prior, the typical American stayed in one house for . . . four years.

The dream of homeownership remains one of the most powerful aspirations in America and probably the most enduring symbol of middle-class life. And for good reason. Homeownership has always been closely associated with rootedness and community, tied to local schools, public safety, environmental stewardship, and more. We may be a pioneer nation, but we've nonetheless long nurtured the conviction that if you own your home, you've made it.

Sixty-four percent of American adults currently own their residence—down only a bit from the historic peak of 69.2 percent in 2004, before the downturn of the housing market and the uptick in foreclosures. Furthermore, Gallup's 2018 "Economy and Personal Finance" poll found that 45 percent of Americans who don't own a home hope to within the next five years. Even among Millennials, who came of age during the worst economic recession since the Great Depression, and who have demonstrated caution when it comes to big purchases, a hefty share of the 67 percent who do not own a home hope to buy in the near term.[1]

Given the argument in Chapter 7 about the need to invest locally, build friendships, and orient oneself toward ultimately settling down, these statistics might suggest we're in better shape than we think. It seems people want to find a place to call home. Isn't this impulse to nest something to celebrate?

In part, yes.

But the massive mismatch between perception and reality is not encouraging; it's worrying. It turns out that at the same time we're becoming less and less rooted, we think we're building castles. Which means that lots and lots of us don't really grasp what is happening around us. Old ways of thinking haven't caught up to new realities.

How does that happen? In no small part, we're telling ourselves a number of things about the good life that probably just aren't true. One example: We nod in agreement as twenty-somethings talk about earning enough money to ditch their roommates and find a place of their own. But there's a good bit of evidence that moving from group living to solitary living ends up making young adults much less happy.

The siren song of solitary housing is new and hasn't received sufficient scrutiny. Americans live much differently now than we did through most of our history. For our grandparents and especially our great-grandparents, extended-family living arrangements—one house with moms, dads, children, grandparents, and maybe an aunt or uncle thrown in for good measure—were the norm. Single-person households were the (*very* exceptional) exception. According to the 1940 Census, fewer than 8 percent of U.S. households consisted of one person living alone. Times have changed, we've grown historically rich, and our expectations about housing structures and about "normal" have ballooned. More Americans live alone today than at any time in our history, by big margins. Between World War II and the 2000 Census, the number of single households more than tripled—to 26 percent. And the curve of those living alone—and aiming to—has increased even more rapidly in the two decades since.[2]

Some of this is an echo of the decline of marriage among young adults. As recently as the mid-1960s, just 17 percent of 21- to 36-year-olds had never been married; today, it's nearly three-fifths. And while in 1940 most of the people who reported living alone tended to be older residents in rural places (with shrinking density as young workers migrated to cities), by the turn of the twenty-first century the population of singles had shifted decisively to urban areas. According to the Census Bureau, 48 percent of households in Manhattan are now single-person residences, and the share of single households in elite college towns like Cambridge, Massachusetts, is booming as well. In other words, the places that are growing are also places embracing atomization.[3]

Many of us are pursuing a new solitary vision of the happy life, but we tend not to have thought fully about whether these ideals are really ideal. Longitudinal studies suggest a significantly higher incidence of antidepressant use among those who live alone. Acknowledging that antidepressant medications have improved, and literally saved, the lives of many Americans, it is nonetheless true that left-behind rural economic areas, often beholden to opioid abuse, and frenzied urban areas, where we see comparatively high rates of antidepressant use, are manifesting the collapse of community in ways that mirror the spike of alcoholism that accompanied American industrialization and urbanization just over a century ago.[4]

The pain of upheaval is real.

Perpetual Homesickness

When Melissa and I first arrived in Chicago as newlyweds, we didn't know what we didn't know. As mentioned in Chapter 2, we chose the Second City because we had dated and grown close there. We didn't have any support system there when we moved; we just assumed that idealism would be enough to carry the day. It turned out that having no connections there to rely on (in particular, older friends who could guide and mentor us) made for thin lives—especially after I began traveling several days a week.

We didn't have a word for what we were experiencing, but twenty years later, psychologists have labeled the widespread angst and lonely disappointment of our twenty- and thirty-somethings the "quarter-life crisis": Is this all there is? Is this really home? Is this job I've taken—marketing trinkets, teaching math, scheduling patients—really what I'm going to "invest" my day-to-day life in?

Many of our young adults feel a hard-to-define, existential ache in their chests: What is my calling? Where is my place? Who are my people? I'm surrounded by humans, but I don't really know any of them. Everything feels alien. How did this happen?

When I first learned about quarter-life crises a few years ago, I thought it was psychologists' oversimple riff on the better-documented, more important phenomenon among older people. But it's clear to me now that the quarter-life crisis is the bigger problem. The midlife crisis, which usually takes place during one's mid-forties to late fifties, is largely about the transition between natural life stages—becoming an empty-nester as children head off, wrestling with shifting callings, and other inevitable changes. In other words, it's about aging and mortality in ways that basically every generation under the sun has known. But after this phase, most Americans will enter what ends up being the happiest period of their lives. The endless frenzy of caring for kids is done, the gift of grandkids arrives, work is more fulfilling and less dictated by ambition and competition. For middle-class families, there tend to be fewer financial stresses than previously. In short, wisdom is arriving and bodily decline is still held at bay. It's a sweet spot of life.

The restlessness of our young adults, on the other hand, is a uniquely modern problem. As I explored in *The Vanishing American Adult*, leaving childhood and becoming an adult used to be conceptually clear. It was a *gift* that older generations gave to the younger. No longer. We have upended almost all the coming-of-age rituals—moving out of one's parents' home, leaving school for the final time, getting a full-time job, becoming economically self-sufficient, getting married, having children, establishing an independent household, etc. There was and is good reason to reevaluate many of these rites of passage—but most of them ended up simply being discarded, with nothing else coming in to fill the void. We've generally set our young people "free" to find meaning on their own—apart from any communities into which they might have been initiated and which could have offered guidance.

Melissa and I were fortunate to be able to make ends meet, and we were learning a lot at work and school, but we were nonetheless feeling a vacuum of community. The mid-1990s were early in the digital revolution, but it was readily apparent that we, like most of the people we got to know in Chicago, were short-termers in each job and short-timers in each city. We spoke with friends from college, and almost every one of them was experiencing the same disorientation. People's experience of place was becoming more transient.

It was (and is) the worry that the hometown-gym-on-a-Friday-night feeling will never return. When I had watched my dad and his coaching buddies in Fremont, I had thought that their fraternity was about sports. I was wrong, of course. It was mainly about the fact that they had taught and coached together for a couple decades already, and they assumed that they would be together for decades more until retirement. They shared together in the work of helping raise the kids of our community. We knew where to deliver the casserole to an athlete with a sprained ankle because Dad had known his aunt since third grade. That sense of organic community can't be replicated simply by going to games at the stadium nearest to your latest apartment. It requires a longer-lasting "we."

In an economy where most of us are likely to change jobs and geography several times, fear of commitment makes a lot of sense. The fact that twenty- and thirty-somethings are becoming more averse to making long-term commitments—to people and places, but also to institutions and even purchases—suggests not so much a generational character flaw but a coping mechanism. Sure, many young adults can cite warm relationships and regular outings, but these aren't feasts with family and friends; they're shotgun meals with other nomads.

We can't fix the problem of thin community individually, and it is especially difficult to invest deeply in a place when we know that many of those around us are also likely to be short-timers. We might admit that this is a sorry state of affairs, but what's the option? It feels like trying to construct a house in a hurricane; before it's finished, it's gone.

The "digital economy," or whatever we end up calling this new stage, because it draws us toward more places, physically and psychologically, draws us away from investing. No one "nests" in a hotel room. No one plants a garden on the shoulder of a freeway. Our new technologies are enabling us to live *wider but shallower*—with more at our fingertips, but with less enduring meaning.

The Wild West Always Comes First

The first years of American life in the nineteenth-century West were unfriendly to sustainable communities. In many gold rush towns, there were ten men for every woman, prostitution was a core business, shootouts stood in for law, and substance abuse was widespread. The "Wild West" was perhaps uniquely rowdy, but the boom phase of many Northeastern and Great Lakes industrial cities was similarly dangerous and undesirable. Even the ugly picture we have of 1880s and 1890s urban life—dismal working conditions, child labor, corrupt machine politics, racial redlining, the ethnic purging of voter rolls—doesn't capture the raw everyday misery of burgeoning city life. Revenue surged (national economic output grew twenty-five-fold from the beginning of the Civil War to the 1920s), and community suffered. To many people, the production explosion was accompanied by a foreboding sense that the strong community of the farm towns had vanished forever. High rates of alcoholism attested to widespread loneliness and unhappiness.

But it didn't last. Eventually, the lawlessness of the frontier town and the churning of the industrial city were tamed. Both places were made hospitable, sustainable, even beautiful. By the 1930s and

1940s, most Americans had moved into or around cities, alcoholism rates had dropped, and a sense of community had returned.

What happened? We found new ways to build community that could accommodate a new economic order.

The challenge that confronted frontiersmen in the West and urban reformers in the East was to discover models of community adaptable to their radically new conditions. It was clear to them that the old models would not do. There were false starts, and efforts that were good steps still usually fell short. It took a great deal of time, which meant a lot of collateral damage. It also required the contributions of millions of people. But eventually they figured out how to create a sense of *home* in the Industrial Age.

We're in a similar moment. The old models no longer work, and we're in need of discovering what it could mean to be *home* in the digital age. What might that look like? I suspect that the new community and the new forms of social capital that we will create will harness the new technologies of the gig economy that have undermined rootedness—but with the goal of putting down roots.

New Community for a Semi-Nomadic Age

New technologies, as we've suggested elsewhere, always have both positive and negative effects. That should be obvious, but sometimes it's hard to keep in mind; we tend to zero in on one side of the equation. Here, we've spent a lot of time discussing how technology has contributed to a significant disruption of contemporary community. But it's likely also to be the case that technology mitigates some of those bad effects.

Let's think more about housing.

It's pretty clear that, in the near term, technology promises to continue undermining relationships and community by making mobility cheaper and easier. Young adults, especially, will find themselves able to pursue the next "gold rush" without too much trouble. (Think, for example, of the thousands of young people who've flooded the Bay Area in recent years, hoping to get in on the Silicon Valley boom.) Technology will liberate them to chase new, lucrative opportunities. Of course, they'll be even less likely to calculate the costs in durable relationships, membership in meaningful institutions, and the rest.

The same technological advances (as we saw in Chapter 2) are likely to displace low-skilled, low-income workers from high-income, high-cost urban areas—again, think of the Bay Area (median house price in San Francisco: $1.6 million). For these workers, two unhappy options will present themselves: join the mobile workforce or become permanently stuck. But they'll struggle to do the first, and they'll dread the second (with all of its attendant social ills: dwindling social capital, declining networks, and intergenerational poverty, etc.). For these workers, homeownership will be one of the big challenges. Being mobile means probably giving up on a permanent address; but being stuck means struggling to afford one. (Recall Chicago's awful Robert Taylor Homes. Public housing and joblessness tend to be mutually reinforcing.) This is simply to say that there's significant uncertainty on its way.

But something else is going to happen, too. The economy will likely change, and people will adapt in ways that are not yet obvious to us. The pessimist's vision of postmodern hunter-gatherers—everyone wandering and rootless—is possible. But it's unlikely. Remember what made it possible for hunter-gatherers to make the transition to a more settled agrarian life: specialization and technology. The Neolithic era was the first great economic revolution in human history and set the stage for the growth of civilization. Specialization and technology will almost certainly help people adapt to the coming disruption, too.

Duke University political economist Michael C. Munger explains how rapid advances in information technology are slashing transaction costs. That's unusual. In the past, innovation has tended primarily to lower the costs of production and acquisition. As production became more efficient, the cost and therefore the price of an item—an ax, or a TV, or a car—fell accordingly. We consumers ended up with more stuff, of both higher quality and lower cost. We also ended up with bigger garages and storage facilities.

What's different now, Munger says, is that technology is making it easier and cheaper not only to "make more stuff" but also to "sell access to existing stuff"—including stuff that twenty years ago nobody would have thought of selling. In other words, in the past, technological innovation has focused primarily on reducing production costs, and therefore making prices cheaper, and therefore making *ownership* cheaper and easier. But today, with so much innovation focused on software that can drive the cost of real-time, geographically aware transactions toward zero, one of the major breakthroughs of our moment is the reduction of what we might think of as *rental* facilitation costs. Hence the rise of the "sharing economy," or the "access economy," or what Munger prefers to call the "middleman economy."

Most of us understand how businesses like Uber and Lyft, the ride-sharing services, or Airbnb, a similar model for temporary housing, work. Not many of us have thought much about moving from ride-sharing to actual car-sharing. But it makes sense to think that this would be the next step. The average privately owned car sits idle more than 95 percent of the time. Wouldn't it be convenient to be able to get access to a Zipcar when you need one, then drop it off when you're finished? (You'll recognize the obvious opportunity here if you've ever tried to park long-term in Manhattan.) Algorithms and global positioning software (GPS) make it possible not only to cater to our consumer preferences but also to quickly and easily find underutilized resources we might want or need. It turns out that there is a lot of value in unused stuff.

"The value proposition in the new economy is selling access to excess capacity," Munger explains. "As transaction costs are driven [down] by new software applications, it is [relatively] more expensive to hold or store consumer and producer durables, precisely because new software applications *make it cheaper to use them*" (my emphasis). Munger uses the example of a power drill to show this dynamic at work:

> I need to drive screws in some wood furniture I'm assembling. I open an app on my smart phone and tell the app

"rent drill." A car—I don't know where it is and I don't need to—picks up a drill that matched my pre-programmed preferences from a hardware store. The car delivers it to a security-coded pod outside my apartment. My phone vibrates "drill delivered." I assemble the furniture and return the drill to the pod. The pod is smart: its software is connected through the "Internet of Things," and the pod tells another car—no particular car, just whomever is nearby, according to the software—that there is a pickup.

The rental costs me $2.50 and no more than a minute spent shopping, obtaining, and retrieving the drill. I got brief access (but that's all I needed!) to a commercial quality power tool. It could have been a saw, a fruit dehydrator, a bread machine, a deep fryer, a sausage grinder, or a collapsible bar to serve drinks at a party . . . I own almost nothing, yet have immediate access to everything.[5]

The drill is just a place holder for his story. When the nice china comes out only once a year, do you really need to own it? Or would it be sufficient—or even better—to be able to get it when you need it, do your entertaining, and send it along? We can think of plenty of other possibilities. The key is the transition from one fixed, traditional sense of "ownership"—because it's simply not necessary.

The reason this business model can be replicated again and again is because it actually doesn't have much to do with the specific item in question. For example, taxi drivers often say Uber is an unregulated cab company that's unfairly taking their business. But Uber isn't a cab company. In reality, Uber is an *information broker*. "Uber makes money not by selling taxi services—the driver sells those—but by selling reductions in triangulation costs, transfer costs, and trust costs," Munger explains. It is the middleman between the driver and rider. "Uber is a pure intermediary."

Uber works because the transaction cost of connecting a driver and a rider is now so small that a market is possible—compared to, say, trying to do the same thing two decades ago, which would have required users to have reliable cellphones (not a guarantee), drivers to have GPS systems (unlikely), and, probably, Uber to have its own satellite (cost-prohibitive, to put it mildly). When we talk about the "uberization" of existing industries, then, what we're talking about is using our ability to digitally map the world in real time to enable the on-demand movement of goods and services at the level of individuals—no longer just at the level of companies moving items in bulk.

The same principle applies to housing. Even though Airbnb markets itself as a low-cost alternative to a hotel, the service isn't really competing with the hotel industry. As it happens, the fastest-growing segment of Airbnb's business is the short-term rental-housing market. The company has not released public numbers, but some analysts estimate that 20 percent of its sales come from rental periods longer than a month. What is happening here? In most cases, these are corporate clients, or consultants in need of a temporary place to live for the duration of a contract. But there are a growing number of young people and people in mobile professions who might make use of such a service. Traveling nurses, for example. A nurse shortage—particularly in specialized fields such as pediatrics, oncology, and neurology—has caused a number of qualified nurses to begin traveling around the country to hospitals where they're needed. A job could last a week or a few months, and hotels are expensive. Short-term rental housing fills the gap, and Airbnb can keep its prices competitive by expanding the supply of available rooms—something that's not possible for the local Holiday Inn.

The likely disruption of housing—and therefore how and where we live and work—will be, I suspect, much more dramatic than we expect. Scholars at the Brookings Institution who study the new "access economy," which was worth $14 billion in 2014, believe it will grow twenty-fold over the next decade—to well over $335 billion by 2026.[6]

We Overlook the Earliest Innovations

When we look back on the problems of community in the old West and in the growing industrial cities of the East and Midwest, we can see—hindsight being 20/20—a variety of attempts to address various crises: attempts that did not always pan out but which were oriented toward the deeply felt, but generally unarticulated, problems of loneliness and anxiety.

The same thing is happening today. There are early experiments in different kinds of housing and living happening all around us. We just haven't tended to see them for what they are—namely, attempts to find better ways to navigate around and through our new rootlessness.

Consider: The average commute in America is now fifty-two minutes (round trip) every day—and it's not uncommon to hear of people spending two or three hours driving to and from work in metropolitan areas like San Francisco, New York, and Atlanta. Naturally, a lot of people are looking for something better. "Mixed-use" developments are one way urban planners and policymakers are trying to mitigate this problem. By creating development zones that blend residential, commercial, and other uses, they hope to make it possible for people to live, work, and shop in roughly the same place.

Or what about the need many people have—especially as the Baby Boomer generation ages—to support parents and extended families? The Great Recession saw a sharp spike in the number of households with more than two generations of a family living under the same roof—from 46.7 million in 2007 to 51.4 million by the end of 2009, according to the nonprofit Generations United. By 2016, the Pew Research Center reported that the number of households with two or more generations had risen to 64 million—or about 20 percent of all U.S. households.[7]

Housing developers, noticing the trend, have begun incorporating in-law suites, backyard cottages, and even multiple master bedrooms into their floor plans. Relatedly, a number of municipalities have seen pushback against local regulations that bar building small structures or parking RVs in backyards. It turns out that many families, looking for ways to accommodate an elderly parent, are trying to create their own "independent living" arrangements on their property.

Other families are looking to downsize or economize—for example, empty-nest parents. They don't need as much space as they once did, they want to free up money for other purposes, or they want to be more mobile, perhaps to move closer to their children when they marry and start families.

The "tiny house" movement—in which people adopt simple living habits in structures roughly 500 square feet or less—is one manifestation of this. Only about 1 percent of homebuyers purchase houses 1,000 square feet or less, according to the National Association of Realtors, but the trend nonetheless gained a bit of traction after the 2008 financial crisis. There are now also, courtesy of manufacturers such as the Colorado Springs–based Tumbleweed, tiny houses on wheels.[8]

There are other intriguing trends in the housing market at present: modular homes, for example, which offer buyers more flexible alternatives to site-built homes. We can point, too, to certain larger-scale movements: for example, the "New Urbanism" of the 1980s, which sought to combat suburban sprawl, promote environmentally friendly habits, resurrect the front porch, and encourage "livability." Obviously, none of these is a silver bullet that will solve the problems of economic and geographic upheaval or restore disintegrating communities. But each is an effort, large or small, more successful or less, to conceive of new ways of living in a time of massive disruption. Technological advances are going to expand opportunities for people to experiment and figure out new ways to navigate between the desire for a rooted home and the contemporary pull toward mobility.

The Blessing of Smaller Backpacks: Go More, but Come Back

One of the more interesting partisan cultural divides in America is about housing. Asked whether they prefer bigger lots and more square footage, or more walkability and closer proximity to restaurants, 75 percent of Republicans choose the square footage, while 75 percent of Democrats prefer the urban proximity.

But what if there could be both more city and more country in a lot more American families' futures?

Many of our ways of thinking are predicated on the ways we've always done things. We maintain, to return to Michael Munger's observations, a deep distinction between "owning" and "renting."

Renting has always been complicated and time-consuming (land-lords or rental agencies, endless paperwork, recurring payments), whereas owning seems easier (a onetime deal, perhaps with cash and a handshake). But, as Munger points out, what technology entrepreneurs do is "change the way we do business."

What if renting things on-demand becomes easier and cheaper in the long run than storing and parking things? As in Munger's rent-a-drill example, we would likely be able to make do with smaller garages and closets, relying instead on those security-coded pods outside our homes. Is it possible that, in that case, the tiny home might become more appealing? Is it possible that we would not only travel light but live light? And what kinds of opportunities would that open up for addressing the mobility/rootedness challenge?

One possibility that I see—although it's certainly not a guarantee, nor the only possibility—is a new vision of home that embraces a "live light" mode without jettisoning entirely the familiar home and garden. Think about it this way: Many of the mobile tend to be born in one place, but then move to City B, and then to City C, and then to City D, and so on, shedding family and friends as they go, and eventually becoming so emotionally exhausted that they stop trying to invest at all in wherever they happen to be.

We know the toll this is taking, psychologically and physically, and it's unsustainable in the long-term. But it's nonetheless true that the new digital economy favors mobility; people are going to be pushed into moving. So, is there a third way?

If Munger and others are right, and we are moving steadily toward more sustainable modes of life that emphasize sharing rather than owning, then it seems there's a possibility that people could strike a compromise between firm rootedness and nomadism—by settling in one place, and returning to it, while continuing to embrace some of the mobility that the digital economy both makes possible and requires. That is, I think that instead of the A → B → C → D pattern we see among the mobile today, it might become possible for people to choose A as a base to which they can return: A → B → A → C → A, et cetera. New technologies, and a sharing-heavy economy that takes advantage of them, will make it possible for people to respond to the demands of a more mobile world without surrendering an anchor, one particular and enduring place they can invest in and call home.

This is just one possibility. No doubt more options will present themselves. Some will be better than others as ways of securing durable forms of community. That's fine. We don't need a one-size-fits-all solution. And, in fact, the nature of the changes we're experiencing should afford greater flexibility to each person and family to strike the balance that suits them.

The key, though, is to start searching. We need to begin now to experiment with institutions that can sustain us as we enter a new era of life and work. This reordering will go far beyond housing—higher education and job retraining will also be restructured amid shorter-duration freelance jobs; retirement will be rethought as people look for second mountains to climb as life expectancy arcs upward. We need to begin now to build the arrangements—and the habits—adequate to a mobile world.

Keeping a Few Friends for a Lifetime

In 1999, five years after college, some buddies and I decided to push back on the transience in our lives. We created a group, which we would eventually call "Cherish" after the (horrible) 1966 song by The Association. The six of us committed to assembling for a few days each year to laugh, to eat and drink, to update each other on our lives, and most important, to hold each other accountable to certain goals in life.

We talk about work aplenty when we're together, but that's not the focus. The goals we're mainly interested in are personal. How can we be better parents and spouses? How can we grow in character? My wife—who loves the group but also enjoys mocking its cheesy name—suggests that we called it "Cherish" only because the "Become-More-Patient-and-Learn-to-Talk-Less-Like-An-@#&hole Group" was too long of a name.

The group is more mobile than America as a whole. I'm the only one of the six who lives in the town where I grew up; only one other guy lives in the same state as his parents; only one lives in the state where he went to college; and none of the six of us married someone from our home state. Going back to Robert Putnam's division of America into the "educationally rich" and the other two-thirds, this group is toward the top of the heap. Nonetheless, I think we're representative of what comes next for most people: namely, trying to create mechanisms for maintaining relationships across employment and geographic changes. Because the reality is that we will succeed in doing this, *or* most people will create temporary social networks that collapse with each move, a surefire recipe for emotional exhaustion and long-term loneliness.

Are our assemblies frequent enough? Nope. Are they a substitute for day-to-day, water-over-the-rock community? Nope. But the group is nonetheless an important part of our lives, and our families' lives. When my wife had a near-death medical event in 2007, three of these guys dropped everything and got there the same day. (The six of us live in four different states.) If any of us fell prey to substance abuse or if one of our marriages was on the rocks, the guys would be there, to help, to advise, to comfort, or to deliver a slap to the face. We've pledged to be there for one another's kids, if something should happen to any of us. Our spouses have become friends. We pray for each other regularly.

Again, this is not the same as rooted community, as working alongside and regularly breaking bread with your closest friends. But *it is something to build on.* It's a foundation of friendship that offers each of us encouragement to invest where we are. Even if we can't see each other *tonight*, this friendship is nonetheless an anchor against high seas. Knowing we have people to turn to who will challenge us and who will keep us honest helps each of us live more purposefully where we are.

Through a Stranger's Eyes

As institutions go, our group of buddies is not much. It's not the YMCA or the Salvation Army. But it's not so different, in this sense: it's part of a uniquely American tradition of joining together to confront a problem, of establishing a community of purpose.

When the French writer Alexis de Tocqueville visited the United States in the 1830s, hoping to explain to himself and to continental Europe just what bizarre thing was unfolding across the Atlantic Ocean, it was precisely this impulse that he pinpointed as the heart of our new, rollicking country.

What Tocqueville discovered, much to his surprise, was that America's power came from the bottom up, in what he called "voluntary associations." He observed that in town after town after town, people discovered something they needed or wanted to do, and they didn't wait for the government to give them permission, or instructions, or funding. They just got together and did it. In the great book he published about his travels, *Democracy in America*, Tocqueville wrote: "Americans come together to hold celebrations, to build hotels, to erect churches, to start libraries, to send missionaries to every corner of the earth; they create hospitals, prisons, schools. They wrestle over difficult questions." He made a pointed comparison: "Every job that in France would be done by the government or in England by some great noble, in America you can bet is being done by a group of volunteers." At the heart of America, he observed, was a twofold spirit: of self-sufficiency and of neighborliness.

For Tocqueville, this spirit was responsible for the success of the country's (small-"r") republican government: "[W]hat is great [in America] is above all not what public administration executes but what is executed without it and outside it." It was not Washington, D.C., that gave America its vitality; it was (updating Tocqueville for the twenty-first century) the Rotary Club, 4-H fairs, and GoFundMe campaigns that raise money online for victims of catastrophes like Hurricane Harvey. "There is scarcely an undertaking so small that Americans do not unite for it," he remarked wryly. Nonetheless, it was these "associations" that oriented people toward "a common goal." Government, especially local government (Tocqueville was impressed by the New England township), was tasked with creating the space for these associations to form.

Tocqueville had seen in flourishing form what the British statesman Edmund Burke, a generation earlier, had called "little platoons"—the basic units of society: family, friends, neighborhood, church. "To love the little platoon we belong to in society," wrote

Burke in his *Reflections on the Revolution in France*, "is the first principle (the germ, as it were) of public affections. It is the first link in the series by which we proceed towards a love to our country, and to mankind."

Community is not easy. As Tocqueville himself saw, the tight-knit communities of New England that he admired were shot through with faults and hypocrisies. Burke, well acquainted with the fierce ethnic divisions in parts of eighteenth-century Great Britain, did not prioritize his little platoons to the exclusion of bigger battalions. But what both men understood was the foundational role of close communities—of the role of love and affection in bonding people together in a particular place. It was this, Tocqueville perceived, that gave America its great energy and splendor. It was this, Burke saw, that made possible any enduring country.

*   *   *

We are in a period of unprecedented upheaval. Community is collapsing, anxiety is building, and we're distracting ourselves with artificial political hatreds. That can't endure—and if it does, America won't.

The alternative is restoring community for our new moment, recognizing that the old modes are obsolete, and that we need to figure out a way to realize a sense of home in a world that looks very different than anything we've seen before. New technologies and experimentation will help with that. But, ultimately, it will require *habits* of heart and mind that introduce neighborliness into a new, more rootless age. It will require us to build new institutions of community that can bond increasingly mobile people together.

There's no formula for how to do that. The only thing we can do is start, wherever we are. Embrace the American genius that Tocqueville identified two centuries ago: come together, and create something new. Even if all you've got at the moment is you and a few buddies and some bad oldies music.

You'll never start building community until you start building community.

A fanatic is one who can't change his mind
and won't change the subject.

—WINSTON CHURCHILL

WE NEED MORE TRIBES

The First Inch: Reject Anti-Identities
The Second Inch: Put Politics in Its Proper Place
The Third Inch: Live Local

MY HOMETOWN OF FREMONT, NEBRASKA, COUNTED AMONG its distinguishing marks a meatpacking plant, a tractor dealership, several grain elevators filled with corn—and a heaping helping of hometown pride. When I was little, my buddies and I would sit in the stands of football, wrestling, and basketball games every week to cheer on the Tigers. I had many reasons to yell—Dad was a coach, for instance—but it was more than that. It felt like the reputation of our town was on the line every game.

But no contest was more important than the one against our rival high school. Columbus's maroon and white uniforms somehow looked meaner to 5-year-old eyes than Fremont's black and gold ones, and the Discoverers' packed visitors' section always seemed to cross the line from cheering to jeering. I watched them with a critical eye, ascribing to them all sorts of malevolence. I never yelled louder than when we played against *them*.

But then, on September 13, 1980, as an 8-year-old, I discovered that the concept of *them* was more malleable than I'd realized. Grandpa Elmer had taken me to my first Nebraska football game, and I climbed the stands at Memorial Stadium in Lincoln, eyes wide, taking in a crowd more than three times larger than my entire hometown. From my seat in the north end zone, I began to cheer for the Huskers and against visiting Utah. That's when I noticed a family from Columbus a few seats over. It took a moment for me to process what I was seeing. These horrible people were polluting my perfect day.

Wait a second . . .

We were on the same side. They were wearing the same color shirt I was—Cornhusker red. And they, too, were yelling against the Utes. It was a bizarre, almost out-of-body experience. Suddenly, I was looking at the bad guys, but they had morphed—almost against my will—into something else. My enemies were also my allies.

Of course, I was eight. I still believed that getting Phantom mag wheels on my Schwinn BMX was the height of worldly attainment, so my "aha moment" had its limitations: for example, the realization that Columbus people weren't evil didn't extend to people from Oklahoma, Nebraska's age-old rival. Those people were *actually* horrible. Even people from Columbus could see that.

A few years later, I was selected for a summer youth program. There I met a kid named Robert, who told me—right away—that he was from Oklahoma. He even admitted he was a Sooners fan, like he didn't know to be embarrassed about it. Since I didn't have any other friends at the camp yet, I didn't have the luxury of scorning him. Over the next many days, Robert and I hung around together, and we realized we saw the world in very similar ways. Robert was smart and I had no doubt he was a good guy, so I was left to wrangle with the fact that—somehow—he was also from Oklahoma.

Odds are, you're pretty mindful of tribalism already, but aren't sure what change could possibly be big enough to reverse the trend. But what if the change doesn't have to be dramatic?

There is a phrase in the Book of Exodus about taking back the land "little by little." A similar concept is at the heart of the 1999 film *Any Given Sunday*, starring Al Pacino as the coach of the struggling Miami Sharks football team. In the movie's most memorable scene, Pacino delivers a pep talk to rally his players before the big game: "Either we heal as a team, or we are going to crumble," he warns. "Inch by inch, play by play, till we're finished."

It might sound like a dramatic analogy for modern America, but I think we can all agree that this nation is a far cry from where it needs to be. "You know when you get old in life, things get taken from you. That's—that's part of life," says Pacino's character:

> But you only learn that when you start losing stuff. You find out that life is just a game of inches. So is football. Because in either game—life or football—the margin for error is so small. . . . The inches we need are everywhere around us. They are in every break of the game, every minute, every second. On this team, we fight for that inch.

The good news for us, too, is that the inches really are everywhere around us. The inches are within the reach of every American, urban or rural, rich or poor, no matter what age, no matter what political party.

America would be a healthier and happier place if we all agreed to set aside those superficial differences more of the time, and instead struggled together for three critical cultural inches.

The First Inch: Reject Anti-Identities

As an adult, it's easy to see how ridiculous it was that people from Fremont hated people from Columbus. How different could two Homestead-era Nebraska towns—46 miles apart, populations 25,000 and 23,000, supported by the same farming industries—actually be?

But that's the thing, isn't it? A good rivalry requires a good deal of similarity. Alabama and Auburn might seem like radically different worlds to the southerners who root for those teams, but they're just as much alike as Texas and Texas A&M. And how different are Ohio State and Michigan, truly? The Packers and Bears? Yankees and Red Sox?

What if those people we dislike so much are more like us than we care to admit? Or, perhaps more accurately, what if there's a higher-order bond that connects us that's prior to and more important than the lower-order schisms that divide us?

Let's go back to the examples we used earlier. It's not the case that a rivalry between Fremont and Columbus was a bad thing. In fact, in some ways it was the impetus for important developments: for example, the skills and character and grit that were built among young men by two-a-day football practices. It was the prospect of that red-letter game against our rivals that drove all those 16-year-old boys to commit to that grueling regimen. The problem arose when, in my mind, the unimportant differences between Fremonters and Columbusites swallowed up the more important things we had in common, among which was that we were all *Nebraskans*. In the same way, it wasn't that the Nebraska-Oklahoma rivalry was bad. (Frankly, it was the best rivalry college football has ever known—see: sellout streaks, winning percentages, national championship counts, "Game of the Century," 1971 . . . I could go on.)

The problem was when "Oklahoma" and "Nebraska" became irreconcilable categories—when I failed to see that they both were also part of an overarching category: *America*.

"You're just not angry enough," said the man at the Valentine grocery store. And the woman at the Lexington baseball field. And the retiree at the Elkhorn town hall. And the group of ladies at the campaign rally.

It's an odd charge to hear regularly—which I do—and I never quite know how to respond. Because, in a way, they're right. I don't share the furious attitude toward Democrats or liberal cable news hosts. Partly, I just don't care much what most media personalities say, because I know what they're often up to (building a fan base, trolling for clicks, etc.).

But more basically, I think the people who level this charge, who want to see policy disagreements accompanied by gobs of outrage and personal contempt, want the wrong thing from politics.

Don't misunderstand me: I'm not advocating for a "mushy middle" on policy, as if just singing "Kumbaya" and "splitting the difference" between conservative and progressive policy proposals would somehow work. I don't think it will. But debating policy and demonizing your debate partner are fundamentally different things.

Saying that "civility matters" is too simple—and too boring. What we need is something bigger: We need to believe that both the dignity of our opponents, and the character we aim to model for our kids, require some basic rules for public debate. We should stop holding the candidates on "our side" to lower standards than we expect from our opponents. This shouldn't be hard. Lying matters, and truth matters. We should stop lazily absolving bad actors on our side by just shrugging and saying, "Well, they all lie." Be skeptical of *any* politician whose statements frame our primary struggle in terms of one group of Americans versus another. Accountability starts at home, and "what-about-ism" is an intellectually vacuous way to live a life—not to mention being a morally bankrupt way to raise our kids.

We have many institutions of trust that need rebuilding. One of the most imperiled is journalism. As we've explored, some of that is because of the technological disruption to the old business model—and we don't yet know what workable economics of great reporting will come next. But much of the problem with current journalism flows simply from our thoughtless consumption—from the "demand signals" we're sending that we want only cotton candy. We need to recover the essential distinction between fact-based reporting and opinion commentary. We need to recover the essential distinction between journalism and entertainment. Why? Because a democracy depends on shared facts. Real journalism isn't a "game"; it's not about the quippiest hot takes. Journalists do not exist to entertain you, confirm your opinions, or support your candidate. In a democracy, we count on journalists to ask hard questions. So when we hear *anyone* powerful, in response to questions about their behavior, attack the media in general—as opposed to merely pushing back on a biased question—we should look more critically at them and their behavior.

Our public square is in bad shape. And the people who want more anger have missed something important. They've come to see the political world through the lens of *anti-tribes*—us versus them, Good versus Evil. They've become so focused on what separates us that they've lost sight of the higher-order bonds that connect us.

The Second Inch: Put Politics in Its Proper Place

I spent the weekend of July 4, 2016, in Waziristan, a jihadi-infested region in northwest Pakistan. (As a summer holiday destination, I don't recommend it.) The U.S. Special Forces and CIA agents stationed near there were briefing me and Joe Donnelly—a Democratic senator from Indiana—on their efforts to clean out a local jihadi cell that had holed up in a particular neighborhood, often using a mosque for cover. Back home, Joe and I disagree on most domestic policy issues. He votes reliably with Chuck Schumer (84 percent of the time), and I reliably . . . don't. But in a context like Waziristan, there is not much difference between hawkish American Republicans and hawkish American Democrats.

Neither Joe nor I was feeling great after all of our travel, which had culminated in teeth-rattling, up-and-down rides over mountainous terrain in a Chinook. It was hot, and our stomachs were churning.

That's when a Pakistani soldier approached us. The Pakistanis are our allies—usually. Many soldiers do brave things to support our troops; but others scheme to undermine our objectives. The soldier held out a tray with two cups and a teapot. The tray hovered in front of us. I caught Joe's eye. On the one hand, the Pakistani soldier was trying to be nice, a clear symbol of hospitality. On the other, was the water in Waziristan treated?

We hesitated.

Back home, Joe and I would be considered "enemies" by some cable news types and their audiences. As we've seen, a whole lot of nutpicking media outlets make their money by convincing Americans that Republicans and Democrats shouldn't agree on anything. When you're in Waziristan, though, it becomes clear just how silly that is.

Joe and I, sitting in what President Obama three years earlier had called "the most dangerous place in the world," were on the same side of everything that mattered. He and I were both for U.S. Special Forces against jihadis. We were both for ensuring that American soldiers were properly fitted out with equipment and munitions. We were both frustrated with the sketchy reliability of the Pakistanis. We were both impatient with the tribal and geographic divisions that continued to plague President Ashraf Ghani's government next door in Afghanistan. We were, in short, both Americans, both people with a calling to support the troops, and both—as the Pakistani soldier approached us with his tray—guys with air sickness hangovers simultaneously worried about being rude and about slurping up an exotic intestinal disease. Political party just didn't matter.

The tray continued to hover. Joe looked at me, and I looked at him. We rolled the dice. Reaching out together, we accepted the tea, expressed our gratitude, and drank.

It turns out that traveling through rural central Asia panicked about hostile locals and debilitating diarrhea puts things in perspective. If I could, I'd recommend it to more Americans. Take that guy you're always yelling at on Twitter and hike the Khyber Pass together. You'll find much more important things to discuss than the latest you-won't-believe-your-eyes headline.

One of the core problems with our public life together is that we're constantly failing to distinguish between politics and civics. Politics is about the use of power—how it is acquired and who wields it. Obviously, politics matters. But civics matters more.

Civics is about *who we are* as a people. A nation requires a framework of shared values, a set of core commitments. Our Framers articulated those first principles in the First Amendment. As shorthand, our grandparents after World War II used the phrase "principled pluralism." That's the beating heart of the whole enterprise. In our system, we don't seek to resolve the most important questions—about this life or the next—through politics. Because we believe that the most important issues are ultimately matters of the heart—that they are rightly matters of free choice, never of coercion—politics is simply the bare-bones instrument we use to protect the freedom to live lives of purpose, service, and love. But if we collapse civics and politics together, as more and more citizens seem to want to do, then we ensure that politics squeezes out community. We give priority to compulsion over friendship, and coerced uniformity over genuine diversity. We're seeing the results of this sort of thinking right now in those partisans who literally despise people on the other side of the policy divide. We have contempt for "them," and we correctly assume that they hate us right back.

This is something altogether different than our former tradition: *Out of many, one.*

Politics is supposed to be downstream from culture, but our anti-tribal zealots are pretending that politics can provide us with meaning. It won't work.

Amid our tribal crisis, many of the people to whom we would typically look to restore balance—trusted leaders in many institutions outside government—seem also to be aligning across a politicized spectrum. We are doubling down on division. We've begun to lose our shared identity as Americans and, I fear, weakening our democracy. Inverting our loyalties—putting politics (the means) before civics (the ends)—makes certain that we don't get either: We sacrifice the fundamental bonds that should unite us across our differences, and we don't get sustainable political or legislative output either.

I'm worried that unless we start to change our behavior, things will get a lot worse. Right now, there is a ton of dry brush out there and too many people—whether for money, fame, or power—are willing to strike a match.

Even under normal circumstances our knee-jerk polarization would be dangerous. But for us, in an America going through the digital revolution that is undermining local community, this is anything but a normal moment. It is a grave threat.

Over the course of this book, we've talked extensively about large-scale trends that are mostly the product of technological developments. The causes have been mostly impersonal. But that is now changing. We cannot ignore the plain fact that *there are also bad actors preparing to exploit, and already intentionally exploiting, these trends for their own gain.*

I talk with the leaders of the U.S. intelligence community nearly every day, and most of them are deeply anxious about information operations currently being conducted by foreign powers who see an opportunity to undermine Americans' confidence in our system, in our institutions, and in our American idea. Put more bluntly: Vladimir Putin loves cable news and the divides it helps to solidify in the American soul.

We mentioned in Chapter 6 the emergence of "deepfakes"—fake videos that look real to the unaided eye. Although at the moment they're mostly confined to the grimy back-alleyways of internet pornography, this technology has the potential to be enormously disruptive to our normal political processes—and to geopolitics. Imagine that, on the eve of a presidential election, video suddenly appears of one of the candidates taking a bribe. Real—or fake? Imagine that audio emerges of a "conspiracy" in the boardroom of a major company. Authentic—or doctored? Imagine that video surfaces online of American soldiers committing a war crime. Genuine—or counterfeit?

How do you know?

Currently, the only way to distinguish a deepfake is by taking a careful look at the technical components of the footage. You have to get down to the level of pixels. It's likely that as deepfake technology advances, so will methods of spotting it. But when breaking news can go viral in minutes—and when viral footage can spark a riot—there won't always be time to consult the lab.

It doesn't require a diabolical imagination to see the ways in which this technology might be used to disrupt our politics—by our adversaries abroad, or by unscrupulous actors here at home. Putin has already demonstrated his interest in sowing confusion and chaos in American politics; and China, which stole confidential information from 21 million Americans in the 2015 Office of Personnel Management hack and where AI capabilities have long been a government priority, might put deepfake technology to use for blackmail purposes. And what happens when cockamamie conspiracy theories, such as 2016's "Pizzagate," which alleged that Democratic party officials were operating a child-trafficking ring out of the basement of a Washington, D.C., pizza parlor, are accompanied by video "proof"? Even without that sort of proof, a North Carolina man drove to D.C. and opened fire inside the restaurant.

I talk regularly with generals and intelligence-community leaders, and I always try to ask them what is keeping them up at night. For more than two years, nearly every single person I've spoken to has told me that they're worried that foreign governments and terrorist groups are going to seize on the extraordinary technological capabilities of our day not to launch an invasion (although there will be plenty of fighting in cyberspace) but to quietly exacerbate the fractures that already divide America internally.

In his 1838 Lyceum Address, Abraham Lincoln famously declared that "all the armies of Europe, Asia, and Africa combined . . . [c]ould not by force take a drink from the Ohio [River], or make a track on the Blue Ridge [Mountains]." That remains true. America's military is superior to any force that could challenge it on the battlefield. But, Lincoln added, that does not mean America is invulnerable: "If destruction be our lot," he remarked, "we must ourselves be its author and finisher. As a nation of freemen, we must live through all time, or *die by suicide*."

Civil discord has always been the gravest threat to America's security. Intentionally, internally destroying the sense of "we" has always been the greatest danger to the future of this republic. And our enemies, fully aware of that, are using the tools at their disposal to give it a nudge.

This is what Vladimir Putin has done to great effect over the past three years. Russian "bots" regularly fuel outrages on social media. More than 50,000 Russian-linked Twitter accounts posted automated election-related messages in 2016. Facebook estimates that 126 million American users were exposed to Russian-created material on its site over the same period. Last year, during the debate over many NFL players' decision to kneel during the national anthem, the viral hashtags #takeaknee (in support of the kneeling players) and #standfortheflag (against them) were both boosted heavily by Russian-backed accounts.

Vladimir Putin, WikiLeaks (his off-the-books disinforma-
tion operation), and many other foreign actors see an America that
is perilously divided, and they are looking for ways to exploit that
vulnerability—not chiefly to help Republicans or Democrats, but to
hurt all *Americans.*

If we can recognize this, we can see not just how important but
how urgent it is to find more constructive ways to fight—to bring
our disagreements on matters of policy under a general agreement
about shared values or core commitments, about what it means to
be American.

Again, I'm not indifferent on policy. I'm an opponent of political
progressivism, because I don't think it works. One-size-fits-all policy
planning models are ill-suited to the profound challenges of our disrupted moment. That's why I'm not a fan of the Affordable Care Act,
which I think is a Rube Goldberg contraption that is neither affordable nor ultimately workable. But I nonetheless have a moral obligation not to despise people who support Obamacare. I have neighbors
down the street who are enthusiastic Obamacare advocates. We disagree vigorously about the government's role in health-care policy.
But at the end of the day, *we're still neighbors.* We live on the same
street, we shop at the same grocery store, our kids play on the same
teams.

When we look around our neighborhoods, we should have eyes
to see that we share common interests and goals that are more important than just about any question of federal policy—chief among
those goals, raising our children to become kind, thoughtful, gritty,
respectful adults who use their skills and talents to serve others. I
don't want to worry that politics is going to prevent my neighbor
from keeping an eye on my kids when they're all playing in the front
yard; and I want my neighbors to know that, even if we disagree on
every policy question from A to Z, Melissa and I will scoop their son
up if he scrapes his knee. There truly are things that unite us above
and before the things that divide us.

We have plenty of actual enemies looking to harm us. We don't
need to add to their ranks. To quote Lincoln once more: "We are not
enemies, but friends."

The Third Inch: Live Local

Our identity cannot be found in anti-tribes. It cannot be found in
politics. And it cannot be found flitting about, here, there, everywhere . . . nowhere. We find lives of meaning and purpose at and
near *home*. Imagine if just 10 percent of the time we spend angrily
tracking national political news were redirected to volunteering at
our kids' or grandkids' school, serving at a soup kitchen, visiting a
nursing home. We'd be community-rich.

So many of our angry partisans miss the fundamental American distinction between our one national community and our many,
diverse local communities. Our national experiment is about defending the individual, with his or her inexhaustible dignity—and
protecting his or her right to freely speak, worship, publish, protest,
and assemble. The District of Columbia is not the center of American life; it exists to maintain a framework for ordered liberty—so
that *your city or town*, the place where you live, can be the center
of the world. D.C. is not supposed to merely tolerate but to actively
encourage a wide diversity of local communities. We don't need to
agree on everything; we simply need to allow the space for communities of different belief and custom to flourish.

As the old saying goes: The American response to speech we
don't agree with is not less speech but more speech. We try to persuade each other, not silence each other. That's how people committed to dignity treat each other.

In the same way, the response to so much of the ugliness of our
moment is not to retreat to our own corners; the prescription is not
less engagement, but more. We should stop hoping that our opponents in this or that cultural dispute will vanish—rather, we should
interact more, in the places where we can meet as something more
than partisans in battle. But that can't happen as long as we continue
to substitute, for the healthy tribes of family, friends, workplace, and
neighborhood, the shallow alternatives of political party and television rage and social media siloes.

So, what's the solution? What should we do? Like all important things, it has to start with you. Let's start here: Turn off the

television. Log out of Twitter or Facebook. Put your smartphone in a drawer. Go outside and throw a ball with your son or daughter. Read a book together. Bake cookies and take them to the new family that just moved in across the street. Invite that coworker you've been meaning to get to know out for lunch. Help clean up after coffee hour at church. Sign up for a shift at the animal shelter. Mow your neighbor's lawn, on the sly, undetected. Visit a widow.

This is where the action is. It's not in Washington. It's not on Instagram. Real, rich, meaningful life is local. It's face-to-face, shoulder-to-shoulder, hand-in-hand. Start—here, now.

I have a long list of identifiers: I'm a husband, a dad, a Christian, an American, a conservative, a Republican, a Nebraskan, a Cornhusker football addict, a historian. For a time, I'm also a public servant. We don't have problems because we belong to too many different groups but rather because we prioritize them wrongly. When we get the order wrong, we cause connections to fray. Husker football is the second-most important religion where I come from, but if somehow my Husker football loyalties took precedence over my being a dad or a husband—well, then I would have messed up.

As a nation, we're messing up.

In the Introduction, I told the story of how my team and I manned a water station at the Lincoln Marathon, and how that picturesque spring day was upset by political activists. "Don't drink it!" they screamed as I handed bewildered runners cups of water. "It's poison!" they shrieked.

These people were angry over various political disagreements. And although I didn't receive an official list of all their complaints, these issues are no doubt important. It may seem naïve to say that merely by turning off cable news and bringing cookies to our neighbors we can make strides toward solving our biggest problems. Take abortion: One group of Americans, and you probably know that I am firmly among this group, believes that abortion involves nothing less than the taking of a life; the other that it's an essential part of a woman's right to control her own body. I must admit that I have a hard time writing about this issue dispassionately.

Or consider the problems of persistent racism in our criminal justice system. Or the breathtaking inefficiencies and inequities of our health-care system. Or the haphazard funding of basic scientific research. Or the absurdities of our immigration and border security regimes. Or the inability of our defense and intelligence communities to modernize for the age of cyberwar. Or our unsustainable budget deficits and the overpromising in our entitlement programs.

All these issues, and many more, require vigorous debate. And we should always worry that calls for civility can be reduced to a demand to accept the status quo, which tends simply to favor those with status. But again, my point is that even as we debate these contentious issues passionately, we have to maintain the republic that allows us to do so. And so *even* on these absolutely essential issues, we must approach our opponents in these debates as people created with dignity—and we must demand that both we and they dig in as sincere, fellow countrymen, rather than as enemies to be trolled.

Having our "identifiers in the right order" doesn't mean we pretend to agree about topics on which we are actually divided. America is more resilient than that. How lucky we are to be alive right now, to have the chance to help tackle these big questions, the answers to which will shape the future of our nation. Glossing over our deep divides might be superficially appealing, but we must resist the urge to water down the debates in the interest of some halfhearted truce. Many of the issues we face today are too important to approach timidly or dishonestly. They are worth arguing over—passionately. The answer is not for everyone to start waving white flags, for faux unity is no unity at all.

What is needed is for people from both sides to agree that political and policy divides *are not our primary identities* or our primary divides. As Americans, we need to agree *first* on the universal dignity of all people, before we descend to the more divisive but less important debates about the prudential use of the levers of government power. If we fail to do that—that is, if we begin by regarding policy divides as ultimate—then we'll inevitably all become the shrieking types. We'll ultimately reduce all community events into platforms for hysterical politics.

This is the recipe for national suicide about which Washington and Lincoln warned us.

The good news is the American idea can be renewed. But it won't happen unless enough of us decide to abandon the path we're on. Politics has always evoked serious emotion. But normal people in the not-so-distant past were able to gather together, discuss politics, and part ways as friends and neighbors. We've let our loneliness, our fears, and our anxieties swallow up the better angels of our nature. A republic can't survive if it's filled with fanatics. We need to be able to identify and then to resist the habits that are driving us toward fanaticism.

We are relational beings, and we're meant for community. We're meant to be rooted, not rootless. We're meant to be together, pursuing goals and dreams in common. But these are much harder to come by in an increasingly transient world. Alexis de Tocqueville defined America by our many associations, but he would barely recognize us today. Our associations and healthy local institutions are withering. The Rotary Clubs—a far more representative picture of America historically than a screaming cable news show—are in collapse. Appalachia is being hollowed out by hopelessness. Exurbia is suffering an anxiety attack.

We're living through an economic and social revolution that is transforming the life we've known for a century and a half. We need to be able to name this moment, and we need to be clear-eyed enough to admit that the challenges this moment presents are not going to be solved by government; they can't be.

Because, ultimately, it's not legislation we're lacking; it's the tight bonds that give our lives meaning, happiness, and hope. It's the habits of heart and mind that make us neighbors and friends.

At the end of the day, it's love. And when a bunch of "them" are joined by love, and by purpose, "they" can become "we."

ACKNOWLEDGMENTS

The only part of writing a book that's painful is ... the writing part.

Every other phase is great: the idea generation, refining the menu of options, reading and research, arguing sections with lifelong friends, trying out riffs in speeches, outlining—and then even the editing that follows the writing. But the writing itself I find to be dreary.

My solution—to minimizing the drudgery, and hopefully also to becoming a better writer over time—is to grow the pre-writing and post-writing phases. In this book, I tried to frame up more of my outline in greater detail before sitting down to write, and I also tried to enlist more friends as critics during the editing phase.

The key to making both of those changes work is a long list of big-brained conversation partners. So here goes ...

The four people who helped me the most with this project were Ian Tuttle, Nancy French, Ben Boychuk, and Joel Gehrke. Even though all of you surely rolled your eyes at me scores of times as I tried and worked and retried and reworked various portions of the argument, thanks for at least not entirely verbalizing your (legitimate) views of how frustrating arguing with me can be. Thanks also for being serious debate partners who take ideas seriously.

I owe a large debt of gratitude to James Wegmann, Jordan Gehrke, and Kari Ridder, who volunteered to read the manuscript multiple places along the way. I genuinely enjoy both intellectual and real-world journeys with all three of you. Your willingness to challenge my ideas is genuinely appreciated. Thanks as well to Dan

Currell for being willing to do a speedread of the manuscript at the time-is-short copyedit stage; you made the argument stronger in a dozen different ways.

The guys from "Cherish" (discussed in chapter 8) are lifelong friends, but you are also quite simply the people I most enjoy arguing with and learning from. Even though I didn't get to discuss every idea in this book with all five of you, I regard all of my thinking as being informed, to a significant extent, by your worldviews. So thank you Mike Horton, Derek Lewis, Dan Bryant, Brian Lee, and Will Inboden, for being people who read deeply and are willing to try on new ideas empathetically, even when you don't agree.

In the same way, there is nothing meaningful that I wrestle with in life that I don't also struggle through with my family—so thanks for being sounding boards (again and again and again . . .) Corrie (16), Alex (14), Breck (7), and Melissa (older than 16). Similarly, I am mindful of the patient forbearance as my thinking develops shown to me by Ray Sass, Tyler Grassmeyer, Shelly Blake, Taylor Sliva, and Raven Shirley.

Finally, thanks to my agents and publisher. Matt Latimer and Keith Urbahn—thanks for genuinely caring not only about the production schedule but also the quality of the output. Tim Bartlett, thanks for being the first to conceive of this as a book unto itself, rather than just a side argument in a book we ultimately decided not to write. You and your colleagues at St. Martin's Press—with a special shout-out to Alan Bradshaw and his hardworking and late-working compatriots—are a gifted crew. Thanks also to Tim's assistant, Alice Pfeifer, for the care and attention she brought to every step of this process, copy editor Jen Simington for her meticulous work, Meryl Levavi for the clean and elegant interior design, Jonathan Bush for the memorable jacket design, and Gabi Gantz for her tireless efforts on behalf of the book.

This is truly a delightful team to co-labor with, whether a steam pipe happens to explode the day before deadline or not. Boom.

North Bend, Nebraska
July 4, 2018

NOTES

Introduction

1. "U.S. Drug Overdose Deaths Continue to Rise; Increase Fueled by Synthetic Opioids," press release, Centers for Disease Control and Prevention, March 29, 2018, www.cdc.gov/media/releases/2018/p0329-drug-overdose-deaths.html; "Suicide Rates Rising Across the U.S.," press release, Centers for Disease Control and Prevention, June 7, 2018, www.cdc.gov/media/releases/2018/p0607-suicide-prevention.html.
2. Sherry Turkle, *Alone Together: Why We Expect More from Technology and Less from Each Other* (New York: Basic Books, 2010).
3. Conor Lynch, "America May Be More Divided Now Than at Any Time Since the Civil War," Salon.com, October 14, 2017, www.salon.com/2017/10/14/america-may-be-more-divided-now-than-at-any-time-since-the-civil-war/.

1

1. Cindy Schreuder, "The 1995 Chicago Heat Wave," *Chicago Tribune,* July 14, 2015, www.chicagotribune.com/news/nationworld/politics/chi-chicagodays-1995heat-story-story.html.
2. "Dying Alone: An Interview with Eric Klinenberg," University of Chicago Press, 2002, accessed July 30, 2018, http://www.press.uchicago.edu/Misc/Chicago/443213in.html; Eric Klinenberg, *Heat Wave: A Social Autopsy of Disaster in Chicago* (Chicago: University of Chicago Press, 2002), xxiv.
3. American Heart Association, "Is Broken Heart Syndrome Real?," last modified December 12, 2017, www.heart.org/HEARTORG/Conditions/More/Cardiomyopathy/Is-Broken-Heart-Syndrome-Real_UCM_448547_Article.jsp#.W1SNOPlKjIU.
4. John Cacioppo and William Patrick, *Loneliness: Human Nature and the Need for Social Connection* (New York: W. W. Norton, 2008), 5.
5. Cited in Jacqueline Olds and Richard S. Schwartz, *The Lonely American: Drifting Apart in the Twenty-First Century* (Boston: Beacon Press, 2009), 136.
6. Cacioppo and Patrick, *Loneliness*.

7. Eric Klinenberg, *Heat Wave.*

8. Felice J. Freyer, "'Loneliness Kills': Former Surgeon General Sounds Alarm on Emotional Well-Being," *Boston Globe,* January 16, 2018, www.bostonglobe.com /metro/2018/01/16/former-surgeon-general-sounds-alarm-hidden-toll-loneliness /GweBtw1woQyll1Tl8CYpVL/story.html.

9. Emily Esfahani Smith, *The Power of Meaning: Crafting a Life that Matters* (New York: Crown, 2017), 55.

10. Sarvada Chandra Tiwari, "Loneliness: A Disease?," *Journal of Indian Psychiatry,* October–December 2013, accessed January 25, 2018, through PubMedCentral, National Institutes of Health, www.ncbi.nlm.nih.gov/pmc/articles/PMC3890922/.

11. Andrew Sullivan, "The Poison We Pick," *New York Magazine,* February 20, 2018, https://nymag.com/daily/intelligencer/2018/02/americas-opioid-epidemic.html; Centers for Disease Control, "Understanding the Epidemic," last modified August 30, 2018, www.cdc.gov/drugoverdose/epidemic/index.html.

12. Robert Putnam, *Bowling Alone: The Collapse and Revival of American Community* (New York: Simon & Schuster, 2000), 265.

13. Ibid., 101.

14. Ibid., 17.

15. Ibid., 352.

16. Cited in Olds and Schwartz, *Lonely American,* 2.

17. Robert D. Putnam, *Our Kids: The American Dream in Crisis* (New York: Simon & Schuster Paperbacks, 2015).

18. Charles Murray, *Coming Apart: The State of White America, 1960–2010* (New York: Crown Forum, 2012).

19. "Pew Social Trends, They're Waiting Longer, but U.S. Women Today More Likely to Have Children Than a Decade Ago," Pew Research, January 18, 2018, http://www .pewsocialtrends.org/2018/01/18/theyre-waiting-longer-but-u-s-women-today -more-likely-to-have-children-than-a-decade-ago/.

20. Putnam, *Our Kids,* 73.

21. Ian Rowe, "Bill Gates Overlooks the Vital Role of Families in Shaping Children's Academic Outcomes," Institute for Family Studies, October 31, 2017, https://if studies.org/blog/bill-gates-overlooks-the-vital-role-of-families-in-shaping-childrens -academic-outcomes.

22. Interview with Robert Putnam on "None of the Above," YouTube, August 24, 2015, www.youtube.com/watch?v=aHN92UbBkFw.

23. Putnam, *Our Kids,* 3–5.

24. Murray, *Coming Apart;* Bill Bishop, *The Big Sort: Why the Clustering of Like-Minded America Is Tearing Us Apart* (Boston: Houghton Mifflin Harcourt, 2008).

2

1. McKinsey Global Institute, "Jobs Lost, Jobs Gained: Workforce Transitions in a Time of Automation," December 2017, www.mckinsey.com/~/media/mckinsey/fea

tured%20insights/future%20of%20organizations/what%20the%20future%20
of%20work%20will%20mean%20for%20jobs%20skills%20and%20wages/mgi
-jobs-lost-jobs-gained-report-december-6-2017.ashx.

2. Ibid.

3. Bill Clinton, *Back to Work: Why We Need Smart Government for a Strong Economy* (New York: Alfred A . Knopf, 2011), ix.

4. Richard Florida, *Who's Your City? How the Creative Economy Is Making Where to Live the Most Important Decision of Your Life* (New York: Basic Books, 2008).

3

1. Cecelia Tichi, *Electronic Hearth: Creating an American Television Culture* (New York: Oxford University Press, 1991), 42.

2. Neil Postman, *Amusing Ourselves to Death: Public Discourse in the Age of Show Business* (New York: Penguin Books, 2006).

3. C. John Sommerville, *How the News Makes Us Dumb: The Death of Wisdom in an Information Society* (Downers Grove, IL: IVP Books, 1999), 15–16.

4. Jeremy Hsu, "People Choose News That Fits Their Views," Live Science, June 7, 2009, www.livescience.com/3640-people-choose-news-fits-views.html.

5. Dan Kahan, "What Is Motivated Reasoning and How Does It Work?," *Science and Religion Today,* May 4, 2011, www.scienceandreligiontoday.com/2011/05/04/what-is-motivated-reasoning-and-how-does-it-work/.

6. Jeffrey M. Jones and Zacc Ritter, "Americans See More News Bias; Most Can't Name Neutral Source," Gallup, January 17, 2018, https://news.gallup.com/poll/225755/americans-news-bias-name-neutral-source.aspx.

7. David Bixenspan, "Media, Twitter and Conservatives Argued about Pickup Trucks for Some Reason," Mediaite, January 4, 2017, www.mediaite.com/online/media-twitter-and-conservatives-argued-about-pickup-trucks-for-some-reason/.

8. Nomination of Robert Bork, Congressional Record—Senate, July 1, 1987. A pdf can be found at https://upload.wikimedia.org/wikipedia/commons/0/02/Robert_Bork%27s_America.pdf.

9. Stuart Taylor Jr., "Justice Stevens, in Unusual Move, Praises Bork as Nominee to Court," *New York Times,* August 1, 1987.

10. Ted Kaufman oral history, https://www.senate.gov/artandhistory/history/resources/pdf/Kaufman_3.pdf.

11. Goldstein quoted at Nina Totenberg, "Robert Bork's Supreme Court Nomination 'Changed Everything, Maybe Forever,'" NPR, December 19, 2012, www.npr.org/sections/itsallpolitics/2012/12/19/167645600/robert-borks-supreme-court-nomination-changed-everything-maybe-forever.

12. U.S. Commission on Civil Rights, "Peaceful Coexistence: Reconciling Nondiscrimination Principles with Civil Liberties," Briefing Report, September 7, 2016, www.usccr.gov/pubs/docs/Peaceful-Coexistence-09-07-16.PDF.

13. Megan McArdle, "Why I Didn't Write About Gosnell's Trial—And Why I Should Have," *Daily Beast,* April 12, 2013, www.thedailybeast.com/why-i-didnt-write -about-gosnells-trial-and-why-i-should-have; Jeffrey Goldberg, "Why Is the Press Ignoring the Kermit Gosnell Story?," *Bloomberg,* April 12, 2013, www.bloomberg .com/view/articles/2013-04-12/why-is-the-press-ignoring-the-kermit-gosnell -story-; Associated Press, "Staffer Describes Chaos at PA Abortion Clinic," *New Haven Register,* April 4, 2013, www.nhregister.com/connecticut/article/Staffer-des cribes-chaos-at-Pa-abortion-clinic-11434458.php.

14. Levi Boxell, Matthew Gentzkow, and Jesse M. Shapiro, "Internet Use and Political Polarization," *PNAS* 114, no. 40 (Oct. 2017): 10612–617, DOI: 10.1073/ pnas.1706588114.

4

1. Matthew Shaer, "How Far Will Sean Hannity Go?," *New York Times Magazine,* November 28, 2017, www.nytimes.com/2017/11/28/magazine/how-far-will-sean -hannity-go.html.

2. Ibid.

3. Kilmeade quoted in Clark Mindock, "'We Don't Even Know Enough to Hate Him': Right-Wing Pundits Responded to the Las Vegas Shooter Being a White Man," *The Independent* (UK), October 5, 2017, www.independent.co.uk/news/world /americas/stephen-paddock-fox-news-response-las-vegas-shooting-struggle-who-he -was-a7985426.html.

4. Dylan Byers, "Donald Trump Has Earned $2 Billion in Free Media Coverage, Study Shows," CNN.com, March 15, 2016, https://money.cnn.com/2016/03/15/media /trump-free-media-coverage/index.html; Philip Bump, "Assessing a Clinton argument that the media helped to elect Trump," *Washington Post,* September 12, 2017, https://www.washingtonpost.com/news/politics/wp/2017/09/12/assessing-a-clin ton-argument-that-the-media-helped-to-elect-trump/?utm_term=.ec8b1884f1ee.

5. Julie Beck, "This Article Won't Change Your Mind," *The Atlantic,* March 13, 2017, www.theatlantic.com/science/archive/2017/03/this-article-wont-change-your -mind/519093/.

5

1. Ronald Reagan, "A Time for Choosing," speech, American Presidency Project, October 27, 1964, www.presidency.ucsb.edu/ws/index.php?pid=76121.

2. Learned Hand, "The Spirit of Liberty," speech, Digital History, 1944, www.digital history.uh.edu/disp_textbook.cfm?smtID=3&psid=1199.

3. Erika Christakis, "Email from Erika Christakis: 'Dressing Yourselves,' email to Silliman College (Yale) Students on Halloween Costumes," Foundation for Individual Rights in Education, October 30, 2015, www.thefire.org/email-from-erika-chris takis-dressing-yourselves-email-to-silliman-college-yale-students-on-halloween -costumes/.

4. Bre Payton, "Watch a Mob of Yale Students Bully a Professor They Say Hurt Their Feelings," *The Federalist,* September 15, 2016, http://thefederalist.com/2016/09/15/watch-a-mob-of-yale-students-bully-a-professor-who-hurt-their-feelings/.

5. Emily Jashinsky, "Brown Students Thought Censoring Guy Benson Would Protect Free Speech," *Washington Examiner,* February 16, 2018, www.washingtonexaminer.com/brown-students-thought-censoring-guy-benson-would-protect-free-speech.

6. Allison Stanger, "Opinion: Understanding the Angry Mob at Middlebury That Gave Me a Concussion," *New York Times,* March 13, 2017, www.nytimes.com/2017/03/13/opinion/understanding-the-angry-mob-that-gave-me-a-concussion.html.

7. Michael Bodley, "At Berkeley Yiannopoulos Protest, $100,000 in Damage, 1 Arrest," *San Francisco Chronicle,* February 2, 2017, www.sfgate.com/crime/article/At-Berkeley-Yiannopoulos-protest-100-000-in-10905217.php.

8. "Spotlight on Speech Codes 2017," Foundation for Individual Rights in Education, n.d., accessed July 30, 2018, www.thefire.org/spotlight-on-speech-codes-2017/.

9. Andrew Sullivan, "We All Live on Campus Now," Daily Intelligencer, *New York* magazine, February 9, 2018, http://nymag.com/daily/intelligencer/2018/02/we-all-live-on-campus-now.html.

10. Abraham Lincoln, "Letter to Henry L. Pierce and Others," April 6, 1859, Abraham Lincoln Online, www.abrahamlincolnonline.org/lincoln/speeches/pierce.htm.

11. W.E.B. DuBois, "Of Our Spiritual Strivings," in *The Souls of Black Folk* (1903), Project Gutenberg edition, www.gutenberg.org/ebooks/408?msg=welcome_stranger#chap00.

12. Martin Luther King Jr., "Letter from Birmingham Jail," April 16, 1963, Online King Records Access, http://okra.stanford.edu/transcription/document_images/undecided/630416-019.pdf.

13. Russ Roberts, "The Three Blind Spots of Politics," Medium.com, June 25, 2017, https://medium.com/@russroberts/the-three-blind-spots-of-politics-c5e8cc7c60b6.

14. "One in Three Americans Fail Immigration Naturalization Civics Test," Xavier University's Center for the Study of the American Dream, April 27, 2012, www.prnewswire.com/news-releases/one-in-three-americans-fail-immigrant-naturalization-civics-test-149209975.html; "Americans' Knowledge of the Branches of Government Is Declining," Annenberg Public Policy Center, September 13, 2016, www.annenbergpublicpolicycenter.org/americans-knowledge-of-the-branches-of-government-is-declining/.

6

1. Nick Bilton, "Steve Jobs Was a Low-Tech Parent," *New York Times,* September 11, 2014, www.nytimes.com/2014/09/11/fashion/steve-jobs-apple-was-a-low-tech-parent.html.

2. Ian Johnston, "Device That Can Literally Read Your Mind Invented by Scientists," *The Independent* (UK), April 18, 2017, www.independent.co.uk/news/science/read -your-mind-brain-waves-thoughts-locked-in-syndrome-toyohashi-japan-a7687471 .html; Rolfe Winkler, "Elon Musk Launches Neuralink to Connect Brains with Computers," *Wall Street Journal,* March 27, 2017, www.wsj.com/articles/elon-musk -launches-neuralink-to-connect-brains-with-computers-1490642652.

3. Adam Greenfield, *Radical Technologies: The Design of Everyday Life* (New York: Verso, 2017), 260–69.

4. Pidcock quoted in Angus Howarth, "Listen: Lost JFK Speech Brought to Life by Edinburgh Firm," *The Scotsman,* March 16, 2018, www.scotsman.com/news/listen -lost-jfk-speech-brought-to-life-by-edinburgh-tech-firm-1-4707398.

5. Darrell M. West and John R. Allen, "Report: How Artificial Intelligence Is Transforming the World," Brookings Institution, April 24, 2018, www.brookings.edu /research/how-artificial-intelligence-is-transforming-the-world/.

6. Smalley quoted in Ed Regis, "The Incredible Shrinking Man," *Wired,* October 2004, www.wired.com/2004/10/drexler/; Mitra information from Lucia Maffei, "How Carbon Nanotubes Could Give Us Faster Processors and Longer Battery Life," *TechCrunch,* August 20, 2016, https://techcrunch.com/2016/08/20/how -carbon-nanotubes-could-give-us-faster-processors-and-longer-battery-life/.

7. Sherry Turkle, *Alone Together: Why We Expect More from Technology and Less from Each Other* (New York: Basic Books, 2010).

8. Adam Alter, "Tech Bigwigs Know How Addictive Their Products Are. Why Don't the Rest of Us?," *Wired,* March 24, 2017, www.wired.com/2017/03/irresistible-the -rise-of-addictive-technology-and-the-business-of-keeping-us-hooked/.

9. Andrew Perrin and Jingjing Jiang, "About a Quarter of U.S. Adults Say They Are 'Almost Constantly' Online," Pew Research Center, March 14, 2018, www.pew research.org/fact-tank/2018/03/14/about-a-quarter-of-americans-report-going -online-almost-constantly/.

10. Tony Reinke, *12 Ways Your Phone Is Changing You* (Wheaton, IL: Crossway, 2017).

11. Stephen Lawson, "Microsoft Patents Body-As-Network," *PC World,* June 23, 2004, www.pcworld.com/article/116655/article.html.

12. Turkle, *Alone Together,* 280.

13. Survey cited in Mark Regnerus, *Cheap Sex: The Transformation of Men, Marriage, and Monogamy* (Oxford: Oxford University Press, 2017), 114–15; Belinda Luscombe, "Porn and the Threat to Virility," *Time,* March 30, 2016, http://time .com/4277510/porn-and-the-threat-to-virility/.

14. "Blue Light Has a Dark Side," Harvard Health Publishing, last modified December 30, 2017, www.health.harvard.edu/staying-healthy/blue-light-has-a-dark-side.

15. Sherry Turkle, *Reclaiming Conversation: The Power of Talk in a Digital Age* (New York: Penguin, 2015).

16. Ryan Browne, "Elon Musk Warns A.I. Could Create an 'Immortal Dictator from which We Can Never Escape," CNBC, April 6, 2018, www.cnbc.com/2018/04/06 /elon-musk-warns-ai-could-create-immortal-dictator-in-documentary.html.

17. Shakya and Vannucci quoted in Markham Heid, "You Asked: Is Social Media Making Me Miserable?," *Time* Guide to Happiness, n.d., accessed July 31, 2018, http://time.com/collection/guide-to-happiness/4882372/social-media-facebook-instagram-unhappy/.

18. Tovia Smith, "A School's Way to Fight Phones in Class: Lock 'Em Up," NPR, January 11, 2018, www.npr.org/2018/01/11/577101803/a-schools-way-to-fight-phones-in-class-lock-em-up.

19. Ibid.

20. Cal Newport, *Deep Work: Rules for Focused Success in a Distracted World* (New York: Grand Central, 2016).

7

1. Schwartz quoted in Dillon Knight Kalkhurst, "Can Too Many Choices Give Millennials Anxiety?," *Huffington Post,* last modified August 22, 2016, www.huffingtonpost.com/entry/too-many-choices-cause-millennials-anxiety_us_57b5e253e4b0cea476e64a66.

2. Tim Herrera, "How to Make Tough Decisions Easier," Smarter Living, *New York Times,* June 4, 2018, www.nytimes.com/2018/06/04/smarter-living/how-to-finally-just-make-a-decision.html.

3. Drew Holcomb and the Neighbors, "Good Light," from the album *Good Light,* lyrics at https://genius.com/Drew-holcomb-and-the-neighbors-good-light-lyrics.

4. "Faculty Charge to Graduates, Veritas School 2017," Veritas School, posted by Sara Kennedy, June 4, 2017, http://veritasschool.com/faculty-charge-graduates-veritas-school-2017/. The charge is an abbreviated version of a longer piece available here: www.circeinstitute.org/blog/honestly-how-hard-should-you-work.

5. C. S. Lewis, *The Weight of Glory,* rev. ed. (New York: HarperCollins, 2001), 32–33.

8

1. Prashant Gopal, "U.S. Homeownership Rate Rises for the Second Time This Year," *Bloomberg News,* October 31, 2017, www.bloomberg.com/news/articles/2017-10-31/homeownership-rate-in-the-u-s-rises-for-second-time-this-year; Jeffrey M. Jones, "U.S. Home Selling and Buying Intentions Point to Sellers' Market," *Gallup News,* May 8, 2018, https://news.gallup.com/poll/233693/home-selling-buying-intentions-point-sellers-market.aspx.

2. Jacqueline Olds and Richard S. Schwartz, *The Lonely American: Drifting Apart in the Twenty-First Century* (Boston: Beacon Press, 2009), 79.

3. Wendy Wang and Kim Parker, "Record Share of Americans Have Never Married: As Values, Economics and Gender Patterns Change," Social & Demographic Trends project, Pew Research Center, September 2014, www.pewsocialtrends.org/2014/09/24/chapter-2-trends-in-the-share-of-never-married-americans-and-a-look-forward/. Manhattan and Cambridge: Cited in Olds and Schwartz, *Lonely American,* 79.

4. L. Pulkki-Råback, M. Kivimäki, K. Ahola, et al., "Living Alone and Antidepressant Medication Use: A Prospective Study in a Working-Age Population," *BMC Public Health* 12 (2012): 236, https://doi.org/10.1186/1471-2458-12-236.

5. Michael C. Munger, *Tomorrow 3.0* (New York: Cambridge University Press, 2018), 1.

6. Niam Yaraghi and Shamika Ravi, "The Current and Future State of the Sharing Economy," *Governance Studies at Brookings* 3 (2017): 5, www.brookings.edu/wp-content/uploads/2016/12/sharingeconomy_032017final.pdf.

7. "Multigenerational Households," Generations United, n.d., accessed July 31, 2018, www.gu.org/explore-our-topics/multigenerational-households/; D'vera Cohn and Jeffrey S. Passel, "A Record 64 Million Americans Live in Multigenerational Households," Pew Research Center, April 5, 2018, www.pewresearch.org/fact-tank/2018/04/05/a-record-64-million-americans-live-in-multigenerational-households/.

8. National Association of Realtors Research Department, "Home Buyer and Seller Generational Trends Report 2017," Exhibit 2.10, National Association of Realtors, March 7, 2017, www.nar.realtor/sites/default/files/reports/2017/2017-home-buyer-and-seller-generational-trends-03-07-2017.pdf.

INDEX

access economy, 227, 229–230
Affordable Care Act, 249
AlphaGo (artificial intelligence), 169–170
Alter, Adam, 175
Amazon, 61, 112, 176
American Civil War, 51, 137, 160
amoralization of America, 155–158
anti-Establishment views, 122, 149
Antifa, 152, 165
anti-majoritarianism, 139, 142, 150
anti-tribes, 13–14, 72, 115. *See also*
    polititainment; polarization business
    model
Any Given Sunday (film), 240–241
Apple, 167, 176
Aristotle, x, 44
artificial intelligence, 52, 55–56, 169–170
associations, 26, 235, 253
augmented reality (AR), 176–178
automation, 52–60, 171
ATMs, 53–55

Baby Boom generation, 59, 115, 230
Bandito (digital content assessment tool),
    112–113
Beck, Julie, 128
Benson, Guy, 152–154
Bezos, Jeff, 112
Biden, Joe, 90–91
Bin Laden, Osama, 109

Bishop, Bill, 43
Bissinger, Buzz, 101
Bixenspan, David, 88
Blitzer, Wolf, 99–101
Boehner, John, 8
Bork, Robert, 89–91
Breitbart, Andrew, 107
Breitbart News, 155
Brooks, Arthur, 65
Burke, Edmund, 235–236
Burns, Ken, 119
Burwell, Sylvia, 96
Bush, George W., 92, 101, 125

Cacioppo, John T., 23
Carr, Nicholas, 184–185
Carter, Jimmy, 13
Castro, Martin, 94
CereProc (speech synthesis company),
    170
Chapin, Harry, 67
Chicago, Illinois, 67–70
    heat wave of 1995, 19–21, 23, 24
    Robert Taylor Homes, 70–71, 226
Chick-Fil-A, 114
Christakis, Erika, 151–152
Christakis, Nicholas, 151–152, 162
Christianity, 93, 95–96, 107, 114, 161,
    205, 215
Churchill, Winston, 50

civil rights
    civil rights movement, 160–162
    March on Washington, 160–161
    U.S. Commission on Civil Rights,
        94–96
Clinton, Bill, 62, 157
Clinton, Hillary, 88, 93, 122, 126
code words, 93–94
Cold War, 2, 76, 137, 177
college campuses, 87, 95, 151–156,
    158–159
common culture, 115–117
community, 11–12, 14–15, 252–253
    associations and, 234–235
    building, 212–213, 236–237
    friendship and, 234
    home and, 219, 221, 223–225, 250
    loneliness and, 22–26
    media consumption and, 82
    political philosophy and, 139, 140, 246
    rootedness as, 187, 206–208
    social capital and, 27–31
    social media and, 178
    Wild West and, 229–230
    work and, 62–63, 66, 68–71
    See also rootedness
confirmation bias, 82–84, 90, 101, 112,
    119
Constitution, U.S., 134–135, 139–140,
    144
    First Amendment, 93–95, 121,
        149–150, 160, 245
    Framers, 135–146, 149, 245
    Reconstruction Amendments, 160
    Second Amendment, 93, 156
Cowen, Tyler, 206
creedal minorities, 142
Cronkite, Walter, 78, 119
Crouch, Andy, 193–194
Crowley, Candy, 100–101
cybersecurity, 123, 248, 252
cyberwar, 248, 252

Dahlem Workshop on Attachment and
    Bonding, 23
death, 203–217
Declaration of Independence, 44,
    138–139, 160
Deep Blue (chess computer program),
    169, 191
deep work, 191–192
deepfake technology, 179, 247–248
DeepMind (artificial intelligence
    company), 169–170, 191
depression, 24–26, 178, 221. *See also*
    loneliness
digital revolution
    digital addiction, 174–178, 186, 193,
        195–198
    digital advertising, 176
    digital friends, 178
    digital memory, 184–185
    digital nomads, 67–69
    digital Sabbath, 190
    disruption and uncertainty of, 55–56,
        60, 61
    happiness and, 167–168
    knee-jerk polarization and, 246
    as new normal, 2, 60
    real friends and, 199
    rootedness and, 190, 206–208, 223,
        225, 232
    sleep and, 180–183
    See also social media
DiNardo, Daniel, 95
divorce, 30, 31, 41
Donnelly, Joe, 244–245
Drexler, Eric, 172
drug overdoses, 3, 25
DuBois, W.E.B., 160
Dugoni, Graham, 190–191
Dunham, Lena, 179–180

Eberstadt, Nicholas, 179
echo chambers, 86–88

education
    age of first pregnancy and, 38
    college campuses, 87, 95, 151–156,
        158–159
    family support and, 33, 36–37
    "*Goodnight Moon* Gap" and, 38–39
    higher education, 30, 32–33, 38,
        41–43, 154
    out-of-wedlock birth rates and, 30–31, 36
    social capital and, 30–33, 36–40, 234
    Success Sequence and, 35
Ekdahl, John, 87
Elauf, Samantha, 94

fact-checking, 99–102
fake news, 92, 109, 128
families
    education and, 33, 36–37
    fatherlessness, xi–xii, 31, 34, 41
    loneliness and, 33–37
    postfamilial families, 182
    as social capital, 33–37, 42–44
    TV "families," 77–81
    See also marriage
Farrow, Ronan, 114
fatherlessness, xi–xii, 31, 34, 41
Federalist No. 10, 140
First Amendment, 93–95, 121, 149–150,
    160, 245
Florida, Richard, 69–70, 206
Foundation for Individual Rights in
    Education, 158
Founders, 139–142, 148–149
    King as modern Founder, 135, 160
    Lincoln as modern Founder, 135
Frankenstein (Shelley), 51, 53, 61
Franklin, Benjamin, 138
Fremont, Nebraska, 10, 12–13, 42–43,
    53–54, 223, 239, 241–242
friendship, ix–x

Gandhi, Mohandas, 160

Gates, Bill, 39, 66
Geftman-Gold, Hayley, 108
Gibbs, Josh, 214–215
Gibson, Charles, 78
Gingrich, Newt, 89, 91–92
Glass, Stephen, 101
Goldberg, Jeffrey, 98
Goldberg, Jonah, 159
Goldstein, Tom, 91
Google, 169, 176, 184
Gosnell, Kermit, 97–98
Great Depression, 115, 220
Great Recession, 4, 220
Greenfield, Adam, 170

Hamilton (musical), 146
Hand, Learned, 147, 150
Hannity, Sean, 105–109, 117, 120–123
happiness
    America's founding principles and, 44,
        135, 143
    choice and, 210–211
    contentment, 214–216
    drivers of, 44–45
    education and, 32
    empathy and, 183
    rootedness and, 14, 168, 187
    solitary living and, 220–221
    technology and, 186, 192–193, 196
    work and, 62, 65
    See also loneliness
Harvard College Faith and Action,
    95–96
Haskins, Ron, 35
hate speech, 96, 128, 151, 158
haves and have nots, 30, 32–33, 35, 42
health care, 78, 93, 249, 252
Hemingway, Mollie, 98
Herrera, Tim, 210–211
Hitler, Adolf, 133, 147
Holcomb, Drew, 212
Holt-Lunstad, Julianne, 23

home and housing
    associations and, 234–235
    friendship and, 233–234
    homesickness, 221–224
    housing trends and innovations,
        229–231
    multi-generation households, 230–231
    New Urbanism, 231
    public housing, 70–71, 226
    quarter-life crisis and, 222
    redefining "community," 225–236
    redefining "home," 224–225
    renting, 227–229, 231–232
    single-person households, 220–221
    technology and, 229–231
    tiny house movement, 231
    See also rootedness
homelessness, 208–209
homeownership, 219–220, 226
homesteaders, 53, 241
hometown-gym-on-a-Friday-night feeling,
    12, 69–72
housing. *See* home and housing
humility, 86, 139, 142–148
hunter-gatherer society, 34, 47, 226

IBM, 169, 172
identity
    anti-identities, 241–244
    identifiers, 251–252
    local living and, 250
    shared identity, 28, 246
    work and, 48, 50, 62, 64, 67
identity politics, 95, 154, 158
inequality, 62
    civil rights movement and, 135
    haves and have nots, 30, 32–33, 35, 42
    technology and, 55
    urbanization and, 49
Industrial Revolution, xi, xiv, 48

Jefferson, Thomas, 138–139, 159
Jim Crow laws, 94, 147, 160

jobs. *See* work
Jobs, Steve, 167
journalism and news
    bias and, 100–102
    echo chambers, 86–88
    fact-checking, 99–102
    fake news, 92, 109, 128
    loneliness and, 80, 102–103
    selective reporting, 88–92
    trust and, 91, 102, 129, 243
    See also polititainment

Kael, Pauline, 88
Kahan, Dan, 85–86
Kennedy, John F., 125, 170–171
Kennedy, Ted, 89–91
Kerry, John, 101
Kilmeade, Brian, 109
King, Martin Luther, Jr., 135, 160–162
Klinenberg, Eric, 20–22, 24
Kling, Arnold, 162–163
Kuhn, Thomas, 83–85
Kurzweil, Ray, 183, 186

labor. *See* work
Las Vegas shooting, 107–109
Lewis, C. S., 216
life expectancy, xii–xiii, 3, 15, 171–172, 233
Limbaugh, Rush, 99
limited government, 143, 149
Lincoln, Abraham, 135, 145, 155, 159,
    248–249, 253
Lincoln, Nebraska
    Marathon, 4–6, 9, 251
    People's City Mission (PCM), 208–209
    University of Nebraska, 64, 239–240,
        251
Little Sisters of the Poor, 95–96
locked-in syndrome, 168–169, 203
loneliness, 253
    broken heart syndrome, 21–22
    depression and, 24–26
    families and, 33–37

"*Goodnight Moon* Gap" and, 37–42
    happiness drivers, 44–45
    health effects of, 21–22
    heat wave deaths and, 19–21, 23, 24
    journalism and, 80, 102–103
    mobility and, 206–207, 234
    pregnancy gap and, 38
    quarter-life crisis and, 222
    relationships and, 211
    social capital and, 27–44
    social connection and, 26–29
    Success Sequence and, 35–38, 41–42
    technology and, 180, 188
    urbanization and, 224, 230
Lunden, Joan, 78
Luther, Martin, 1, 217

machine learning, 56, 170
Madison, James, 139–146
Manyika, James, 55–56
marathon water station protests, 4–6, 9
marriage, 212
    divorce, 30, 31, 41
    intermarriage (educational levels), 33
    male death statistics and, 23
    out-of-wedlock birth rates, 30, –31,
        36, 40
    rates for young adults, 221
    Success Sequence and, 35–38, 41–42
McArdle, Megan, 97–98
McCain, John, 89
McKinsey Global Institute, 55–59
McLuhan, Tony, 175
McPherson, Miller, 28–29
media. *See* journalism and news;
        polititainment; social media
megachurches, 26, 95
Merantix (medical device company), 171
Microsoft, 178
middleman economy, 227–228
Millennial generation, 220
Miranda, Lin-Manuel, 146
Mitra, Subhasish, 172

mobility, 62
    housing and, 15, 229–233
    mobile, rooted, and stuck (categories),
        69–72, 206–207, 226
    work and, 62, 69–72, 225–226, 229
Moonves, Les, 127
Moore, Roy, 128, 156–157
motivated reasoning, 82, 84–86, 148
Moynihan, Daniel Patrick, 36
Munger, Michael C., 226–228, 231–232
Murray, Charles, 41, 43, 116, 152
Murthy, Vivek, 24
Musk, Elon, 169, 183

Neuralink (neurotechnology company),
    169
neuroscience, 22, 183–186, 193, 196
Newport, Cal, 191–193
NFL kneeling controversy, 248
Nixon, Richard, 88
Norat, Rick, 64–65
nostalgia, 11–12, 61, 64, 67
nursebots, 173
nutpicking (cherrypicking nuttiest
        comments), 106–109, 244

Obama, Barack, 95, 100–101, 125, 153,
    157, 244
Obamacare (Affordable Care Act), 249
Olds, Jacqueline, 24
opioid abuse, xii–xiii, 25, 51, 221
optical character recognition technology,
    183
out-of-wedlock birth rates, 30–31, 36, 40

Palin, Sarah, 89
Patrick, William, 23
Pelosi, Nancy, 8
Petraeus, David, 125
Pidcock, Chris, 170–171
Piepenbring, Dan, 114
Pizzagate (conspiracy theory), 129,
    247–248

Plato, 44, 78
pluralism, 14, 141, 245
polarization business model
    clicks, 112–120, 126, 129–130, 135
    common enemies, 115–117
    conservative radio, 120–122
    distribution of information, 118–120
    future of, 127–130
    goals of, 110–112
    Hannity and, 105–109, 117, 120–123
    nutpicking, 106–109, 244
    psychology of enemies, 108–109
    Trump and, 124–127
polititainment, 75–77, 110, 120, 125
    confirmation bias, 82–84
    echo chambers, 86–88
    fact-checking, 99–102
    motivated reasoning, 82, 84–86, 148
    origins of polarization, 88–92
    pro-life movement and, 97–99
    religious liberty and, 92–96
    television viewing habits, 102–103
    TV "families," 77–81
porn-induced erectile dysfunction
    (PIED), 179
postfamilial families, 182
post-industrial economy, 61–62
Postman, Neil, 78, 193
post-truth, definition of, 104
Powers, Kirsten, 98
prescription drugs, 25, 221
presidential election of 2016, 12, 92–95,
    121, 126–129, 138, 247–248
Pressman, Sarah, 23
Prohibition, xiv, 48–49
pro-life movement, 89, 97–99, 128,
    251
public square, 95, 117, 138, 243–244
Putin, Vladimir, 247–249
Putnam, Robert
    "Goodnight Moon Gap," 38–39, 43
    repotting hypothesis, 207
    savvy gap, 43–44, 234

scissors graphs, 29–31
social capital theory, 26–34

racism, 35, 70, 94, 107, 126, 160
    criminal justice system and, 252
    institutional racism, 152, 154–155
rage-peddlers, 136–137
Rather, Dan, 101
Reagan, Ronald, 13, 89, 138
Reid, Harry, 8
Reineke, Tony, 175–176
religious liberty, 92–96
republicanism, 126, 142–143, 147, 159,
    235
Riley, Naomi Schaefer, 181
Roberts, Russ, 163
Romney, Mitt, 99–101
rootedness, 12, 15, 190, 205–208, 253
    happiness and, 14, 168, 187
    home and, 13, 219–220, 225, 231–234
    mobile, rooted, and stuck (categories),
        69–72, 206–207, 226
    rootlessness, xiii, 15, 67, 190, 207–208,
        214, 226, 230, 236, 253
    technology and, 190
    uprooted, 13, 15, 207
Rowe, Ian, 39–40
Russia, 247–249
Rust Belt, 71
Ryan, Paul, 8

Saarikivi, Katri, 183
Sandler, Adam, 188–189
Sandy Hook shooting, 109
Sawhill, Isabel, 35
Scalia, Antonin, 90
Schumer, Chuck, 8, 62, 244
Schwartz, Barry, 210
Schwartz, Richard S., 24
scissors graphs, 29–31
Sebelius, Kathleen, 96
Secure Compartmented Information
    Facilities (SCIFs), 190

segregation, 27, 71, 89, 115, 135, 160
Shaer, Matthew, 108
Shakespeare, William, 21, 23
Shakya, Holly, 186
sharing economy, 56–57, 227, 232–233
Shelley, Mary, 51, 53, 61
Silver, David, 170
Singh, Simratpal, 94
slavery, 1, 135, 159–160
Smalley, Richard, 172
social capital
    change and, 135
    decline of, 27–29
    definition of, 27
    family as, 33–37, 42–44
    heat wave deaths and, 19–21, 23, 24
    homelessness and, 208–209
    inequality and, 29–33, 41–44
    loneliness and, 27–45
    mobility and, 206–207
    Success Sequence and, 35–38, 41–42
social isolation, 24. *See also* loneliness
social media, 140–141
    addiction to, 174, 176, 195–198
    connectedness and, 11, 28, 66
    Facebook, 2, 89, 108, 128, 179, 181,
        186–187, 192, 248
    ghost-posting, 111
    interactive television and, 78
    journalism and, 87–88
    limits and rules for, 196–200
    loneliness and, 186–188
    news and, 77
    nutpicking and, 108–109
    polarization business model of,
        108–111, 126, 128, 130
    quitting social media, 192, 196
    #Resistance, 15
    Russian bot influence, 248
    Twitter, 2, 79, 88–89, 108–109, 126,
        130, 139–142, 151, 192, 195–199,
        248
Socrates, 1, 200

Solzhenitsyn, Aleksandr, 147–148
Sommerville, C. John, 79
SpaceX, 169
Stanger, Allison, 152–154
Statue of Liberty, 134
Stevens, Christopher, 100
Stevens, John Paul, 90
Success Sequence, 35–38, 41–42
suicide, 3–4, 23, 26
    Lincoln's Lyceum address ("die by
        suicide"), 132, 145, 248, 253
Sullivan, Andrew, 25, 154, 158
Supreme Court, 89–95

Tea Party, 107, 157
technology, 167–169
    Click (film) and, 188–189
    cloud technology, 168, 198
    digital addiction, 175–176, 195–198
    digital revolution, 2, 56, 60, 190,
        206–208, 223, 246
    happiness and, 186, 192–193, 196
    healthcare and, 171
    home and, 229–231
    implants, 169, 177, 198–199
    inflection points, 171–172
    inevitability and irresistibility of,
        169–171
    loneliness and, 180, 188
    mental health and, 186–188
    opportunity costs, 177–178
    robots, 173–174
    sexuality and, 178–180
    singularity, 183–186
    sleep and, 180–182
    tech skepticism, 193–195
    wise use of, 190–200
    work and, 48, 50–62, 171
    See also social media
television
    cable networks, 118–119
    common culture and, 115–117
    television viewing habits, 102–103

television (*continued*)
  TV "families," 77–81
Thomas, Clarence, 91
Tichi, Cecelia, 77–78
Tocqueville, Alexis de, 13, 235–236, 253
Tolstoy, Leo, 21, 23
traffic light debate (Sasse's father and
  grandfather), 81–82
transhumanism, 183–184
Trump, Donald
  birtherism and, 125
  media and, 88, 107–109, 120n,
    122–123, 125–128
  reluctant supporters of, 98–99
  role of political polarization in election
    of, 88–89
trust, 15
  anti-tribes and, 122
  journalism and, 91, 102, 129, 243
  neighborhood trust, 30–31
  social capital and, 27–33, 44
  Uber and, 228
Tubman, Harriet, 1
Turkle, Sherry, 11, 173–174, 178, 181–182

Uber, 50, 227–229
Uberization, 56. *See also* sharing economy
Ungar, Rick, 164
urbanization, 15, 48–49, 51, 60–61, 221

VandeHei, Jim, 88–89, 91–92
Vannucci, Anna, 186

Wang, Wendy, 35
Warren, Elizabeth, 8
Warren, Rick, 95
Washington, George, 142–146, 155, 253

West, Darrell, 171
what-about-ism, 243
WikiLeaks, 123, 249
Wilcox, Brad, 41
Wild West, 224–225, 229
Williams, Brian, 101–102
work
  agriculture, 2, 51–52, 60–61
  artificial intelligence and, 52, 55–56
  automation and, xi, 52–60, 171
  commute, 50, 230
  connection and, xi, 65–67
  drivers (jobs), 49–51
  future of, 55–63
  history of, 47–49
  identity through, 48, 50, 62, 64, 67
  industrialization and, 2, 15, 48, 52
  loneliness and, 65–67
  manufacturing, 52, 60
  mobility and, 62, 69–72, 225–226,
    229
  place and, 67–69
  post-industrial economy, 61–62
  Prohibition and, 48–49
  sharing economy, 56–57, 227, 232–233
  specialization, 226, 229
  technology and, 48, 50–62, 171
  upskilling, 54–55
  urbanization and, 15, 48–49, 51, 60–61
  value and purpose of, 62–65
World War II, 27, 50–52, 147

Yiannopoulos, Milo, 155–156, 158
Yondr (mobile phone pouch), 190–191

Zeleny, Jeff, 107–108
zero-sum thinking, 161

Matthew DeBoer

U.S. senator BEN SASSE is a fifth-generation Nebraskan. The son of a football and wrestling coach, he attended public school in Fremont, Nebraska, and spent his summers working soybean and corn fields. He was recruited to wrestle at Harvard before attending Oxford and later earning a Ph.D. in American history from Yale. Prior to the Senate, Sasse spent five years as president of Midland University and was one of the youngest college presidents in the country. As perhaps the only commuting family in the U.S. Senate, Ben and his wife, Melissa, live in Nebraska, but are homeschooling their three children as they commute weekly to Washington, D.C.